Linking Research and Teaching in Higher Education

Edited by

Simon K. Haslett

and

Hefin Rowlands

Proceedings of the Newport NEXUS Conference 2009

**Centre for Excellence in Learning and Teaching
Special Publication No. 1**

Published by the University of Wales, Newport.

Published 2009 by the University of Wales, Newport
Lodge Road, Caerleon, South Wales, NP18 3QT, UK.

© 2009 University of Wales, Newport.

Typeset in Myriad Pro.
Printed by MWL Print Group Ltd, Units 10-13, Pontyfelin Industrial
Estate, New Inn, Pontypool, South Wales, NP4 0DQ, UK.

Cover photographs supplied with thanks by (from left to right):

Peter Brabham (Cardiff University)
Alan Rowse (University of Wales, Newport)
Carolyn Roberts (University of Gloucestershire)

ISBN 978-1-899274-38-3

Contents

| University of Wales, Newport | Prifysgol Cymru, Casnewydd | *Linking Research and Teaching in Higher Education*
Simon K. Haslett and Hefin Rowlands (eds)
Proceedings of the Newport NEXUS Conference
Centre for Excellence in Learning and Teaching
Special Publication, No. 1, 2009, pp. 5-6
ISBN 978-1-899274-38-3 |

Linking research and teaching in Higher Education: an introduction.

Simon K. Haslett[1] and Hefin Rowlands[2]

[1]Centre for Excellence in Learning and Teaching, University of Wales, Newport, Lodge Road, Caerleon, South Wales, NP18 3QT, United Kingdom. Email: Simon.haslett@newport.ac.uk

[2]Research and Enterprise Department, University of Wales, Newport, Allt-yr-yn Avenue, Newport, NP20 5DA, United Kingdom. Email: Hefin.rowlands@newport.ac.uk

Like many other institutions, the University of Wales, Newport, has set itself strategic targets to promote research-informed teaching and to encourage further links to made between research and teaching (*i.e.* the research-teaching nexus). In the response to this, in December 2008 the University launched the Centre for Excellence in Learning and Teaching (CELT) as a research centre to provide a focus to bring research and learning and teaching (L&T) closer together. The CELT's activities have been to:

1. publish a journal, the *Newport CELT Journal*, the first volume of which was published in December 2008,
2. recruit PhD students (all of which have papers or abstracts in this volume),
3. co-ordinate themed research networks for University staff and students, including Technology Enhanced Learning (TEL), Education for Sustainable Development and Global Citizenship (ESDGC), and Community Education, Distance Learning and Outreach (CEDLO), all of which have contributed to this book,
4. run monthly workshops on themes such as applying for educational research funding, academic writing for publication, professional academic standards, TEL, ESDGC, and linking research and teaching,
5. to internationalise the research activity through, for example, Pedagogic Research Expeditions (ExPedR), the first of which involves a team of five Newport academics visiting Australia in July 2009, all presenting at the Higher Education Research and Development Society of Australasia (HERDSA) Annual Conference, as well as visiting a number of Australian universities,
6. manage institutional Learning and Teaching Grants, and establish awards for recognising and rewarding teaching excellence, of which a number have been made,
7. to organise the Annual Learning and Teaching Conference to disseminate good practice.

It is this last area of activity that has directly led to this volume. In order to bring research and L&T closer together, to blur if not break down barriers between these two often separated academic areas, the 2009 conference is jointly convened by both the CELT and the Research and Enterprise Department (RED) and focuses on the research-teaching nexus and research-informed teaching; hence it is titled the *Newport NEXUS Conference* (15-16th June).

Although initially envisaged as a vehicle through which Newport academics and students could come together, the organisers were very pleased with the interest from external colleagues, from the UK and abroad, not only to attend but to present papers. This reflects, we feel, the interest in the linkages between research and teaching currently in academia. The conference is made up of ten themed symposia, five keynotes, a plenary and an exhibition.

The format of this volume loosely follows the provisional conference programme. It comprises 20 full written papers and 43 abstracts. Each full paper is presented separately, whilst the abstracts of the remaining papers are collected together at the end. Although each paper falls within a symposium, it has not been possible to present them as such in this volume, other than as a way of deciding the running order of the full papers, and the grouping of abstracts. However, such a pigeonholing is, in any case, relatively artificial, as many of the papers are interdisciplinary and cross several of themes represented by the symposia. We are also very pleased to see authors from every level of the University represented in this volume, from undergraduate and postgraduate students, to academic staff up to the level of Deputy Vice Chancellor. To have students publishing in the volume is particularly welcoming and sits very well within a conference that aims to promote linking research and teaching.

We are very fortunate to have, to open, a paper by Professors Mick Healey and Alan Jenkins, who are eminent scholars in the research-teaching field having written numerous journal papers, and monographs for the Higher Education Academy on the subject. Their paper explores ways in which students may be developed as researchers. A symposium on Research-informed Teaching, chaired by Professor Stuart Hampton Reeves, includes papers from the Centre for Research-informed Teaching at the University of Central Lancashire, and a keynote from Professor Hefin Rowlands.

A number of papers examine aspects of ESDGC, including embedding it within the curriculum, the role of science, institutional strategies, the role of local media and the visual arts. For the CELT, it is pleasing to see a symposium being organised by the newly established ESDGC Research Network. A number of these papers are actually presented within a Professional Development symposium, where others look at what it is like to be a new researcher and the role of the lecturer.

Student engagement is very topical at present and a number of papers, and a keynote by David Gibson, are related to this theme, including the benefits and dangers of engaging with students on social network sites, and examples of curriculum developing, such as how to engage non-law students in the law subject.

By far the most papers delivered at the conference are those related to TEL, including a keynote by Professor Gilly Salmon, again springing from the CELT Research Network. Papers here include examining 3D virtual learning environments, digital inclusion, and podcasting, but papers in other symposia are also clearly linked to this area where technology is employed.

The internationalisation of research activity is an important priority and the symposium on International Scholarship highlights some of the exciting collaboration that can result. Papers here include ERASMUS funded projects with, for example, partners in the Czech Republic, Romania, Sweden and Finland.

As an example of subject-based L&T research, a Hazard and Geoscience symposium presents case studies of how research may be embedded within teaching at undergraduate and postgraduate levels, with students both as recipients and producers of research, often in collaboration with academics. Papers include a case study from South Wales, the Indian Ocean tsunami of 2004, and water hazards in Tunisia.

Finally, Newport is currently championing entrepreneurialism, enterprise and knowledge transfer within the curriculum, and a symposium chaired by Professor Carolyn Roberts contains papers linking teaching and knowledge transfer, including a paper on developing the use of customised dice games.

We hope that this volume goes some way to capturing the activity that is currently going on in this area, and will excite and encourage both academics and students to come together to form academic learning communities of research and enterprise.

University of Wales, Newport

Prifysgol Cymru, Casnewydd

Linking Research and Teaching in Higher Education
Simon K. Haslett and Hefin Rowlands (eds)
Proceedings of the Newport NEXUS Conference
Centre for Excellence in Learning and Teaching
Special Publication, No. 1, 2009, pp. 7-11
ISBN 978-1-899274-38-3

Developing students as researchers.

Mick Healey[1] and Alan Jenkins[2]

[1]Centre for Active Learning, University of Gloucestershire, Swindon Road, Cheltenham, GL50 4AZ, United Kingdom. Email: mhealey@glos.ac.uk

[2]Emeritus Oxford Brookes University, Room D106, Wheatley Campus, Oxford, OX33 1HX, United Kingdom. Email: alanjenkins@brookes.ac.uk

Abstract

Our intellectual starting point is Humboldt's vision for higher education which arguably recently finds its strongest current manifestation in the US undergraduate research programmes which are frequently for selected students. We argue the task now is to 'reinvent' the curriculum to ensure that *all* undergraduate students in *all* higher education institutions learn through some form of research or inquiry. This argument follows from the international research evidence of the student experience of research and inquiry. We illustrate the argument with initiatives by curricula teams, departments and institutions who have attempted to 'mainstream' undergraduate research and inquiry for most or all students.

"We want all students to access the benefits exposure to teaching informed by research can bring. ... We believe an understanding of the research process – asking the right questions in the right way; conducting experiments; and collating and evaluating information – must be a key part of any undergraduate curriculum." (Bill Rammell, UK Minister for Higher Education, 2006, p. 3).

Introduction

Our argument can be simply stated: *all* undergraduate students in *all* higher education institutions should experience learning through and about research. This applies to all students in higher education, including those taking higher education courses in Further Education Colleges. While recognising that there are other goals the curriculum should support (*e.g.* student employability, civic engagement), students learning in 'research mode' should be *central* to the curriculum. Unfortunately, the Research Assessment Exercise (RAE) has both devalued the importance of teaching and effectively moved many undergraduate students and academic staff out of the worlds of research.

Our interest in developing students as researchers originated through our explorations over the last few years into ways to enhance the linkage between teaching and discipline-based research. Our conclusion is that one of the most effective ways to do this is to engage our students in research and inquiry; in other words, to see them as producers not just consumers of knowledge.

In attempting to do this we feel that there is a lot we may learn from the undergraduate research programmes in the US, which started by providing research opportunities for selected students in selected institutions and were often outside the formal curriculum *e.g.* in summer enrichment programmes. However, for us the key to mainstreaming undergraduate research is to integrate it into the curriculum.

Is Undergraduate Research for all Students?

Your answer to this depends on how you define undergraduate research. If you restrict it to the creation of new knowledge, often through working with staff, such as part of a laboratory research team, then the experience is likely to be limited to a few select students. However, if you conceive undergraduate research as students learning through courses which are designed to be as close as possible to the research processes in their discipline then it can be for all students. The focus then is on student learning and on being assessed in ways that mimic how research is conducted in the discipline, for example, through undergraduate research journals and student research conferences and exhibitions. In these cases, what is produced and learned may not be new knowledge *per se*; but it is new to the student and, perhaps more significantly, transforms their understanding of knowledge and research. In terms of Figure 1 the emphasis is on the student learning in 'research-based' and 'research-orientated' modes.

The argument as to whether undergraduate research is for all or selected students is in part a political question - to whom and for what, do national systems and institutions allocate resources, in particular staff time? But for us it is largely an educational and/or philosophical question as to the nature of *higher* education. We are persuaded by the arguments of those, such as Ron Barnett, that what distinguishes *higher* education is the emphasis on helping students to live in a supercomplex world and that the curricula task is for "lecturers (to) adopt teaching approaches that are likely to foster student experiences that mirror the lecturers' experiences as researchers" (Barnett, 2000, p. 163).

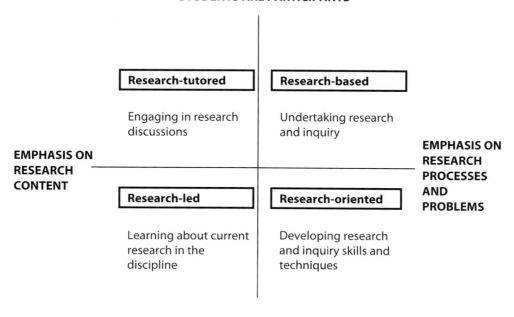

Figure 1. The nature of undergraduate research and inquiry.
Source: Healey and Jenkins (2009a, amended from Healey, 2005, p. 70).

The Research Evidence

There is growing international research on teaching and discipline-based research relations. In brief this shows that the asserted close interconnection between research and the curriculum is professed more than it is delivered, and in Brew's (2006, p. 52) powerful phrase too often undergraduate students are "at arms length" from the worlds of university research.

Coordinated interventions in zoology at University of Tasmania, Australia (Edwards *et al.*, 2007)

- *Years Two and Three.* All invited to participate in Student Research Volunteers program (http://www.zoo.utas.edu.au/volunteers/summvolunteer3.htm). Volunteers are matched with mentors, usually Postgraduate or Honours students, for short-term, in-house research placements that may offer either laboratory or field experiences.
- *Years One, Two and Three.* 'Reach into Research' seminars held several times each semester (www.zoo.utas.edu.au/rir/rir2&3.htm). Speakers from industry, collaborating institutions and PhD students present their research, and then all non-undergraduate audience members, except the facilitator, leave the room.

Miami University Ohio, US, are embedding inquiry into the largest courses (Hodge *et al.*, 2008)
They have instituted a Top 25 project in which over a four-year period the largest recruiting courses, mainly at first year level, are being supported to convert to inquiry-based learning.

Undergraduate research at University of Gloucestershire begins at induction
In 2007 over 650 students in the Faculty of Education, Humanities and Science undertook discipline-based inquiry projects during induction week. This involved them working in small groups to collect information from the library and in the field, analyse it, present it to tutors in novel ways, and receive formative feedback. For example, the human geographers and the sociologists researched the experience of Gloucester residents of 'the Great Flood of 2007'. The Biologists and the Psychologists investigated primate behaviour at Bristol Zoo, while English Literature students visited an arboretum and explored the use of trees in literature. Social and academic activities were integrated, the students had fun, and, importantly, they made friends. The approach was developed, and initially supported, by the Centre for Active Learning (http://resources.glos.ac.uk/ceal/pre-induction/index.cfm). It has proved a significant staff development activity both for the many academic tutors and the library staff who changed their approach to library induction to support the specific student research projects. Over the next two years other Faculties in the University are developing their versions of developing undergraduate research as part of induction.

Academic journal writing in geography at Oxford Brookes is part of course requirements (Walkington and Jenkins, 2008)
The geography programme at Oxford Brookes has developed a set of linked requirements that support all students learning to write research articles. In the second year all students undertake field-based research in a range of venues. A third-year compulsory first semester course 'Geography Research and Practice' has as its main assessment students writing an article of up to 4,000 words from the data collected in the second-year fieldwork (http://www.brookes.ac.uk/ schools/social/geoversity/index.html).

Undergraduate research programmes at University of Michigan, US, support racial diversity and widening participation (Huggins *et al.*, 2007)
While the University had been successful in recruiting Afro–American students from inner-city Detroit their drop out rate was high. Special programmes were targeted at these students in years one and two to enhance their integration and academic success with significant positive impacts.

Table 1. Examples of 'interesting' curricula interventions

Particularly important to our argument here is the research of Baxter Magolda. Based on a detailed interview-based study of students' intellectual development during and after university, she has argued that university curricula need to support student and citizen development from *"absolute knowing* (where) students view knowledge as certain; their role is to obtain it from authorities (to) *contextual knowing* (where) students believe that knowledge is constructed in a context based on judgement of evidence; their role is to exchange and compare perspectives, think through problems, and integrate and apply knowledge" (Baxter Magolda, 1992, p. 75). However, too often curricula "frame learning as the passive acquisition of knowledge" (Baxter Magolda, 2008).

We have gathered a large collection of 'interesting' international examples of mainstreaming undergraduate research from a range of disciplines, institutions and national systems (Healey and Jenkins, 2009a, 2009b). A small selection is shown in Table 1.

Where Next?

We know of many examples of interesting practices for engaging students in research and inquiry in individual modules, but far fewer cases where undergraduate research has been mainstreamed across a course, department, institution or national system. More strategic interventions to reinvent the curriculum, such as Miami University Ohio is attempting, are needed.

We believe that undergraduate research and inquiry should be an important part of the curriculum from the day students start studying at University, and perhaps before then, as the example of the University of Gloucestershire suggests. Undergraduates should be included in the research community, as happens with Zoology students at Tasmania, and not kept 'at arms length'.

Developing students' competencies to engage in research and inquiry and to begin to think like discipline specialists is a significant way of meeting many graduate attributes and the government's employability agenda, as is well illustrated by The Scottish Higher Education Enhancement Committee approach to developing research-teaching links.

Finally, we echo the perspectives of Angela Brew (2007, p. 7) that:

"For the students who are the professionals of the future, developing the ability to investigate problems, make judgments on the basis of sound evidence, take decisions on a rational basis, and understand what they are doing and why is vital. Research and inquiry is not just for those who choose to pursue an academic career. It is central to professional life in the twenty-first century."

In other words, as David Hodge (2007, p. 1), President of Miami University, says, "undergraduate research should … be at the center (sic) of the undergraduate experience".

NOTE

This article was originally published in *University College Magazine* (October, 2008, 17-19). It draws on a chapter in Rust, C. (ed.) (2009) *Improving Student Learning through the Curriculum.* Oxford: Oxford Centre for Staff and Learning Development and is reproduced here in a slightly modified and updated form with permission. The full article is available from the authors.

SOME USEFUL WEBSITES

- Council on Undergraduate Research: www.cur.org
- Higher Education Academy Research and Teaching: www.heacademy.ac.uk/ourwork/research/teaching
- Learning Through Enquiry Alliance: www.ltea.ac.uk/
- The Scottish Higher Education Enhancement Committee Enhancement Themes: Research-Teaching Linkages: www.enhancementthemes.ac.uk/themes/ResearchTeaching/default.asp
- University of Gloucestershire: NTFS Project 'Leading, promoting and supporting undergraduate research in new uni-

versities' http://resources.glos.ac.uk/tli/prsi/current/ugresearch/index.cfm; and Centre for Active Learning 'Undergraduate Research case studies': http://resources.glos.ac.uk/ceal/resources/casestudiesactivelearning/index.cfm

- Universities of Warwick and Oxford Brookes, The Reinvention Centre for Undergraduate Research: http://www2.warwick.ac.uk/fac/soc/sociology/research/cetl/ugresearch/

REFERENCES

BARNETT, R. 2000. *Realising the university in an age of supercomplexity*. Buckingham: Society for Research into Higher Education and Open University Press.

BAXTER MAGOLDA, M. B. 1992. *Knowing and reasoning in college: gender-related patterns in students' intellectual development*. San Francisco: Jossey-Bass.

BAXTER MAGOLDA, M. B. 2008. Educating for self-authorship: Learning partnerships to achieve complex outcomes In C. Kreber (ed.) *The university and its disciplines: teaching and learning within and beyond disciplinary boundaries*. Oxford: Routledge.

BREW, A. 2006. *Research and teaching: beyond the divide*. London: PalgraveMacmillan.

BREW, A. 2007. Research and teaching from the students' perspective, *International policies and practices for academic enquiry: An international colloquium* held at Marwell conference centre, Winchester, UK, 19–21 April, portal-live.solent.ac.uk/university/rtconference/2007/resources/angela_brew.pdf.

EDWARDS, A., JONES, S. M., WAPSTRA, E., RICHARDSON, A. M. M. 2007. Engaging students through authentic research experiences, *UniServe Science Teaching and Learning Research Proceedings* 168, science.uniserve.edu.au/pubs/procs/2007/33.pdf.

HEALEY, M. 2005. Linking research and teaching exploring disciplinary spaces and the role of inquiry-based learning. In: R. Barnett (ed.) *Reshaping the university: new relationships between research, scholarship and teaching.* pp. 30-42. Maidenhead: McGraw-Hill/Open University Press.

HEALEY, M., JENKINS, A. 2009a. *Developing undergraduate research and inquiry*. York: HE Academy.

HEALEY, M., JENKINS, A. 2009b. *Linking discipline-based research and teaching through mainstreaming undergraduate research and inquiry*. resources.glos.ac.uk/ceal/resources/index.cfm.

HODGE, D., PASQUESI, K., HIRSH, M. 2007. From convocation to capstone: developing the student as scholar, Keynote address. *Association of American Colleges and Universities Network for Academic Renewal Conference*, April 19-21, Long Beach, California, http://www.miami.muohio.edu/president/reports_and_speeches/pdfs/From_Convocation_to_Capstone.pdf.

HODGE, D., HAYNES, C., LEPORE, P., PASQUESI, K., HIRSH, M. 2008. From inquiry to discovery: developing the student as scholar in a networked world, Keynote address, *Learning through enquiry alliance inquiry in a networked world conference*, June 25-27, University of Sheffield, http://networkedinquiry.pbwiki.com/About+the+LTEA2008+keynote.

HUGGINS, R., JENKINS, A., SCURRY, D. 2007. *Undergraduate research in selected US universities: report on US visit - institutional case studies*. Coventry: The Reinvention Centre, University of Warwick and Oxford Brookes, http://www2.warwick.ac.uk/fac/soc/sociology/research/cetl/ugresearch/.

RAMMELL, B. 2006. *Innovations: exploring research-based learning*, University of Warwick Conference 25 October 2006, http://www.dfes.gov.uk/speeches/media/documents/Rammell_speech_warwickrbl_25.10.06_internet.doc.

WALKINGTON, H., JENKINS, A. 2008. Embedding undergraduate research publication in the student learning experience: ten suggested strategies, *Brookes E-journal of Learning and Teaching*, 3(1), http://bejlt.brookes.ac.uk/.

Linking Research and Teaching in Higher Education
Simon K. Haslett and Hefin Rowlands (eds)
Proceedings of the Newport NEXUS Conference
Centre for Excellence in Learning and Teaching
Special Publication, No. 1, 2009, pp. 13-19
ISBN 978-1-899274-38-3

University of Wales, Newport

Prifysgol Cymru, Casnewydd

The greening of computing and ICT curriculum: challenges and directions.

Brendan D'Cruz[1] and Andy Phippen[2]

[1]Newport Business School, University of Wales, Newport, Allt-yr-yn Campus, Allt-yr-yn Avenue, Newport, NP20 5DA. Email: Brendan.dcruz@newport.ac.uk

[2]School of Computing, Communications and Electronics, University of Plymouth, Drakes Circus, Plymouth, PL4 8AA, United Kingdom. Email: Andy.phippen@plymouth.ac.uk

Abstract

Higher Education Institutions have a responsibility to produce graduates who will contribute to the future workforce in a manner that extends knowledge and better practice. In the case of Information and Communications Technology, the next generation need to be more socially aware and have knowledge regarding the impact of their industry on the planet and society, to help address the shortcomings of many within the industry at present. However, given the focus of the majority of Computer Science and Information Systems curricula, examining issues of sustainability presents significant challenges to the curriculum. How might we best articulate these 'social' issues to technically focused undergraduates? Case-based approaches with final year students at the University of Plymouth considered sustainability in the curriculum, and qualitative analysis of coursework submissions enabled an assessment of the impact of these issues to help identify trends in perceptions and attitude. Conclusions drawn so far demonstrate the willingness of a subset of students to engage with sustainable issues, and allowed us to reflect on the appropriate models for delivery of such materials. Computing provision at University of Wales, Newport, is only just beginning to consider 'Green IT' within the curriculum, and comparisons are made with the work undertaken at the University of Plymouth.

Introduction

Modern organisations of different sizes across all sectors now face intense political and social pressures to be more environmentally responsible, but at the same time must remain competitive in order to maintain their profits or revenue streams (Cook, 2008). More recently recessionary influences have dramatically changed the global economic landscape, and it can be argued that they have helped place a greater emphasis on 'green issues' as a potential driver to help reduce costs and develop business sustainability. Information and Communication Technologies (ICT) are considered a significant contributor to operational costs, therefore when taken in parallel with consumer concerns about the environment have naturally led to greater awareness and need for response by mainstream ICT vendors, users and developers (Murphy, 2007). The IT industry contributes around 2% of global greenhouse gas emissions, equivalent to the aviation industry, but its emissions are actually growing at a much faster rate (Sparkes, 2008). The IT industry has therefore experienced justifiable criticism for its attitude towards sustainability and social responsibility given its significant carbon footprint and social impact. While the industry can be seen in some areas to be acknowledging the need for more accountable behaviour (for example

13

the corporate social responsibility outputs of BT, GSK, IBM) this is still in the minority.

The main issues in the greening of ICT include the need to reduce energy consumption and use of natural resources, reduce travel and transportation, lower carbon emissions, and generate less waste. New legislation was introduced in the United Kingdom (UK) in 2007 to help minimise the impact that ICT and other technologies have on the environment, including the EC Directive on Waste Electrical and Electronic Equipment (WEEE) and the EU's Energy Using Products (EUP) Directive. However, Boccaletti *et al.* (2008) argue that computing and ICT have the potential to reduce far more emissions than they generate, assuming that technology manufacturers and users fully understand how this can be facilitated and enabled.

Although the popularity of traditional computing courses in the UK has declined in recent years, globally there are still large numbers of students that are moving into the computing and ICT industry having first studied on relevant university undergraduate and postgraduate courses to give them the required knowledge, skills and understanding. These graduates will help to develop the digital economy and contribute to global economic and social productivity (Whetstone, 2009). The emergence of 'green collar' jobs as a phenomenon suggests that future graduates with environmental awareness and sustainable development capability will be much in demand, especially with the need to develop greener and cleaner technologies, and to build ICT applications to help tackle climate change and meet global targets on reducing carbon emissions (Ashford, 2008). It can however be argued that UK universities have been slow to consider revising their computing and ICT curriculum to accommodate these 'green issues', and it should be noted that professional bodies for computing and ICT such as the British Computer Society (BCS) have only recently launched a 'Green Specialist Group' as of March 2009.

This paper will consider the developing curriculum at University of Plymouth and at the University of Wales, Newport with a particular emphasis on the computing and ICT programmes in the departments where staff, students and resources relating to these programmes are located. The paper will look at current practice with respect to assessment (Plymouth), and at staff perceptions on the nature and location of the learning outcomes in the curriculum (Newport). Comparisons will be made with respect to the emerging approaches to tackling the issues of Education for Sustainable Development and Global Citizenship (ESDGC).

Growing a Green ICT Sector

There are approximately one million people currently working in the IT industry and eSkills UK, the sector skills council for information technology (IT) and telecommunications in the UK, predicts that the industry is growing at such a rate that there will be a further 120,000 job opportunities created by 2012 (eSkills UK, 2008). According to the Society of IT Management (a professional body representing IT professionals in the public sector) expenditure in IT continues to grow (SOCITM, 2009). There is now an interesting tension between an industry that is not perceived to be addressing its professional responsibility and is failing to demonstrate effective practice, yet one which will continue to grow and make an even more significant impact upon our world. Recent technical advances will move applications into "the cloud" (for a non-technical description, see Wikipedia, 2009), migrating functionality and data storage away from organisations and into massive, centralised data centres controlled by huge technology companies and accessed by their clients via high speed networks, which will generate even greater power consumption. Therefore, it is not surprising that there have been moves by some larger technology suppliers and consumers to start to embrace the 'Green Agenda'. However, it can be cynically observed that those within the sector that are embracing 'Green IT' are doing so for primarily for cost savings, competitive advantage and brand image rather than for the benefits that it can bring to the environment and global citizenship.

Until recently those recruited into the IT industry were recognised for their technical ability and logical thinking, and not for their environmental and social awareness. IT originally manifested itself as an entity that could hide deep inside an organisation, and there was little need for reflective practitioners to consider the broader societal implications of their newly developed systems. It should therefore be no surprise that we currently have a profession that is struggling to keep up with the impact of what they now do, in a highly inter-connected business and social world.

The beginnings of an ICT-related career will start in school, and will be developed through a computing or ICT-related degree at University into a job in the industry. However, when we examine the coverage of ICT education in schools, we see the age-old technical focus. Therefore those who wish to embark on an ICT career will apply to go to university with little grasp of the wider social implications of ICT. Certainly from the authors' experiences, the "average" Computer Science[1] undergraduate applicant will apply to such a degree because of an interest in computers and technology, but with little awareness of the wider industry. Last year the University of Plymouth surveyed all applicants at open and preview days to gain a snapshot of their understanding of the industry. The vast majority of the approximately 300 applicants were aware that the industry was a lucrative one, and that technical skills were important, yet had little grasp of the professional, legal or social skills required by the modern profession.

Therefore, we have to conclude that it is the responsibility of Higher Education Institutions (HEIs) to ensure that those graduating into the ICT industry are aware of the social implications of the technologies they develop and manage, with a clear appreciation of the wider impact of the

systems they use. However, if we anecdotally examine the majority of Computer Science degrees, we see they are still embedded in the technical aspects of the discipline, with much coverage of mathematical and algorithmic theory, architecture, communications, programming and data management. Coverage of social, environmental or legal aspects is very much in the minority.

There is now a growing awareness among ICT educators of the need to work towards understanding what is needed to produce a more socially and environmentally aware graduate. Whilst the mainstream ICT industry is still very much focused upon 'technical' training and education, there are pockets of emerging academic practice that attempt to integrate key issues and reflective learning into the Computer Science and ICT curriculum. This pedagogy aims to explore how curriculum and learning/teaching approaches need to be modified to facilitate a greater social awareness in learners who are typically keen to write code, develop games and websites, and create new technology. Research is needed to understand how such capability can be embedded in curriculum to ensure that graduates leave university appreciating the responsibility they will face in their professional careers. Two examples of evaluating academic practice at the University of Plymouth and at the University of Wales, Newport are discussed below.

Evaluating Current Practice at University of Plymouth

At the University of Plymouth the green agenda is embraced within a wider curriculum that focuses upon professional practice and social responsibility. In 2008 a strategy was put in place to embed this in all stages of degree programmes in specific credit bearing modules which are formally assessed. A first year module examines the social and ethical aspects of ICT in a broad sense. These are related back to social technologies such as social networking and gaming, and examine the more extreme examples of technology such as the sex offenders websites that exist

---

[1] The term "Computer Science" is used here as a generic term to relate to all manner of computing related degrees in the UK

in the United States (US)[2], so as to make students realise the potential impact of the technologies that are developed. The environmental impact of IT is also introduced at this stage by considering aspects such as the scale of power consumption in the industry by examining the scale of a large IT system (for example, the current University of Plymouth infrastructure consists of more than 100 servers and 5,500 desktop systems).

In the second year, a more detailed ethical and legislative examination of the social and environmental aspects of the industry is carried out, considering the "carrot" of ethical practice against the "stick" of legislation. Within this context, the growing body of environmental guidelines and legislation is explored (for example, the UK Government's aim to make the public sector IT carbon neutral by 2012[3]). The assessment requires students to evaluate the social and ethical implications of a proposed software system they develop within another part of their second year. The final year embarks on a more detailed examination of students' perceptions and attitudes towards the environmental aspects of the profession into which they are about to enter. In the final term of their degree, students take on a module that gets them to reflect upon their own position within the industry and their career aspirations against the topics of Globalisation, Green IT, and Social Responsibility. Each topic is supported by lectures in the topic area. In the case of Green IT, the context is put in place by a more general lecture about the global implications of sustainability (delivered by staff from the University's Centre for Sustainable Futures[4]), prior to examining key issues faced by the industry, such as power and waste material management. In each area, the students are asked to pick a recent news story and to write an essay on why they selected the specific article, and whether they believe the issues raised in the story are important for the industry as a whole and,

more importantly, for their own career aspirations. It should be stressed that as the cohort in this study would not have had detailed coverage in the first two years of their degree around aspects of sustainability in the IT curriculum, for the majority this subject material was effectively new to them.

For the Green IT assessment, this was evaluated by an analysis of 55 coursework submissions. The objectives of the evaluation were:

- To examine the choice of story – topic, focus and "bias" (i.e. for or against the green agenda)
- To identify key themes that are drawn from the personal reflection

A sample of the essays was randomly selected to develop a coding scheme of terms that was then used to code up all of the submissions. Analysis of the coding responses allowed us to identify key themes to address the evaluation objectives. The findings from this analysis are presented below, with anonymised quotes from some of the submissions to support these.

1. A lack of awareness of green issues in the IT sector

"I must admit that all of these issues surrounding 'Green IT' and sustainability never occurred to me as relevant or something that I should consider within my career"

The most significant finding from this analysis was that green IT issues were not familiar to the students. Many stated that the lectures delivered and articles they researched were the first time they had reflected upon the environmental implications of the IT industry in detail. Some had come across these issues on placement, but none stated a familiarity with the issues from previous University work.

2. Students are environmentally aware and can relate green IT to their wider beliefs

"The article makes me think about the type of company that I would like to work for. I did not know that IT companies were such a big factor

---

[2] For example, see http://www.georgia-sex-offenders.com/maps/offenders.php
[3] http://www.cabinetoffice.gov.uk/media/66177/greening_government_ict.pdf
[4] http://csf.plymouth.ac.uk/

in the poor health of the environment. I would not like to be part of a company that did nothing to try and lessen their environmental impact"

However, what is also apparent is that an awareness of sustainability within the IT industry causes a strong reaction to the theme. Many students reflected on their awareness of green issues in their social lives, but had not really considered its relevance to IT. Having learned about these issues in lectures, and then developed their under-standing through subsequent research, the fact that they could relate their career to their social beliefs formed strong opinions regarding their choice of company. In some cases, as in the case highlighted above, students stated they would not work for a company without a green IT policy.

3. Green IT is a hardware problem

"I plan to go into web development, there is no way you can make software greener, it is the hardware that needs to be improved to run the software more efficiently"

Interestingly, among some of the more technically minded students who had stated they wished to enter into software develop-ment careers, there was a feeling that they could not do anything in their jobs to address energy efficiency, therefore it was not their problem. Given that *any* IT professional will use hardware as part of their daily operational functions, and their awareness and choice of such could have serious implications for the company. More importantly, efficient software development, that which will be able to be effectively scaled, can result in a significant reduction in the amount of hardware required to run them.

4. Green IT is good PR!

"While I feel there isn't anything major that I can do to improve my carbon footprint as a self employed web designer I do feel that if I was to try and keep my business green I could possibly increase my clientele"

The PR perspective of green IT was reflected upon both personally and in the sector as a whole. It was interesting to see many comments related to the positive "spin" that companies were receiving from having green strategies, as well as comments such as the one above, where students were considering being perceived as "environmentally friendly" might be a good thing personally as well as professionally!

5. Power management is the most visible aspect of green IT

"I do consider power efficiency and controlling costs to be an important issue"

The vast majority of articles selected by students focused upon the issues of power management to achieve cost savings, therefore achieving a green IT strategy. There was very little discussion around other aspects of sustainable IT such as waste management and this would suggest (given that students were given free reign to select any article they felt appropriate) that power management is currently the most visible aspect of green IT.

Evaluating Current Practice at the University of Wales, Newport

At the University of Wales, Newport in the Department of Business & Computing, all staff members were asked to respond briefly to three questions. Only the responses from seven staff (out of nine) in the Division of Computing are considered here, and the questions with a summary of responses are given below:

1. Do you cover sustainability, environmental or global citizenship issues in any of the modules you teach, and if so where?

Interestingly, the answer to this question was almost entirely 'No' except for one respon-dent who covered battery technologies and their environmental implications in a postgraduate Mobile Computing module, and another respondent who covered sustainabil-ity issues in the first year Professional Skills module. However, it was argued that there was not enough space to cover skills-related curriculum in the module, and so some important sustainability content and discussion was unfortunately omitted to focus on the development of transferable skills.

2. Are any of these issues articulated in the learning outcomes for your modules, or in the indicative content?

Again the answer to this question was almost entirely 'No' except for one respondent who stated that ethical rather than sustainability issues were articulated in the learning outcomes. Another respondent suggested there was scope to include such issues in Software Engineering implications when considering more general engineering.

3. Do you think these issues are important in the modules that you teach, or should be better covered by other modules or at a programme level (such as in PDP activity or skills development sessions)?

Most staff stated that the issues are important and should be embedded and integrated into the modules. However one respondent was of the opinion that sustainability was a PDP issue and not for the modules, but acknowledged that s/he could be wrong. This is in contrast to another respondent who said:

"I think these issues would be better addressed within the modules rather than as a separate module in itself. I found a lot of students do not wish to fully engage in modules that they do not feel fit with their core study area (despite the efforts of lecturing staff to explain the importance of such a module)"

Conclusions

Inferences drawn so far at Plymouth demonstrate the willingness of a subset of students to engage with sustainable issues, and allowed reflection on the appropriate models for delivery of such material. It is clear that these issues need to be integrated into the assessments if they are to be fully developed, and this is contingent on them having been articulated in the learning outcomes which has been facilitated systematically at Plymouth at all of the levels of study, with the support of the Centre for Sustainable Futures. Computing provision at Newport is only just beginning to consider 'Green IT' within the curriculum, and the main finding to date is that staff believe that there should be an embedding of the issues in each of the modules rather than as 'peripheral' to their studies in a dedicated module, which some staff believe is counter-productive. This would suggest that it needs to be explicit in learning outcomes in the core modules, but clearly this needs to be tested out from research on students (and there is an ongoing ESDGC project funded by Newport's Centre for Excellence in Learning and Teaching to consider this), and necessitates further discussions within the Division of Computing in terms of what are the core modules, what are the key issues, and how best to achieve this.

Some computing lecturers at Newport are still unable to see the relevance to their 'technical' module area, so these issues are not considered at all, thus there is already a potential conflict in terms of developing approaches to ESDGC in this area. At postgraduate level, sustainability is considered in a module called Strategic Planning for Technology Management which is taught by one of the authors of this paper, and during assessment students each choose a different organisation and evaluate their strategic directions to include sustainability issues, in a similar way to the Plymouth approach. However, there is limited personal and career reflection, and much scope for further enhancement which can only be facilitated through incremental change processes to modify the intended learning outcomes that are linked to the assessments. There is opportunity for further work at Plymouth to evaluate the perceptions of staff teaching the computing and ICT modules and to consider how this relates to better assessment practice and outcomes for ESDGC.

In conclusion, one useful student quote from a Plymouth essay poignantly demonstrates the bigger challenge facing all institutions that teach computing and ICT:

"How are we supposed to develop skills to address the needs of Green IT when we are being taught current, not future, practice at University? The solution is to teach sustainable IT at University along with the rest of the course to incorporate new skills and ideals that are necessary to make a beneficial change in corporate IT".

REFERENCES

ASHFORD, W. 2008. Climate Change Act will have impact on IT. *ComputerWeekly.Com*. Available at www.computerweekly.com/articles/ (accessed 1/12/08).

BOCCALETTI, G. LOFFLER, M. OPPENHEIM J.M. 2008. How IT Can Cut IT Emissions, *The McKinsey Quarterly*, October, pp.1-5.

COOK, I. 2008. Green ICT: Economically Sound, Ecologically Sustainable, *National Computing Centre Guidelines for IT Management*, August, Issue 317, pp. 3-15.

ESKILLS UK. 2008. Industry Insights. Available at http://www.e-skills.com/cgi-bin/orad.pl/565/e-skillsUK_ ProfilesoftheIndustryandWorkforce_ Insights20082.pdf (accessed 20/4/09).

MURPHY, C. 2007. The Role of the IT Professional in Slowing Climate Change. *IT Adviser*, 51, Sept/Oct 2007, pp. 20-23.

SOCITM. 2009. News. Available at http://www.socitm.gov.uk/socitm/News/Press+Releases/20090123.htm (accessed 30/4/09).

SPARKES, M. 2008. Top 10 Tips for Green IT. *IT Pro*. Available at www.itpro.co.uk/608193/top-10-tips-for-green-it/ (accessed 13/11/08).

WHETSTONE, S. 2009. Eco Opportunities Come Knocking. *Computing*. 30th April, p.18.

WIKIPEDIA. 2009. Software as a Service. Available at http://en.wikipedia.org/wiki/Software_as_a_service (accessed 30/4/09).

University of Wales, Newport

Prifysgol Cymru, Casnewydd

Linking Research and Teaching in Higher Education
Simon K. Haslett and Hefin Rowlands (eds)
Proceedings of the Newport NEXUS Conference
Centre for Excellence in Learning and Teaching
Special Publication, No. 1, 2009, pp. 21-26
ISBN 978-1-899274-38-3

Sustainability and global citizenship as part of curriculum design in Higher Education: what approach works in changing the actual behaviour of today's students/tomorrow's decision makers?

Mary Hedderman, Alexandra Dobson and Brendan D'Cruz

Newport Business School, University of Wales, Newport, Allt-yr-yn Campus, Allt-yr-yn Avenue, Newport, NP20 5DA, United Kingdom. Email: mary.hedderman1@newport.ac.uk; alexandra.dobson@newport.ac.uk; brendan.dcruz@newport.ac.uk

Abstract

This paper outlines a research project currently underway to evaluate the specific contribution being made by Higher Education to Education for Sustainable Development and Global Citizenship (ESD&GC). The eighteen month project which commenced in January 2009 is collaborative involving the business schools of three diverse Higher Education institutions – Newport, Northampton and East London. The project aims to build on continuing work in the area of ESD&GC (known as ESD in England) through research focused on the area of curriculum design, delivery and assessment. The project will evaluate current practice and perceptions regarding issues of sustainability and global citizenship relating to four key groups of students across the three institutions: first year undergraduates, continuing undergraduates, postgraduates and part-time students. Areas for particular consideration will include recycling, corporate governance, ethical trade, tolerance, community engagement and power/energy, and be informed by the curriculum directions of professional bodies and public policy. The aim of the research is to inform curriculum design and contextual assessment that will impact on students' future behaviours in the workplace and the wider community. In this sense the project will endeavour to link students' actual and intended behaviours to ESD&GC rather than simply considering the location of ESD&GC within the curriculum. It is hoped that the research will not only instigate effective curriculum change across the participating business schools, but also help to re-evaluate practice across the wider HE sector.

Introduction

It is widely acknowledged that in order to ensure an acceptable quality of life for the current generation and the generations that will follow, there is a need for considerable change in the behaviour of both individuals and their respective nations. The United Nations declared 2005–2014 the Decade of Education for Sustainable Development (ESD) with the aim of facilitating behavioural change through a transformation within education (United Nations, 2009). Known as ESD in England and ESD&GC in Wales to incorporate Global Citizenship, the goal is to develop the knowledge, skills and understanding of individuals at all stages of education, from primary school onwards, to inform their future actions with regard to global citizenship and sustainability. According to ESD&GC Wales (2002): *"The role of Higher Education Institutions within ESD&GC is pivotal in that they educate a great number of professionals and leaders of tomorrow's society."*

In recognition of this important contribution to be made by Higher Education to ESD&GC, a collaborative research project between three Higher Education institutions, Newport, Northampton and East London is underway to determine the most effective practice within the sector in driving the required behavioural change in today's students. This paper will outline how this research project will build on the work of the ESD&GC, discuss the key issues to be investigated, and present the methodological aspects of the research.

Building on progress in terms of ESD&GC

Sibbel (2009) believes that sustainability education to date has been inadequate, primarily concerning itself with encouraging individuals to change their patterns of resource consumption and waste management. Sibbel (2009) suggests that as the professionals of the future, Higher Education students will be the 'designers' of the options from which consumers make choices and will therefore be in a position to influence real change. Sibbel (2009, p. 68) concludes that:

"To actualise the potential requires that Higher Education curricula offer experiences which develop graduates of self–efficacy, capacity for effective advocacy and interdisciplinary collaboration, as well as raise awareness of social and moral responsibilities associated with professional practice."

Moore (2005) researched existing university curriculum models and raised many questions about their effectiveness. It is, however, apparent that limited research has been done at the level of curriculum design and delivery and not in a form that allows direct comparison across a range of institutions. The crucial questions to be answered are firstly, whether current approaches within Higher Education are making any measurable difference in communicating an understanding of global citizenship and sustainability; and secondly,

whether this education and experience is leading to a change in behaviour. Arbuthnott (2009) argues that many ESD&GC programmes are designed to change attitudes, but her research indicates that there is a weak correlation between attitudes and behaviour; she suggests that teaching and learning must go beyond attitude change and actively encourage individuals to alter their behaviour. This research will, therefore, extend beyond an investigation of where ESD&GC is included within Higher Education programmes and examine how the learning experience at these institutions impacts upon the behaviour of students within a real world context. This will facilitate understanding of whether wider community and societal benefits are actually being realised or are likely to be realised in the future.

Like many other Higher Education institutions within the UK, each of the collaborative partners is engaged in implementing global citizenship and sustainability issues into the curriculum to a lesser or greater degree. However, practice does differ amongst the partners in that some institutions must conform to a central skills curriculum in which they use case studies to highlight sustainability issues (*e.g.* East London) whilst other institutions choose to embed the issues into specific module content and link these to intended learning outcomes (*e.g.* Northampton). Alternative approaches include extensive use of technology to help develop better cross-cultural awareness of the issues, or thematic approaches that are indicative of the needs of specific professional bodies and subject areas (*e.g.* Newport).

In 2002, a Welsh Assembly Government paper entitled *Education for Sustainable Development and Global Citizenship* (ESD&GC, 2009) outlined the key concepts for ESD&GC as: *interdependence* (between people, the environment and the economy - both locally and globally); *citizenship and stewardship* (recognising the importance of taking individual responsibility and action); *needs and rights* (including that of future generations); *diversity* (both human and biodiversity); *sustainable change* (understanding that resources are finite); *quality of life* (that basic needs must be met universally and that global equity and justice are essential elements of sustainability); *uncertainty and precaution* (embracing different approaches and the need for flexibility); *values and perceptions* (of less developed parts of the world); *conflict resolution* (an understanding of how conflicts are a barrier to development).

To bring some tangibility and measurability to the above concepts and to gain true insight into the experience of students and their intended behaviour, the research project will explore seven key areas:

1. Recycling – studying student perceptions and their current use, re-use and recycling behaviours.
2. Global citizenship – exploring student understanding of what is meant by global citizenship and the actions and behaviours required to become a global citizen.
3. Corporate Governance – investigating student awareness of current regulation and legislation and student views on the role of organisations with regard to corporate social responsibility.
4. Ethical and fair-trade purchasing – gaining insight into student behaviour regarding their own purchases and their perception of organisations with/without an ethical policy. It will also be interesting to discover whether the ethical position of an organisation affects students' choices when deciding which organisations that they would like to work for (*i.e.* their actual behaviour).
5. Tolerance – exploring student awareness and understanding of religious, cultural and political values.
6. Community engagement – to explore current student participation in and perception of volunteering, community participation and social activities and the contribution this makes to society.
7. Power/Energy – to investigate awareness of and intended actions regarding energy resources and climate change.

The research will consider whether an early introduction to the above issues and the associated curriculum beneficially impact upon the perceptions and behaviours of learners. Interestingly, Blaze and Wals (2004) stress the importance of graduates being able to contextualise their knowledge in an increasingly globalised society. It will, therefore, be important to evaluate whether embedding the issues into modules and programmes (including assessments) assists in contextualising the issues thus leading to better outcomes. It will also be of interest to investigate whether the incorporation of different types of skills could assist in encouraging a change in behaviour. In fact, Stephens *et al.* (2008) suggest that a curriculum that is intended to promote sustainability should incorporate skills of synthesis and integration. The project will also examine whether there are factors that influence the effectiveness of ESD&GC such as the mode of study, social background, demographic factors, entry standards and institutional approach. Considering ongoing changes in curriculum delivery, the use of technology-enhanced learning will also be examined to determine whether this can help promote access and raise awareness of the issues, thereby actively influencing behaviours.

There is likely to be considerable overlap between the areas under consideration within this research project and so care will be taken to triangulate the findings from the research. Since these institutions collectively embody a diverse range of students with varying entry qualifications, backgrounds and characteristics, this will enable the experience of all types of students to be considered. However, to manage the research effectively, four key (broad) groups have been identified: first year undergraduates, continuing undergraduates, postgraduates and part-time students. Within each of the target groups there will be broad age spectrum and students not only from within the UK, but also from the EU and International students. It will become evident that the research methods selected will allow different cultural perspectives to be examined. Since the project aims to determine if the Higher Education experience has driven a change in behaviour, it will also be important to explore the views and experience of the alumni at each of the business schools. This group will be considered separately as part of the ongoing research.

Methodological aspects of the research project

The implementation phase of the research will take place between September and December 2009. Whilst one of the aims of this research is to go beyond a discussion of where sustainability and global citizenship issues are included within the curriculum, it is essential to first 'audit' all of the information that is readily available. As Smith and Fletcher (2001, p.188) suggest:

"Critical to the holistic approach to the analysis of data is making sure you have a fully rounded understanding of how your problem 'nests' in the various 'contexts' and builds on existing management tuition and knowledge."

Sufficient background information must, therefore, be obtained to provide a firm foundation against which the student experience and intended behaviours can be considered. Since curriculum design and effectiveness aspects are key to this project, the first stage of the research will be to closely examine the differing institutional approaches and structures.

The members of the collaborative team will be assigned as project leaders for their respective institutions, charged with collating the necessary information. Liz Beaty, cited in Bourn *et al.* (2005) suggests that for graduates to perceive themselves as global citizens, institutions need to promote a culture that values sustainability and global human development. It is, therefore, of value to the research to consider whether the institutions actively promote their commitment to the issues under discussion. Evidence of this could include reference to sustainability and global citizenship within their mission statement, inclusion of the issues within the main communications tools employed such as the website(s), prospectuses and handbooks. Another area of interest will be to identify specific institutional initiatives in the area – perhaps an award scheme or links with external organisations within the field of sustainability and global citizenship.

Shephard (2008) discusses how, within Higher Education institutions, the teaching and assessment of sustainability and global citizenship tends to centre on the required knowledge and understanding, rather than on actual outcomes and behaviours. Since this research project aims to link the learning and teaching to actual behaviours, a comprehensive audit of the content of the programmes and modules at the respective institutions will need to take place, including the articulation of learning and assessment outcomes, and the extent to which real-world application is brought into the learning and assessment process.

It is also of great importance to gain insight into how lecturers at the participating institutions perceive and understand sustainability. Reid and Petocz (2006) describe varying ways in which lecturers view sustainability within their own subject areas, and the different type of suggestions they make for embedding sustainability into their modules. According to Reid and Petocz (2006, p.63):

"Real change in thinking about sustainability requires creative pedagogy which acknowledges the different ways that people think about sustainability and provides spaces in which their ideas can be developed."

Once the position and practice of each of the institutions has been established, this information will provide a firm foundation against which the student experience at each of the institutions can be considered. Since this research project aims to relate understanding of sustainability and global citizenship issues to everyday perceptions and behaviours of students, it will be essential to investigate whether current practice at the respective institutions is likely to lead (or has already led) to a measurable change in behaviour. A student survey will, therefore, be conducted across the three participating institutions to explore the views of the students in terms of their current actions and future intentions. This student survey is a complex undertaking in that there are four different target groups to be questioned across three diverse institutions. Research conducted by Roberts and Charles, cited in the National Foundation for Educational Research (2004), suggests that online surveys are an appropriate tool when the survey is large-scale, when respondents have easy Internet access and when up to date email addresses are readily available. Since this particular survey appears to fit these criteria, an online survey has been selected as the most effective method. There also tend to be fewer missing entries in web-based rather than paper surveys, and a reduction of researcher effects (Cohen *et al.*, 2007, p. 231). Additionally, it is useful to appreciate the 'cool factor' in that in trying to encourage participation of student groups, it could be argued that contemporary technological tools have more appeal and are more likely to result in an increased response rate when compared with more traditional research methods.

An initial investigation of the online surveys currently available and testimonies of past users would indicate that *Survey Monkey* would be an appropriate choice, allowing the survey to be constructed and distributed with relative ease and speed. The survey could generate a specific link that can be emailed to all target students with an invitation to participate, and a brief explanation of the research. This would allow the research team to view results as they are collected and 'drill down' to obtain individual answers – this will be important in understanding differing perceptions between the various groups participating and to monitor cultural differences. Since this is a collaborative research project, it is also useful that the survey results can be shared amongst the representatives of the various institutions. It will be necessary to include a combination of open and closed questions to effectively address the seven key areas. Closed questions will facilitate the provision of quantitative data for coding and cross-tabulation of results across the three institutions whilst open-ended questions will facilitate insight into

participants' attitudes and their understanding of the key issues (Proctor, 2003, p. 188).

It is anticipated that the online survey will provide comprehensive and valuable data. However, online surveys do not allow for further exploration of emerging themes. Of particular interest will be to explore the link between student attitudes as expressed in the survey and their ensuing behaviour in the real world. In other words, should the survey reveal that students' attitudes to sustainability have changed as a result of their learning experience then will this actually translate to a change in their behaviour in the workplace? Smith and Fletcher (2001) discuss this 'attitude behaviour link' and suggest that one-to-one interviews are an appropriate research method for exploring such connections. Localised interviews will, therefore, be organised to ascertain whether there has been or will be a real change in behaviour as a result of the student experience at the respective institutions. It is anticipated that this further investigation will add credence to the online student survey results.

In addition to the one-to-one surveys, focus groups - a growing area in educational research (Cohen *et al.*, 2007), will also take place to further explore the pertinent issues and to allow for triangulation with the other research methods. According to Proctor (2007, p. 210) focus groups will encourage free discussion of some of the key issues and the interaction between students has the potential to generate innovative ideas and suggestions.

As earlier discussed, since this research project places such emphasis on students' behaviour in the real world, it will be of great value to the research project to engage the alumni of the various institutions in the research project. It is anticipated that a questionnaire link will be sent via the alumni mailing lists at all three institutions. The questionnaire will aim to obtain quantitative data regarding the types of employment and roles and responsibilities of the alumni, and also qualitative information regarding their views on the Higher Educational experience and the extent to which it informs their decision making.

The analysis and interpretation phase of the research will take place between January and August 2010, and it is hoped that draft findings will be presented at Learning and Teaching conferences at the participating institutions.

Conclusion

The final report will be completed in December 2010 and will include findings and recommendations to influence the learning and teaching strategies at the respective institutions and, hopefully, within the wider Higher Education sector. It is hoped that the ultimate consequence of this research will be that, in keeping with the objectives of the ESD&GC agenda, an increasing number of students will leave Higher Education equipped with the knowledge, skills and ability to function as responsible global citizens within the workplace and beyond, building a sustainable world for future generations.

REFERENCES

ARBUTHNOTT, K. 2009. Education for sustainable development beyond attitude change. *International Journal of Sustainability in Higher Education*. **10** (2), pp.152-163.

BLAZE, P. and WALS, A. 2004. *Higher Education and the Challenge of Sustainability: Problematics, Promise and Practice*. Dordrecht, The Netherlands: Kluwer Academic Publishers.

BOURN, D., MCKENZIE, A. and SHIEL, C. 2006. *The Global University*. London. The Development Education Association.

COHEN, L., MANION, L., and MORRISON, K. 2007. *Research Methods in Education*. 6th edn. Oxon: Routledge.

ESD&GC WALES. 2009. Education for Sustainable Development and Global Citizenship. www.esd-wales.org (accessed 26/04/2009)

MOORE, J. 2006. 'Universities understanding of sustainability'. *Journal of Higher Education*. **51** (1). pp.105-123.

NATIONAL FOUNDATION FOR EDUCATIONAL RESEARCH. 2004. http://www.nfer.ac.uk/publications/other-publications/downloadable-reports/pdf_docs/AnnRep20032004.PDF (accessed 23/04/09)

PROCTOR, T. 2003. *Essentials of Marketing Research*. 3rd edn. Essex: Pearson Education.

REID, A and PETOCZ, P. 2006. University lecturers' understanding of sustainability. *Higher Education*. **51** (1), pp 105-123.

SHEPHARD, K. 2008. Higher Education for sustainability: seeking affective learning outcomes. *International Journal of Sustainability in Higher Education*. **9**(1), pp.87-98.

SIBBEL, A. 2009. Pathways towards sustainability through Higher Education. *International Journal of Sustainability in Higher Education*. **10** (1), pp. 68-82.

SMITH, D.V.L. and FLETCHER, J.H. 2001. *Inside information: Making Sense of Marketing Data*. Chichester: John Wiley & Sons.

STEPHENS, J., HERNANDEZ, M., ROMAN, M and SCHOLZ, R. 2008. Higher Education as a change agent for sustainability in different cultures and contexts. *International Journal of Sustainability in Higher Education*. **9** (3), pp.317-338.

UNITED NATIONS. 2009. Welcome to the UN. It's your world. http://www.un.org/ (accessed 18/04/09).

University of Wales, Newport

Prifysgol Cymru, Casnewydd

Linking Research and Teaching in Higher Education
Simon K. Haslett and Hefin Rowlands (eds)
Proceedings of the Newport NEXUS Conference
Centre for Excellence in Learning and Teaching
Special Publication, No. 1, 2009, pp. 27-33
ISBN 978-1-899274-38-3

The role of science within education for sustainable development and citizenship: sustainable development and citizenship within science education.

Ronald A. S. Johnston

School of Education, University of Wales, Newport, Lodge Road, Caerleon, South Wales, NP18 3QT, United Kingdom. Email: Ronald.johnston@newport.ac.uk

Abstract

The importance and difficulties of delivering science education for citizenship is considered in a curricular and wider life long learning context. The results of a pilot study, surveying students to identify reservations and opinions about science in this context, are considered and research questions for a wider study are identified on the basis of these results. The most effective approach for education for sustainable development and global citizenship (ESDGC) in a curriculum based context is also considered.

Introduction

This paper considers the (essential) role of science teaching and learning in the context of citizenship education and education for sustainable development (ESD) in the secondary, Further Education (FE) and Higher Education (HE) sectors. It identifies the difficulties which limit the use of science as a vehicle for enhancing the understanding of sustainable development and global citizenship issues. The intent here is not to separate the sciences from other disciplines but rather to identify the ways in which scientific understanding may complement and be complemented by these other disciplines.

The revised curriculum for Wales (2008) couples issues of sustainable development with issues of *global* citizenship (ESDGC) thus, linking local, regional and national issues within a global perspective (DCELLS, 2008). England, Scotland & Northern Ireland each have similar themes in their curricula, identified as Education for Sustainable Development (ESD) within which GC is also addressed to a greater or lesser degree.

However, it is the role of science education within the theme of *citizenship* and *global citizenship* that forms the central interest of this paper. Over the past two decades there has been a decline in interest in the sciences as evidenced by a reduction in number of students undertaking science courses. In this paper care has been taken not to become too involved in this parallel but separate question. Nevertheless, some consideration must be given to the potential social consequences for a scientifically illiterate society as a result of this decline.

The goals of ESDGC

Element A2 (Standard AS **2**) of the application guide to professional standards for teachers embedding Education for Sustainable Development and Global Citizenship advises that the teacher should:

"Understand that a goal of ESDGC is to enable action via informed discussion and debate which may inform lifestyle changes choices and so positively influence both the individual and society" (LLUK, 2009, p. 10).

It (LLUK, 2009) further notes in Element A4.2 that teachers of ESDGC should *"recognise the responsibility to present balanced information from a range of sources in order to enable critical thinking and informed debate"*.

These guidelines clearly show how ESDGC aims to contribute to the development of informed opinions, decision making processes and the taking of appropriate actions based on these decisions. With reference to science education this necessarily entails considera-tion of socio-scientific issues (SSI's); being those issues which "have a basis in science and which have a potentially large impact on society" (Ratcliffe and Grace, 2003, p. 1). Since citizenship implies participation in decisions made by society, scientific literacy is, therefore, essential to enable effective participation in many of the decisions necessitated by a heavily scientific and technologically dependent society. Waghid (2005), referring to citizenship education in a wider more general sense, identifies its important role in preparing students for informed participation in public dialogue about questions of justice and morality. It follows then that the greater the understand-ing of socio-scientific issues that an individual or group has, the better equipped they will be to make such decisions or adopt/oppose policies relating to these issues.

The problems/difficulties of science education for citizenship – or is it citizenship education for scientists.

So, it seems clear that science education is an excellent vehicle for citizenship issues and that everyone should welcome the role it has to play. Nevertheless, embedding citizenship education into science teaching is not without its problems. For most people the association between science as a subject and sustainable development is obvious in terms of efficient resource consumption, environmental management and conservation programmes. It is also clear how applied science relates to a wide range of environmental management strategies, risk management, energy policies, and to increased personal and social well-being through medical advances. This comparative ease of understanding may result from the fact that ESD has grown out of a blend of environmental studies and development studies curricula (Ratcliffe and Grace, 2003). However, it is not always so obvious how science learning may underpin citizenship issues. Whilst the link may be obvious in the minds of academics and educationalists, there may not be such a clear association in the minds of the general public, students and pupils. In fact, science may often be perceived as being the root cause of many non-sustainable and anti-social developments especially when its findings conflict with opinion, faith or are simply unpleasant truths.

One problem is that scientific information is communicated by means of a complex technical language. This in itself has the capacity to exclude and disenfranchise students and the public from a democratic role in socio-scientific decision making processes. In comparison with most humanities or social studies subjects, where there is in the main a commonly understood vocabulary, science uses a highly complex and technical language which must be learned first before personal understanding and effective communication of ideas can take place. This is often outside the comfort zone of many learners (particularly true of mature students returning to study) who find it difficult to know where to start learning this "obscure" language. Consequently, many people hold views informed by the media which itself often suffers from incomplete alarmist reporting and misinterpretation of the facts. As an example of this one only needs to note the controversy surrounding the MMR vaccine where in the first instance public response occurred more in response to alarmist reporting and misreported facts, rather than scientific fact (Deer, 2009). The issues here are of course not clear cut (Jardine, 2008), but what is clear here is that the science underpinning this SSI is greatly misunderstood and muddied by reportage to a confused and confusing degree. A survey reported in the *British Journal of General Practice* asking the source of parental information abut MMR established the TV as the major source (Pareek and Pattison, 2000).

So, here is an example where science for citizenship is also science for "self interest" and also a good driver of science self - education.

One of the key findings of the UNI-CEF2000 survey of Citizenship in UK Schools (Mackenzie, 2000) was that Religious Education, History and Geography and Personal, Social and Health Education at Key stages (KS) 3 and 4 are the most likely areas for teaching citizenship issues; perhaps because the terminology of the subject is familiar. An unintentional effect of this can be the development of a polarised understanding of the natural world (and perhaps society), where science and SDGC are viewed as belonging to separate conceptual frameworks (Johnston, 2002). Surprisingly, science would appear not to be the "natural home" for the teaching of citizenship related issues. Surprisingly, because in the context of the type of socio-scientific issues referred to above, a basic understanding of science would seem essential in order to appreciate the social and political impacts of developments in science and technology. In the absence of such an understanding many learners are effectively excluded from the decision making process and having a voice in the application of these developments (Hodson, 2003). Science teaching at KS3 and 4 in the 21st Century Science Curriculum (OCR) emphasises skills and enquiry and caters for all pupils. It recognises that only a small proportion of students will progress on to a career in science but that the great majority will also have a need to have an understanding of science and technology. This is important since as Ryder (2002) notes "school science is only the beginning of the process of learning to engage with science as an adult".

From a `life-long learning' and citizenship perspective it is important that individuals continue to learn (about?) science beyond school age. This raises a fundamental question when considering "embedding" citizenship studies in the science content: are we teaching science with the emphasis on scientific knowledge in order to understand more fully the implications of socio-scientific issues or are we teaching "about" science

which suggests that SSI's take precedence themselves; as perhaps has happened with he climate change as enshrined in most citizenship curricula. To make the importance of this distinction more evident it is worth noting the following extract from the Relevance of Science Education (ROSE) survey in Scotland (Finlayson and Roach, 2007, p. 6):

"Although pupils express concern about the environment and generally think that they can make a contribution to solving issues they show a general lack of interest in learning about causes of environmental damage such as the greenhouse effect and the ozone layer. ...."

Of course, the best answer is "both" but this pre-supposes that non-scientists concerned about SSI's are willing to and have the opportunity in a crowded curriculum to engage with the world of science. It is proposed that a useful exercise lies in identifying the gaps that exist in learners understanding of the joint concepts of science education and education for citizenship. A pilot study to explore this was undertaken recently and is reported below. A larger and more comprehensive study based on this is planned in the near future.

Pilot Survey of Attitudes and Perceptions Towards Science and Citizenship.

Methods

Likert survey data has traditionally been regarded as ordinal data (Likert, 1933) and there is much (unresolved) debate surrounding the treatment of Likert survey data as interval data (Jamieson, 2004). However, Lubke and Muthen (2004) suggest that true parameter values may be found in Likert survey data with certain assumptions; Wu and Tsai (2007, pp. 120-122) note that "it has become common practice to assume that Likert-type categories may constitute interval-levels of measurement". This assumption has been adopted here and in the pilot survey presented here. The ROSE survey (Finlayson and Roach, 2007) treats Likert data most effectively as interval data and this study was used as a template for the pilot survey discussed here.

The sample group consisted of 28 mature students enrolled on the Access course 2008/2009 at the University of Wales, Newport. The group was chosen on the basis of their engagement in a multi-disciplinary educational programme and the wide range of ages and backgrounds represented. Respondents were asked about the importance of science to themselves and society and their understanding of the terms sustainable development and citizenship. A four point Likert scale (ranging from very negative to very positive) was used in order to estimate the intensity of the respondent's point of view. On the 4-point scale the lowest two values (1.0 and 2.0) represent negative responses, whilst the highest two values (3.0 and 4.0) are weak and strong positive

responses. Where opinion is evenly divided, (negative responses being held as strongly positive responses) the mean Likert score will be 2.50. So values above 2.50 can be interpreted as 'net positive' and values below 2.50 as 'net negative' responses (Finlayson and Roach, 2007). Table 1 provides the specific questions with mean scores and associated standard deviations (Stdev). Figure 1 shows the variability of response for each question using a plot of the means against their standard deviation. Data points towards the top of the plot represent a high degree of variation in opinion across all respondents whereas points in the lower section part show strong levels of agreed with reduced variation. On the x–axis, negatively biased responses occur with mean scores <2.5 and positive ones >2.5.

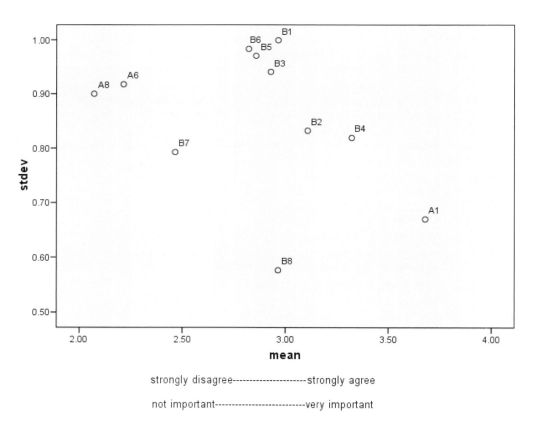

Figure 1. Means plotted against st.dev of Likert data in response to questions identified in Table 1.

		mean	Standard deviation
{A1}	Science and technology are important for society.	3.68	0.67
{A6}	Science and technology are the cause of problems in the world such as climate change.	2.21	0.92
{A8}	We should always trust what scientists have to say.	2.07	0.90
{B1}	How well do you understand the term: sustainable development?	2.96	1.00
{B2}	How well do you understand the term: citizenship?	3.11	0.83
{B3}	How well do you understand the term: global citizenship?	2.93	0.94
{B4}	How important to your quality of life are concepts of sustainable development?	3.32	0.82
{B5}	How important to your quality of life is the concept of citizenship?	2.86	0.97
{B6}	How important to your way of life is global citizenship?	2.82	0.98
{B7}	How important to your way of life is a good understanding of scientific issues?	2.46	0.79
{B8}	How important to society is a good understanding of science issues?	2.96	0.58

Table 1. Likert survey questions shown in Figure 1.

Results

- There was generally strong agreement about the importance of science to society with the results for {A1} gaining a strong positive response with a mean of 3.68 and a proportionally low Stdev 0.67. However, there was an extremely negative response to the trustworthiness of scientists themselves.
- Science and technology were not considered to be the cause of world problems {A6}, however, no great trust in scientists was shown {A8, mean 2.07}, although a varied response to this is suggested by the relatively high Stdev of 0.9. Considering, these responses together, if science is not responsible for the world's troubles then why are the scientists perceived as the problem?
- Questions {B7} and {B8} raise an interesting question in that while there was a high level of agreement that "a good understanding of science was necessary

for society" {B8, mean 2.96, Stdev 0.58} the importance of a good personal understanding of science was not so important in relation to the individual's way of life {B7, mean 2.46, Stdev 0.79}!
- Responses to {B1} and {B2} suggest that the terms SD and GC are only tentatively understood although with much variability across the sample, however, everybody seems confident about the term *citizenship* with high level of agreement with low Stdev.

In view of the small sample size conclusions cannot confidently be drawn from the responses returned. Nevertheless, certain broad considerations have shown up in the data which may be associated with some of the points made above and from which useful research questions may be generated for testing by more rigorous methods.

In general the results suggest that only slight importance was attached to the importance of GC to an individual's *quality* of life whereas SD was quite strongly viewed as a positive influence. The terms themselves however, were only slightly understood {B1, B2, B3} and this in itself merits revisiting in a future study. The acceptance of the essential role of science in society and rejection of science as the source of more problems than it solves {A6} is encouraging but at odds with the view that scientists should not always be trusted.

The importance of scientific issues being understood by society appears to take priority over personal understanding of the scientific issues. This is similar to the ROSE extract noted above where a SSI may be identified but followed by any desire to identify the facts which underpin it. To an extent this constitutes a relinquishment of responsibility for decision making and policy development. A further study will attempt to find the underlying reasoning for this response. Is this through lack of information, lack of choice or lack of interest?

Conclusions

It is proposed that most people are generally aware of the impacts of socio- scientific issues but frequently do not have the knowledge to understand their origin or their resolution. For science education to be effective as a vehicle for (global) citizenship studies it must associate SSI's with key concepts in science and this requires a curriculum shift at secondary FE and HE levels of education.

For the reasons noted above, science teaching and the inclusion of subject specific citizenship education in the form of ESDGC has a number of problems to overcome. Perhaps the concept of embedding ESDGC in discrete subject areas is not enough to introduce citizenship associated with SSI's to a wider audience and more informed audience since, this may also serve to reinforce the divisions that can exist between subject areas and fuel the mutual suspicion that the sciences and humanities can often be capable of. Instead, it is proposed that SSI's should be taught across all areas of the curriculum with clear supporting links between disciplines for a more inclusive approach to understanding

and resolving citizenship issues. For this reason it is suggested that as well as being subject orientated in a curriculum, citizenship studies should continue to maintain its own identity in secondary, FE and HE contexts. Certainly, the policy of embedding citizenship studies in all subjects has great merit but it is proposed that this should be an "as well as" rather than an "instead of" policy since the levels of impact that science can make on society in recent centuries demands inputs from all disciplines and vocations and a high developed social conscientiousness for the application of scientific advances to be considered real "progress".

REFERENCES

DCELLS, 2008. *Education for Sustainable Development and Global Citizenship: A Common Understanding.* Cardiff: Welsh Assembly Government.

DEER, B. 2009. MMR doctor Andrew Wakefield fixed data on autism. *Times [Online]* www.times online.co.uk/tol/life_and_style/health/article5 683671.ece (accessed 11/5/09).

DELLS, 2006. *Education for Sustainable Development and Global Citizenship – A Strategy for Action.* Cardiff: Welsh Assembly Government.

FINLAYSON, M., ROACH, A. 2007. *The Relevance of Science Education (ROSE) Survey.* The Scottish Executive, Transport, Enterprise & Lifelong Learning Department: STEM-ED Scotland.

HODSON, D. 2003. Time for action: Science education for an alternative future. *International Journal of Science Education*, 25, 645–670.

JAMIESON, S. 2004. Likert scales: how to (ab)use them. *Medical Education,* 38, 1212-1218.

JARDINE, C. 2008. MMR: The debate that won't go away. *Daily Telegraph* [online] www.telegraph. co.uk/health/children_shealth/3354907/MMR-The-debate-that-wont-go-away.html (accessed 11/5/09).

JOHNSTON, R. A. S. 2002. Wild Berwyn or coy nature reserve: a changing landscape. *Canadian Journal of Environmental Education*, 7 (2), pp. 166-178.

KERLINGER, F. N., LEE, H. B. 2000. *Foundations of Behavioural Research* (4th edition). Fort Worth, TX: Harcourt College Publishers.

LLUK (Life-Long Learning, UK) 2009. *Application of the professional standards for teachers embedding Education for Sustainable Development and Global Citizenship*. Cardiff: Welsh Assembly Government, in press.

LUBKE, G. H., MUTHEN, B. O. 2004. Applying Multigroup Confirmatory Factor Models for Continuous Outcomes to Likert Scale Data Complicates Meaningful Group Comparisons. *Structural Equation Modeling*, 11, 514-534.

MCKENZIE, A. 2000. *Citizenship in Schools: a baseline survey of curriculum & practice in sample English, Welsh & Northern Irish Education Authorities in Spring 2000*. London: UNICEF.

PAREEK, M., PATTISON, H. 2000. The Two-Dose Measles, Mumps and Rubella (MMR) Immunization Schedule: Factors Affecting Maternal Intention to Vaccinate. *British Journal of General Practice,* 50, 969-971.

RATCLIFFE, M., GRACE, M. 2003. *Science education for Citizenship: Teaching Socio-Scientific Issues*. Maidenhead, Philadelphia: Open University Press.

WAGHID, Y. 2005. Action as an educational virtue: toward a different understanding of democratic citizenship education. *Education Theory*, 55 (3): 323–343.

WELSH ASSEMBLY GOVERNMENT 2008. *Education for Sustainable Development and Global Citizenship Guidance for teacher trainees and new teachers in Wales*. Cardiff: Welsh Assembly Government.

WU, Y., TSAI, C. 2007. Developing an information commitment survey for assessing students' web information searching strategies and evaluative standards for web materials. *Educational Technology & Society,* 10(2), 120-132.

University of Wales, Newport

Prifysgol Cymru, Casnewydd

Linking Research and Teaching in Higher Education
Simon K. Haslett and Hefin Rowlands (eds)
Proceedings of the Newport NEXUS Conference
Centre for Excellence in Learning and Teaching
Special Publication, No. 1, 2009, pp. 35-41
ISBN 978-1-899274-38-3

Autocatalysm: a visual call to environmental action.

Milo Newman[1] and James Thomson[2]

[1]47 Yanley Lane, Long Ashton, Bristol, BS41 9LR, United Kingdom.
Email: milo_newman@hotmail.com

[2]21 Wingate Way, Cambridge, CB2 9HD, United Kingdom.
Email: james.thomson@students.newport.ac.uk

Abstract

Autocatalysm emerged as an open collaboration of ideas and work between two photographers Milo Newman and James Thomson. Its aim was to find new ways in which the visual arts, photography in particular, could be used to communicate the urgent issue of anthropogenic climate change. In January 2009, the authors held an exhibition of photographs at the Create Centre for the Environment in Bristol, during which time they also put together a symposium of talks and discussion, introducing the scientific concepts and discussing the way various artists have communicated the concepts in a variety of mediums. For the purposes of this paper, the text has been divided between the authors and each discusses their own projects, what inspired them and the exhibition itself.

Introduction by Milo Newman

Autocatalysm is a project undertaken by James Thomson and myself. Both James and I have studied on the undergraduate Documentary Photography course at the University of Wales, Newport, in the past few years, James graduating in 2009, myself in 2008. By using the visual arts we both realised that we could bring attention to the issues involved in anthropogenic climate change in an accessible way and try to affect change. Various films released during the past few years have attempted to bring people to focus their actions on the twin issues of anthropogenic climate change and the peak oil crisis. For example, Al Gore's engaging *An Inconvenient Truth* (2006), Basil Gelpke and Ray McCormack's *A Crude Awakening* (2006), as well as the recent *Age of Stupid* (2009) by Franny Armstrong. The increasing number of cinematic releases only serves to show the increasing urgency with which the creative industries are realising that they have a responsibility to attempt to draw attention to this subject. Acting individually to begin with, both James and I undertook our own photographic projects to try and contribute to this awareness building movement, later coming together to jointly exhibit our work.

Autocatalysm emerged as an open collaboration of ideas and work between us both. Its aim was to find new ways in which the visual arts, photography in particular, could be used to communicate the urgent issue of anthropogenic climate change. In January 2009, we held an exhibition of photographs at the Create Centre for the Environment in Bristol, during which time we also put together a symposium of talks and discussion, introducing the scientific concepts and discussing the way various artists have communicated the concepts in a variety of mediums. For the purposes of this paper, in a change perhaps to the traditional paper formats, we have divided the text between us and will each be discussing our own projects, what inspired them and the exhibition itself.

Milo Newman

Till the Slow Sea Rise

Beginning my project about eighteen months ago I have undertaken a series of journeys in winter along areas of the British coast. The areas picked in which to photograph were low-lying areas of shoreline, which provided a conceptual integrity for the subsequent photographs as these landscapes are threatened by the rise in sea levels promised by anthropogenic climate change. The decision to photograph in winter was mainly an aesthetic one, the wintry light provided a suitably melancholic backdrop for the feelings and concepts I was trying to portray, although as I later realised, the winter weather blowing in from the sea came to represent the threat of increasing number of violent storms predicted by scientists as oceanic temperatures rise.

The subsequent images are direct responses to these landscapes, as well as to vernacular objects found within them, speaking of the wider social and environmental themes involved. The photographs are meditations on the concepts of transience and fragility, shattering the illusions of permanence that we have built up around our social and architectural endeavours. They speak of change and what may become of our society should we continue our unsustainable practices, aiming at the goal set by landscape photographer Robert Adams (1996, p. 20), who wrote that "the main business of landscape art is a rediscovery and revaluation of where we find ourselves".

Robert Adams is an environmentally aware photographer, whose vernacular innovations provided a great inspiration for my project. His photographs deal with the areas where human civilization and the natural environment collide. For example, his book *Turning Back* (2005) deals with clearcutting in his home state of Oregon.

His work showed me that scenes of environmental degradation could by captured with dignity and intelligence, as well as conveying strong emotions and at the same time remaining beautiful and thus engaging to the viewer. The question of engagement is key; considering the severity and urgency of our problem I realised that any artistic endeavour dealing with it must be accessible and it must be engaging so as to encourage the viewer to try and do something about it.

Adams' work follows in a photographic lineage from that of another American, Walker Evans. Both photographers being interested in the vernacular and also in the links between photography and literature; Adams himself took up the camera after working as an English teacher for many years and has subsequently written several volumes of essays on the subject of photography. Walker Evans often pointed out the links between photography and literature in interviews and described his own work as "lyric documentary" (Hill, 1993). Another photographer, Alec Soth (2007, p. 2) elucidates this idea when talking about his own work "I draw more from poetry than anything else. For me it is the medium most similar to photography. I take a lot from the way these poets assemble images, incorporate vernacular and invent rhythm." The sequence of photographs from the beginning of Soth's (2004) book *Sleeping by the Mississippi* is a good example.

The opening image of the houseboat leads into the second image of Charles due to the similar atmosphere of the two pictures, the identical backgrounds of skeletal winter trees continue the narrative flow, as do the wood clad buildings that are depicted in each image. The link between the photograph of Charles and the image of Charles Lindebergh's boyhood bed is of a different, more conceptual kind. The key to the narrative are the two planes held by Charles. These link to the fact that Charles Lindebergh was the first man to fly solo across the Atlantic in the Spirit of St. Louis in 1927. The rest of the book follows in a similar vein, with each picture leading on to the next one; this idea of the narrative is something I find very exciting both within my own work and that of others. When I look through a book of well-sequenced photographs I am reminded of the words written by Nobuyuki Yuasa (1966, p. 14) to explain the narrative flow of linked verse Japanese haiku poems:

"Note how each poem takes up the suggestion of the preceding poem and yet opens up a new world of its own, so that the reader is carried through the whole series as through the exquisitely arranged rooms of a building, always entertained by delightful changes but never arrested by sudden contradictions."

During my initial research for the project I came across numerous examples of writers or poets whose work deals with, or can be read as dealing with some of the concepts of anthropogenic climate change. Also, the poem *A Forsaken Garden* by the Victorian poet Charles Algernon Swinburne has provided a great inspiration for my project and eerily predicts the issues we face today (Findlay, 2002).

It is not only poetry though that provides such strong imagery, *The Peregrine* by the English writer J. A. Baker (1966) follows the author as he wanders the flat coastal landscape of Essex near his home during the cold months of one winter. The book chronicles month by month his attempts to reconnect with his environment as he pursues a Peregrine Falcon, which haunts the sky above the marshes. The book deals fundamentally with the increasing disconnection between our modern society and the environment, for example:

"at three o'clock, a man walked along the sea-wall flapping with maps. Five thousand dunlin flew low inland, twenty feet above his head. He did not see them. They poured like a waterfall of shadow on to his indifferent face" (1966, p. 46).

After reading passages such as this in the book, described with a sense of profound sadness by the author I realised that my life too, was tragically distant from its environment. This disconnection seemed to be one of the key factors in our continuing degradation of our planet, for if there is a connection between man and his environment there develops affection, or even a love for it, and thus a desire to look after it. It became clear that if my project was to be successful I needed to reconnect with the landscape in which I was to work and the subsequent

journeys I undertook, walking as a nomadic photographer along areas of low lying coastline allowed me to re-establish a vital personal connection with the landscape and the natural environment.

Further, by walking the distance of shoreline, not only was the ethical integrity of the project upheld (walking does not emit carbon dioxide into the atmosphere), but also added a further conceptual dimension into it. The photographs themselves act as an imagining of the future, so the method of the project, of walking, and camping outside without comforts became a sort of macabre vision of a future of wandering refugees in a world without civilization.

The photograph of the road (Figure 1) is a continuation of this thought. The road depicted was submerged twice a day by the rise and fall of the tide, the tarmac broken and crumbling from the erosion caused by this cycle, the water lingers from the flood reflecting the light from the sky above as the storm clouds pass and the tide recedes. In the distance the sand dunes stand tall but fragile. It reminds me of some of the passages from Cormac McCarthy's stunningly bleak book *The Road* (2007).

Figure 1. Untitled photograph by Milo Newman.

The main characters of McCarthy's novel are a man and son who wander as nomads through the landscape of a burnt and empty world. No clue is given to what catastrophe befell civilization and the book is all the more ominous for it; for it could be a landscape of a world post-global warming. At various points in the book the father has flashbacks, in one of which is described the scenes of refuges abandoning the cities and taking to the road:

"In those first years the roads were peopled with refugees shrouded up in their clothing. Wearing masks and goggles, sitting in their rags by the side of the road like ruined aviators. Their barrows heaped with shoddy. Towing wagons or carts. Their eyes bright in their skulls. Creedless shells of men tottering down the causeways like migrants in a feverland. The frailty of everything revealed at last" (2007).

There is a connection here with a quote taken from the feature film documentary *Age of Stupid*. In an interview in the film Alvin DuVernay, a survivor of Hurricane Katrina describes the aftermath of the catastrophe and its effect on him:

"I lost everything. Everything that I owned. From family heirlooms to the paper towels sitting on the kitchen counter. And the grief that comes with that is just, it's, it's profound" (Armstrong, 2009).

In both cases the tremendous fragility of civilization becomes clear, McCarthy (2007) writes of the frailty of everything being revealed, of people homeless and dispossessed, but such terrible things are already being seen in our climatically unstable world as proved by the destruction of New Orleans at the hands of a violent hurricane. The terrifying thing is that the bleak fiction imagined by McCarthy in his novel is

becoming a reality. Using photographs I have tried to depict this destructive force waiting to be unleashed on our society. For example, by sequencing a series of images together (Figures 2-4) a house is turned to rubble at the hand of the sea.

It is not however only humanity that is threatened by anthropogenic climate change; much of the diversity of the natural world faces extinction due to our actions and the unpredictability of a changing planet. The image of the skeins of pink-footed geese (Figure 5) describes this thought; it provokes a feeling of tremendous fragility. I remember standing on the shore in a frozen December dusk watching the huge flocks flying out over the mud flats of the Wash in Norfolk from a distance they looked as thin and as a fragile as a wisp of smoke pulled apart by the wind. The following morning as they flew back inland to feed through the mist I made this photograph. I was reminded of the words of Vladimir Norbokov who wrote:

"Beauty plus pity – that is the closest we can get to a definition of art. Where there is beauty there is always pity for the simple reason that beauty must die: beauty always dies" (Soth, 2006, p. 101).

Seen from a different angle however, the thin lines continue to evoke feelings of fragility but then as it emerges overhead the very shape of the skein seems as an arrow pointing forward suggesting a society striving towards a higher purpose and it becomes an image of fragile hope.

Figure 2. Untitled photograph by Milo Newman.

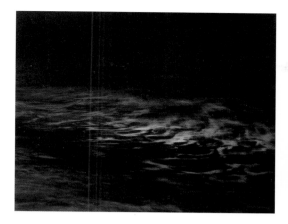

Figure 3. Untitled photograph by Milo Newman.

Figure 4. Untitled photograph by Milo Newman.

The project remains a work in progress; the narrative I wish to construct requires pictures that I have so far been unable to capture. As to the more important question of whether humanity can work its way out of the mire it has immersed itself in I swing violently between optimism and mournful pessimism. At my worst and most doubtful I believe that the ugliness we have wrought over the face of the planet far outweighs the beauty we have created and perhaps the world will be better off without our corrupt and malignant form of stewardship. But on the other hand, as if balanced on a fragile scale I find there is art, and the remaining fragile beauty of the world, and its inhabitants. At such times I often ask myself what use is photography or art when facing such seemingly insurmountable issues and I become morose at what seems like the pointlessness of it all. But I take solace from something Robert Adams (1996, p. 70) once wrote in one of his essays:

"Photography as art does address evil, but it does so broadly as it works to convince us of life's values; the darkness that life combats is the ultimate one, the conclusion that life is without worth and is finally better off ended. And though poems and pictures cannot by themselves save anyone – only people who care for each other face to face have a chance to do that – they can strengthen our resolve to agree to life."

Figure 5. Untitled photograph by Milo Newman.

In the end I realise that there is no point in negativity. We have to try, it is our duty to try, all of us as individuals to do what we can, to do what we love and do the best we can do with what we have and to strive together for our planets future.

James Thomson

The apocalyptic imagination is a strange thing to deal with, but for artists like us making steps to take on the subject in question – it has been a necessary right of passage towards change. What it offers, in relation to the practice of photography; is the chance to live out the very worst within the subjectively broken world around us and provide the option of avoiding it in the landscape of reality. A quote that inspired the making of the body of work is one by Michael Ortiz Hill (2004, p. 53) who wrote that:

"we are far more likely to participate in the world's destruction by clinging to the fiction of our innocence than if we have a conscious and living relationship with the darker aspects of our own nature."

Given the depressing nature of the subject matter it was a relief and a weight off my shoulders to be working with Milo exchanging visual ideas and combining our research from the last year. This process was an inspiration to both of us. It soon became clear that if a visual arts campaign of any significance were to be mounted to draw public awareness to the race against runaway climate change then it would have to be made together. It seemed necessary and urgent to work together to get the ideas freely flowing between us. In light of the enormous problem we face with the issues of climate change it seemed that nothing was going to get done if we worked alone as individual artists.

Within the venue for the exhibition in Bristol we discovered a small lecture theatre that was available to hire alongside the gallery space, which we decided to make use of for an afternoon of talks. From our research we gathered that very few institutions have decided to hold a symposium event to discuss representation of climate change through the visual arts. One that was held at Cambridge University charged £20 for student entry, limiting the amount of people that would come and be inspired by the talks.

Without any money behind us, our proposed keynote speakers were less than eager to leave London to talk for us. But fortunately a small minority of people cared enough, and were willing to speak for nothing, allowing us to stick to our guns and hold the event for free. These generous people included our chair, Ed Gillespie, Creative Director of Futerra. With Ed's knowledge of the advertising industry and Professor Simon Haslett's in depth understanding of the science at the heart of the anthropogenic climate change debate an action plan was galvanized.

On the day of the talks we became aware that many of those that turned up were not fully aware of the scientific process underlining the issue. To this point Haslett's lecture was invaluable, as he explained the fundamentals in an easily accessible way. While Birgit Muller, an artist from Bristol talked about her experience as an artist attempting to deal with the issues in her installation 27 Kilos.

Filling the seats at the symposium were policy makers, members of independent think tanks, photographer's (both amateur and professional alike), lots of art students, bicycle route planners – all sorts. We were fortunate to have with us Lauren Muchan and Joe Sharpe from the BA Documentary Film course at Newport who kindly documented the proceedings for others benefit (the films have since been uploaded to the Autocatalysm Youtube channel where they can be watched for free).

Scrawling through the database that is YouTube I became quickly aware of the growing number of Universities – particularly in America – that are now broadcasting lecture series for free onto Youtube for the benefit of others. We value this altruism for it is this type of behaviour that will help bring about change. The University of California has spearheaded this movement with their collaboration with the Center for Information Technology Research in the Interest of Society (CITRIS). Between the Berkeley, Davis, Merced and Santa Cruz campuses over 400 individual lectures have been uploaded on relevant issues such as Professor Grey Niemeyer's thesis that computer games can be used to invoke thought about climate change with its users:

"They see solutions to many of the concerns that face all of us today, from the environment and finding viable sustainable energy alternatives to healthcare delivery and developing secure electronic medical records and remote diagnosis, ultimately boosting economic productivity. CITRIS represents a bold and

exciting vision that is leveraging one of the top university systems in the world with highly successful corporate partners and government resources." (CITRIS – SOURCE: Youtube)

Perhaps one conclusion that can be made from the experience is that if artists and students are to become engaged in the issues of anthropogenic climate change they need to be encouraged to do so through events, films, photographs and the arts.

REFERENCES

ADAMS, R. 1996. *Beauty in Photography: Essays in Defence of Traditional Values.* New York: Aperture.

ADAMS, R. 2005. *Turning Back: A Photographic Journal of Re-exploration.* U.S: Distributed Art Publishers.

ARMSTRONG, F. 2009. *The Age of Stupid*

BAKER, J. A. 1966. *The Peregrine.* New York: The New York Review Books.

CITRIS (Center for Information Technology Research in the Interest of Society) 2009. Available at http://www.youtube.com/user/citrisuc .

CRASSH 2008. Representing Climate Change: Ecology, Media and the Arts. Available at http://www.crassh.cam.ac.uk/events/546/.

FINDLAY 2002. *Selected Poems of Algernon C Swinburne.* London: Routledge.

GELPKE, B. 2006. *A Crude Awakening: The Oil Crash.*

GORE, A. 2006. *An Inconvenient Truth.*

HILL, J. 1993. *Walker Evans: The Hungry Eye.* New York: Henry N. Abrams.

HILL, M. O. 2004. *Dreaming the End of the World: Apocalypse as a Rite of Passage.* Connecticut: Spring Publications.

McCARTHY, C. 2007. *The Road.* Picador.

SOTH, A. 2004. *Sleeping by the Mississippi.* Gottingen: Steidl.

SOTH, A. 2006. *Niagara.* Gottingen: Steidl.

SOTH, A. 2007. *Fashion Magazine.* New York: Magnum Photos.

YUASA, N. 1966. *Matsuo Basho The Narrow Road to the Deep North and Other Travel Sketches.* Harmondswoth: Penguin Classics.

University of Wales, Newport

Prifysgol Cymru, Casnewydd

Linking Research and Teaching in Higher Education
Simon K. Haslett and Hefin Rowlands (eds)
Proceedings of the Newport NEXUS Conference
Centre for Excellence in Learning and Teaching
Special Publication, No. 1, 2009, pp. 43-52
ISBN 978-1-899274-38-3

The role of local media as an educational tool in sustainable community development: Aylesbury Estate in South East London.

Tatiana A. Diniz

Centre for Excellence in Learning and Teaching, University of Wales, Newport, Lodge Road, Caerleon, South Wales, NP18 3QT, United Kingdom.
Email: Tatiana.araujodiniz@students.newport.ac.uk

Abstract

Council estates with high levels of social housing situated close to London South Bank University, in South London, are targeted to go through complex regeneration schemes during the next decades. According to the official campaigns, some neighbourhoods will be knocked down and rebuilt to become "sustainable communities". This work examines the process of change experienced by residents in the Aylesbury Estate, in South East London, home of approximately 7,500 people, and tries to explore an intersectional zone between EfS, urban planning and communication. Methods included sampling 50 residents with a face-to-face questionnaire and analysing the contents of two sources of information distributed in the estate. Results verified a lack of dialogue between the local people's understanding of issues related to sustainability and the official intentions advertised by those running the regeneration plans, and revealed that local media is not properly contributing to clarification of the residents' uncertainties. Findings highlight a room for future action of educators and policy makers and unveil the possibility of future partnership with Higher Education institutions in the implementation of educational models of participatory media in the studied area, as well as in other neighbourhoods that are to face similar transitions.

Introduction

Calls for "sustainable communities" highlights the current intentions of British urban planning. This paper focuses on the context of urban regeneration and tries to verify possible opportunities for introducing Education for Sustainability (EfS) as a complementary approach to the official goals of redeveloping metropolitan housing areas, considering its potential to future implementation of community-based learning agendas. In addition, a dialogue between EfS and the media field is attempted, claiming a possible role to be played by local media as an educational tool to enhance participation and awareness regarding issues that are to affect communities' realities throughout their change to become sustainable.

The investigations here presented were concentrated in the case study of the Aylesbury Estate, in South East London, home of approximately 7,500 people. Official targets agreed for this area are to knock down and rebuild all the existing blocks during the next 15 years in order to create a "sustainable community" (Southwark Council, 2007). The chosen council estate seems emblematic for some historic reasons. In 1997, former British Prime Minister Tony Blair chose it as the backdrop of his first speech as an illustration of the challenge in regenerating Britain's inner cities (Leftly, 2007). In 2002, a local ballot pointed out that most of the tenants preferred refurbishment to demolishing the buildings (Dennis, 2005). By the time the research was carried out, I had been living in the estate for 14 months.

The purpose of this study was to investigate how Aylesbury Estate residents were relating to the official aims of making the area become a "sustainable community" through 15 years of regeneration. Furthermore, it tried to assess similarities and differences between the local people's ideas of sustainability and the ones presented by two local sources of information.

Literature Review

Barton (2002, p. 5) defines community as "a network of people with common interests and expectations of mutual recognition, support and friendship". For him, the term is not a synonymous with neighbourhood, which, according to this author, "is essentially a *spatial* construct, a place".

In the late sixties, the idea of community went through some severe conceptual enquiries when authors within the sociology field argued that the overuse of the term had led to a loss of its meaning (Stacey, 1969). However, along with the aims for sustainability applied to neighbourhoods, behavioural aspects of community life have been recalled.

Gilchrist (2002) advocates that the exchange among friends and neighbours equips them to consume less non-renewable resources once they gain the possibility of sharing, borrowing and bartering. He also believes that this exchange influences personal decisions to be made taking a sense of collectivism and avoiding "wasteful and distressing mistakes" (Gilchrist, 2002, p. 148).

Taking globalization, migration and citizenship into account, multiculturalism comes up as an aspect that calls for attention in contemporary community settlements, and despite the fact that a proper approach to multiethnic societies remains unknown, past experiences have shown that participation enhances the feeling of belonging to a place (McCarney, 2006).

Regeneration plans often happen through gentrification, defined in the literature as "rehabilitation of working-class or derelict housing and the consequent transformation of an area into a middle class neighbourhood" (Smith and Williams, 1986, in Bridge, 1993, p. 1). Criticisms were addressed to this approach of urban planning by the supporters of the Chicago School of Sociology who faced it as a process in which "the metabolism of the city was most out of balance" (Park, 1926, in Bridge, 1993, p. 5).

Between 1987 and 1989, Bridge (1993) carried out research in the district of Sands End, in West London, while the neighbourhood experienced the gentrification of its Victorian terraces and the transformation of its riverside into a luxury residential and commercial zone (today named Chelsea Harbour and Sans Wharf). Throughout the mixing of different social classes in the area, the author verified a lack of involvement and some social tension between old residents and newcomers, but argued that the traditional "yuppie invader/working-class resistor explanation" was inadequate. He calls for a city-wide scale analysis able to reach concerns about work and workplace as well as residence and home (Bridge, 1993, p. 26). Apparently, urban regeneration often places face-to-face those who are and those who are not "doing well" in an economy oriented to profit and to wealth accumulation, rather than promotes expectations regarding a common future.

Many of London council estates carry a reputation for crime and social problems and, therefore, face severe prejudice within British society (Reeves, 2005; Hall and Knight, 2007). This impacts in the inhabitants' self-esteem and such effect can become worse if regeneration pushes them into segregation. Agenda 21 recognizes that any plan willing to reach sustainability needs to take into account local people's needs (UNCED, 1992). Similarly, the relevance of local people's engagement in urban planning is claimed by different authors (Colenut and Cutten, 1994; Fagan, 1996).

Media and Voice

This paper tries to suggest that Media and EfS are intrinsically linked and, therefore, can be approached as interrelating fields of study. Many authors point out the predominance of an "elite consensus" in the news and advocate that the worldwide transmission of neo-liberal core values operates as a complex structure of ideological domination (Herman and Chomsky, 1998, in Clarke-Patel and Parker, 2001, p. 20).

Conversely, other commentators focus on changes that have been impacting communication processes throughout globalization and consider them potential accelerators for local activism. For them, in the information age and with the development of new technologies, we are witnessing the rise of more autonomous and participative approaches of news making that can divert and even challenge the predominant mainstream influence (Coyer, 2005). Atton (1999) defines alternative media as those "conceived as methods of achieving social and political action" and, therefore, the ones that assume a social role that is beyond simply delivering information.

Indeed, both media's top-down ideological imposition and bottom-up engaging possibility currently coexist and this could justify the effort to explore participatory media as an educational tool in urban settings to be regenerated, giving voice for those who will have their lives transformed by the plans.

Reflecting on housing, the terminology "voice" is presented in the literature as a capacity that can directly contribute to the empowerment of the local people. Glennerster and Turner (1993) argue that voice can be an effective form of pressure and "the only realistic option for deprived estates" (Glennerster and Turner, 1993, in Stuart and Taylor, 1995, pp. 25-26). Chamber's (1997, p. 118) comments on how giving a voice to excluded locals can be "putting the first last": "those who are powerful have to step down, sit, and listen, and learn from and empower those who are weak and least".

Methodology

This work tried to provide elucidative numbers regarding the study of a chosen sample, but the main characteristics of social science research are largely predominant. Henwood and Pidgeon (1993, p. 18) observe that traces of quantitative approach hold the possibility of strengthening qualitative research, and mention simple counting techniques as an example.

Moreover, critical theory is a paradigm that contributed to the choice of the adopted research design. Fay (1987, p. 33) defines a critical theory as the one that "wants to explain a social order in such a way that it becomes itself the catalyst which leads to the transformation of this social order." According to critical theorists (Habermas, 1973; Hillcoat, 1996), theory is assessed to generate political action and, therefore, knowledge is never neutral. As I was a resident in the estate, my neighbours talked to me as "one of them" as we shared common concerns, which added a political emphasis to my role.

Choosing the Aylesbury Estate as a case study allowed me to look for "human-scale" data that could be gathered as a sample of the wider sociological experience of targeting deprived areas to become sustainable communities (Cohen *et al.*, 2007, p. 255). The fact that I have lived in the estate also allowed me to adopt an ethnographical approach by collecting "whatever data are available to throw light on the issues that are the focus of the research" (Hammersey and Atkinson, 1983, p. 1).

Methodological Approaches

Two different approaches were applied during the investigations. The first was surveying a sample of 50 residents with an in-depth questionnaire to assess how people were dealing with the idea of regeneration, how they understood "sustainability" and "sustainable community" and how they related to the local media coverage of the plans to the area.

I adopted a convenient sampling method (Cohen *et al.*, 2007, p. 176) in which the main parameter was to approach residents explaining the purposes of my survey and welcoming those who were happy to take part. Therefore, participation was non-selective.

Generalising findings is a complex issue in social research as results can often fail to represent a whole heterogeneous population (Schofield, 1989). Aiming to ensure a reasonable level of generalizability of the sample's results within the estate, I did the survey in different blocks, tried to achieve some balance between gender and age groups and followed different timetables to reach those who worked full-time, studied or were mostly at home.

The applied questionnaire was divided in three parts. The first focused on interviewees' ideas about the estate in the present and as "sustainable community" in the future. The second aimed to rank the local priorities amongst different topics related to sustainability. The last part recorded reactions and impressions about the two sources of information delivered in the area covering issues related to the planning intentions. Most of the questions had multiple choices answers, which were combined to open questions in order to ensure triangulation.

During October 2008, I piloted the questionnaire with five residents of different age groups and improved it based on their feedback. Ethical concerns were addressed at this point, and after listening to parents/guardians I decided to require verbal consent or the supervision of a responsible adult to interview those aged between 10 and 17 years old. This procedure also followed the ethical guidelines published by the British Educational Research Association (BERA, 2004, p.7).

The quantitative data was transformed in charts based on the general responses. The topics related to the local comprehension of sustainability; however, analysis demanded specific graphics demonstrating results within age groups. Dealing with the answers to the open questions was complex, as my intention was not simply reproducing the best comments but also systematically congregate the most mentioned issues. For this reason, I assembled comments according to themes and tried to summarize general views highlighting predominant arguments.

The second approach of the investigation complemented the face-to-face survey. During 12 months, I collected printed information delivered in my flat about the proposed regeneration. Two types of publications caught my attention: a regularly delivered collection of glossy magazines entitled *Aylesbury Regeneration News*, published by local authorities Aylesbury New Deal for Communities/Creation and South-wark and a couple of informal leaflets done by the Tenants' Association without any patterns of regular distribution.

After recording and analysing the questionnaire results, I focused on the content of this local media material, searching for features advertised as "sustainable" and comparing them with the views on sustainability unveiled by the survey. This coding system equipped me to go beyond any initial "predictions" that had motivated my work, helping me to better deal with unexpected results (Gage, 1991).

Research Findings

The survey was carried out in November and December 2008 and 50 people were interviewed, of which 27 were female and 23 male. Seven residents were aged between 10 and 18 years old; 11 were from 19 to 32; 15 were between 33 and 45; 8 were 46 to 55; and 9 were over 55 years old. The time of residence in the area varied from less than one year to more than 20 years, with approximately half of the sample had been living in the estate for more than 10 years.

The majority of interviewees declared they did like living in the estate, as 39 participants declared so. The number was more than three times larger than those who said they did not like it or they did not know it. Similar results came up regarding safety, with 37 people who said they felt safe in the area. Focusing on regeneration and its communication, most of the interviewees affirmed they did hear about the plans of regenerating the area, although a high number declared they did not receive enough information about it. In addition, the slight preponderance of participants who believed rebuilding the estate could make their lives better was closely followed by numbers of those who said they did not know it or they did not believe it, demonstrating regeneration is still synonymous with uncertainty for many.

The survey verified if interviewees knew what "sustainability" means, without asking them to explain the meaning of the term. The aim was to check if they would declare having any subjective views related to sustainability or would mention the word was meaningless for them. The amount of people who declared they did not know what sustainability means (26) was larger than those who said they knew it (see Figure 1). Results were similar within almost all age groups, but amongst those who were more than 55 years the number of residents who said the word was meaningless was twice higher than those who declared knowing it.

An open question helped me to gather details on how people imagined the estate as a "sustainable community", and comments are summarized bellow:

"The Aylesbury Estate will be a sustainable community with people who care and who can rely on themselves. There will be more interaction between neighbours to fight together for the community so that it will be less dependent on the government. There will be facilities around and more jobs in the area. The environment will be friendly, with parks and playgrounds. The buildings will look more like houses and they will be different one from each other. They could be eco-friendly and the common areas could be equipped with recycling community bins and routes to cycle. Also, we could have a system to locally recycle water and waste. Transport links could be better so that people would not need to use their cars as much as they do now. The estate will not be so dense anymore, there will be more space inside the flats and outside the buildings will look nice. It will be safer and cleaner, there will be proper

maintenance, the heating will not stop and we will not need electric heaters on. There will be less problematic families and more polite people will come. Even still, the house prices will remain affordable. Finally, there will be no more knife crime and gun crime in the Aylesbury."

The content of the open answers were impressive for their practical approaches, showing that the local people were concerned about environmental issues as well as presented a willingness to foster empowerment and participation. Additionally, most of the respondents (31) affirmed they believed the estate could become sustainable through regeneration, taking into account their own ideas of a sustainable community (see Figure 2). Within all age groups, more than a half of interviewees shared this opinion.

In the News

The presence of articles/information related to sustainability in the two local publications was restricted. In both magazines and leaflets analysed, there was almost no room given to coverage reflecting on how the estate could become a sustainable community or what steps would be necessary to achieve this target. Each publication explored a setting of opponent views, with the magazines campaigning for the regeneration and the leaflets, against it.

A discreet column is dedicated to the topic "Sustainable Development" in issue 13 of *Aylesbury Regeneration News*, and the "key points" listed as strategic measures to create a sustainable community are: aiming zero carbon growth; homes with insulation; individual control of heating and encouraging wild life (Aylesbury New Deal for Communities/Creation/Southwark Council, 2008,13, p. 3). Compared with the practical topics pointed out by residents, the official strategic aims to reach sustainability are somewhat abstract.

"Do you know what the word *sustainability* means?"

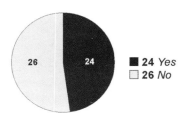

■ 24 *Yes*
☐ 26 *No*

Partial results within age groups

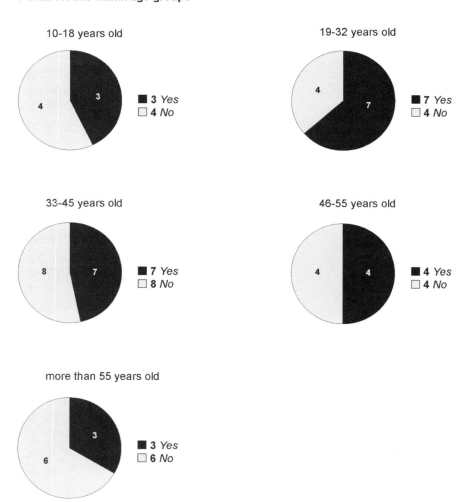

Figure 1. Survey responses to "do you know what the word sustainability means?"

"Do you believe the estate can become sustainable (as you understand it) through the regeneration?"

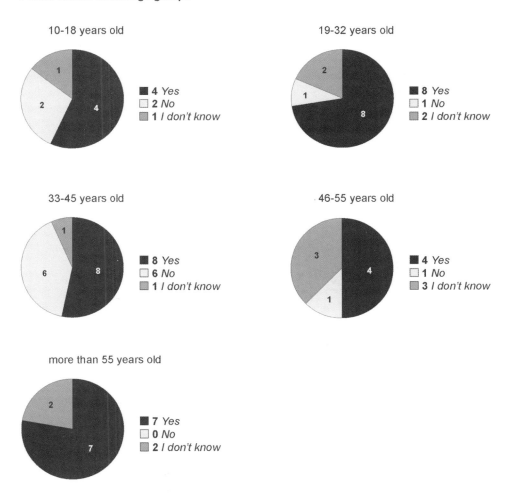

Figure 2. Survey responses to "do you believe the estate can become sustainable (as you understand it) through regeneration?"

In the leaflets distributed by the Tenants' Association, most of the space is dedicated to the campaigning against the plans. Nevertheless, some of the priorities identified by the surveyed residents are present in this material. For instance, claims against downsizing homes and for enhanced green areas.

Results have shown that the visibility achieved by *Aylesbury Regeneration News* was predominant: while 24 interviewees declared they had saw this publication but not the Tenants' Association's leaflets, 20 affirmed they had seen both of them and 6 said they could not recognize any of the two. Even though majority saw the magazine, 28 people assumed not reading them, against 22 who said doing so.

A Language Gap

The issue of language command and its relevance to allow participation came up as serendipity during the interviews. Four interviews were carried out in Spanish and two in Portuguese, and two questionnaires could not be answered because residents spoke Vietnamese only. Children in a Bengali and in an Arabic families helped their parents to understand the questions and translated their answers. Oslo (2005, p. 12) points out that even though citizenship is usually understood as a status, it also involves feeling, "the degree to which individuals feel they belong, and citizen participation and engagement, what can be termed the practice of citizenship". Drawing on that, the language gap observed during the interviews seemed to reflect a citizenship gap in which residents are not able to take part in decisions in their community and, therefore, assume a status of political isolation.

Conclusions

Findings indicated opportunities for introducing EfS as a complementary approach to the official aims of developing metropolitan housing areas to make them become "sustainable communities". Additionally, how to better take local knowledge into account in

these processes is an aspect that calls for future research. This work revealed patterns of how the local people in the Aylesbury Estate understood concepts like "sustainability" and "sustainable communities" and these notions could be incorporated to create and implement educational programmes designed to cope with the needs of residents in their journey towards a future as a "sustainable community", following Fagan's recommendation for using locals' reference to create knowledge and celebrating their views "as researchers and activists" (Fagan, 1996, pp. 138-139).

Furthermore, the conflicting aspects between the local views and the official advertisements to the area provide evidences of a mostly imposed top-down agenda of "sustainable development". The most evident local challenge seems to be allowing residents to become actors within this change, which requires an educational approach able to provoke what Brazilian educator Paulo Freire called "coscientization" (Freire, 1980, 1983): using learning to encourage people to free themselves from oppressive situations and contribute to decisions.

Results also pointed out that there is a role to be played by local media as a tool to enhance participation and awareness regarding issues that affect the Aylesbury Estate community throughout its transformation to become sustainable, as a lack of clarification regarding the plans was evident. Therefore, one of the recommendations to be made by this study is that the Aylesbury Estate's neighbour Higher Education Institution, London South Bank University (LSBU) could become a potential stakeholder in the effort to structure an innovative scheme of community-based learning.

This scheme could involve students of LSBU Education for Sustainability Programme and Media Studies Programme as well as this institution's Widening Participation Unit in designing and implementing participatory media workshops orientated to EfS to be offered for residents. By doing so, students could gain relevant experience, and social responsibility towards a deprived population living close to this HE institution could be brought to the agenda. The ideal structure of this educational approach, however, invites for further discussion and could motivate future research work focusing on facilitating not only the process of change experienced in the studied council estate as well as in other similar contexts.

ACKNOWLEDGEMENTS

This research was undertaken at London South Bank University as part of an MSc study. I must say a very warm thank you to: my children João and Ingá, my husband Cuquinha and my brother Rui, for living with me in the Aylesbury Estate; my supervisor Róbinson Rojas and my LSBU course-director Ros Wade, for encouraging my journey; Girafa Não Fala Design Gráfico (Sao Paulo, Brazil), for designing the charts in the originals of this work; the British Council, for funding my MSc; and the CELT (University of Wales, Newport), for giving me the opportunity to carry a PhD research related to the theme here presented.

REFERENCES

ATTON, C. 1999. A reassessment of the alternative press. *Media, Culture and Society,* 1(1), pp. 51-76.

AYLESBURY AND AREA TENANTS AND LEASE-HOLDERS FIRST 2008. *Who exactly is the regeneration for?* [Informal leaflet distributed in the Aylesbury Estate].

AYLESBURY NEW DEAL FOR COMMUNITIES/ CREATION/SOUTHWARK COUNCIL 2008. Plans firm up for the new area. *Aylesbury Regeneration News,* August (13), p. 11.

BARTON, H. 2002. Conflicting perceptions of neighbourhood. In*:* H. BARTON (ed.) *Sustainable communities – the potential for eco-neighbourhoods.* London: Earthscan, pp. 3-17.

BRIDGE, G. 1993. *Gentrification, class and residence: a reappraisal.* Working paper 109. Bristol: SAUS Publications/School for Advanced Urban Studies, University of Bristol.

BRITISH EDUCATIONAL RESEARCH ASSOCIATION (BERA) (2004) *Revised ethical guidelines for educational research.* Available at www.bera.ac.uk/files/2008/09/ethica1.pdf [accessed 31/01/2009].

CHAMBERS, R. 1997. Us and them: finding a new paradigm for professionals in sustainable development. In: WARBURTON (ed.) *Commu-*nity & sustainable development – participation in the future.* London: Earthscan pp. 116-147.

CLARKE-PATEL, A., PAKER, J. 2001. Globalisation: setting the context. *Local and global with a focus on NGO education (study guide).* London: Distance Learning Centre/South Bank University, pp. 9-21.

COHEN, L., MANION, L., MORRISON, K. 2007. *Research methods in education.* Oxon and New York: Routledge.

COLENUTT, B., CUTTEN, A. 1994. *Community empower in urban regeneration.* London: The Barrow Cadbury Fund Limited and The Docklands Consultative Committee, pp. 15-35.

COYER, K. 2005. If it leads it bleeds: the participatory news making of Indymedia. In: W. DE JONG, M. SHAW, N. STAMMERS (eds) *Global activism global media.* London; Ann Arbor: Pluto Press, pp. 165-178.

DENNIS, A. [issue 1970] 2005. *Housing democracy denied by demolition plan.* [Online] Socialist-Workeronline. Available from: http://www.socialistworker.co.uk/art.php?id=7 476 (accessed on 22/11/2007).

FAGAN, G. 1996. Community based learning. In: J. HUCKLE, S. STERLING (eds) *Education for Sustainability.* London: Earthscan, pp 136-148.

FAY, B. 1987. The elements of critical social science In: M. HAMMERSLEY (ed.) *Social research – philosophy, politics and practice.* London; Newbury Park; New Delhi: Sage Publication and The Open University.

FREIRE, P. 1983. *Pedagogia do oprimido.* Rio de Janeiro: Paz e Terra.

FREIRE, P. 1980. Acción cultural libertadora. In: TORRES, C. A. (ed.), *Paulo Freire: Educación y conscientización.* Salamanca: Sígueme.

GAGE, N. L. 1991. The Obviousness of social research and educational results. In: M. HAMMERSLEY (ed.), *Social research – philosophy, politics and practice.* London; Newbury Park; New Delhi: Sage Publication and The Open University.

GILCHRIST, A. 2002. Design for living: the challenge of sustainable communities. In: H. BARTON (ed.) *Sustainable communities – the potential for eco-neighbourhoods.* London: Earthscan, pp. 147-158.

HABERMAS, J. 1973. *Theory and practice.* London: Heinemann.

HALL, P.G., KNIGHT, B. 2007. *London voices, London lives: tales from a working capital.* Bristol: Policy Press.

HAMMERSEY, M., ATKINSON, P. 1983. *Ethnography: principles in practice.* London; New York: Routledge.

HENWOOD, K., PIDGEON, N. 1993. Qualitative research and psychological theorizing. In: M. HAMMERSLEY (ed.) *Social research – Philosophy, politics and practice.* London; Newbury Park; New Delhi: Sage Publication and The Open University.

HILLCOAT, J. 1996. Action research. In: M. WILLIAMS (ed.), *Understanding Geographical and Environmental Education.* London: Cassel Education.

LEFTLY, M. 2007. Aylesbury and after. Available at: www.building.co.uk/story.asp?sectioncode=32&storycode=3087131&featurecode=11917&c=1 (accessed 28/12/2007).

OSLO, A. 2005. Education for democratic citizenship: new challenges in a globalised world. In: A. OSLER, H. STARKEY (eds) *Citizenship and language learning: international perspectives.* Stoke on Trent; Sterling: Trentham Books, pp. 3-20.

REEVES, P. F. 2005. *An introduction to social housing.* Oxford; Burlington: Elsevier Butterworth-Heinemann.

SCHOFIELD, J. W. 1989. Increasing the generalizability of qualitative research. In: M. HAMMERSLEY (ed.), *Social research – philosophy, politics and practice.* London; Newbury Park; New Delhi: Sage Publication and The Open University.

STACEY, 1969. The myth of communities studies. *British Journal of Sociology,* 20 (2), pp. 134-147.

SOUTHWARK COUNCIL 2007. *Interim sustainability appraisal – Aylesbury Area Action Plan.* Cm:2623

STEWART, M., TAYLOR, M. 1995. *Empowerment and estate regeneration.* Bristol: The Policy Press.

UNITED NATIONS CONFERENCE ON ENVIRONMENT AND DEVELOPMENT (UNCED) 1992. *Earth Summit 1992.* Rio de Janeiro, Brazil, 1992. United Nations.

University of Wales, Newport

Prifysgol Cymru, Casnewydd

Linking Research and Teaching in Higher Education
Simon K. Haslett and Hefin Rowlands (eds)
Proceedings of the Newport NEXUS Conference
Centre for Excellence in Learning and Teaching
Special Publication, No. 1, 2009, pp. 53-57
ISBN 978-1-899274-38-3

Institutional strategies for education for sustainable development and global citizenship in Wales.

Alison Glover

Centre for Excellence in Learning and Teaching, University of Wales, Newport, Lodge Road, Caerleon, South Wales, NP18 3QT, United Kingdom. Email: Alison.glover@newport.ac.uk

Abstract

Global Issues such as climate change, poverty, health, education and environmental degradation are very topical, with substantial media coverage. The Welsh Assembly Government has published several policies prioritising sustainability in Wales across all sectors. Higher Education Institutions provide future citizens, who will lead, design and create change within society and it is, therefore, desirable for students to be empowered if they are to be effective. In 2008 the Welsh Assembly Government funded audits to establish the situation of Education for Sustainable Development and Global Citizenship (ESDGC) within the higher education sector in Wales. Now the question arises as to whether institutions are developing the policies and strategies to tackle sustainability issues and whether staff and students perceive that they have a role to play. Considerable research has been carried out within pre-university education and their delivery of the ESDGC agenda. However, there appears to be limited scholarly literature regarding the implementation and impact of institutional strategies in the higher education sector, particularly as far as sustainability is concerned. This research will develop a conceptual and analytical framework as a guide for case studies in order to examine the implementation process and impacts at twelve Welsh Higher Education Institutions.

Introduction

In 1999 power devolved to a Welsh Assembly in Wales, approved by voters. Since being established the Welsh Assembly Government has demonstrated a strong commitment towards sustainability. Sustainability is written into the constitution and evident in the publication and implementation of several policy documents. These include:

- A Sustainable Wales, 2000,
- The Sustainable Development Action Plan, 2004-2007,
- Education for Sustainable Development and Global Citizenship, 2006,
- One Wales One Planet, 2009.

During 2008 the Welsh Assembly Government endorsed their conviction towards sustainability when they funded audits to determine evidence of sustainability at all Higher Education Institutions (HEIs) in Wales. There were two strands to the audit; (i) environmental management systems and (ii) the curriculum; using the STAUNCH tool.

STAUNCH was developed by the Centre for Business Relationships Accountability Sustainability and Society (BRASS) at Cardiff University (module descriptors were searched for breadth and strength of sustainability content using set criteria). Alongside the audits an *Analysis of Good Practice in the Higher Education Sector in Wales* (HEFCW 2009) was also commissioned. Around the same time the English Higher Education Funding Council and the Higher Education Academy in

Scotland also reported on sustainability within the sector. The reports identified gaps in evidence available; particularly in the appraisal of the mechanism of corporate planning and incorporating sustainable development into mission statements, strategic plans and policies. (HEFCE, 2009, p. 21; HEFCW, 2009, p. 17; Ryan, 2009, p. 21).

It is relevant to acknowledge that the political context of Education for Sustainable Development and Global Citizenship (ESDGC) is perceived differently in England and Scotland. Greater government priority is given to ESDGC in Wales and the terminology used differs. England and Scotland both use Education for Sustainable Development appearing to make the assumption that Global Citizenship is incorporated within the term. Whereas Wales have made a specific point of placing Global Citizenship alongside Education for Sustainable Development, ensuring it is viewed as equally important and not to be subsumed within the term 'sustainability'.

Research Aims

The question has, therefore, emerged as to whether the high profile of sustainability at the national government level is resulting in changes in policy development and implementation at the local level, in this case in HEIs. According to Jenkins and Healey (2005) mission statements of institutions do help develop a sense of shared purpose and influence planning, but 'most institutions attempt to deliver a range of semi-structured strategies' (Healey and Jenkins, 2005, p. 25). The outcomes of the research will, therefore, establish the current position of Welsh HEIs within the spectrum of change towards the necessary transformative learning (Sterling, 2001, p78). 'Transformative learning' involves a complete cultural shift in education and public awareness and this theoretical basis underlies the possibility of re-evaluating what education is for. In agreeing with Sterling's (2001) vision for a shift in perception; from education for socialization and employability the main function of education should be to contribute to a sustainable and just society.

This mirrors third order learning, as proposed by Bateson's hypothesis of learning (1972, p. 293), whereby true consideration of the learning process, not simply the content, is evident if transformative learning is to take place.

Key Questions

The purpose of the research is to determine the current position of ESDGC in the Welsh Higher Education sector by reviewing and analysing institutional policies and strategies, in light of Welsh Assembly requirements.

1) How do Welsh HEIs define ESDGC?
2) What are the approaches to strategy and policy development in Welsh HEIs?
3) What evidence exists of the impacts of policy implementation?
   a) On campuses?
   b) And within curricula?
4) What do students and staff expect is Higher Education's role in promoting the value and effectiveness of ESDGC?
5) What are the lessons to be learnt and shared between HEIs, both nationally and internationally as they strive to implement policy changes effectively?

The resultant findings should provide benefit to the Higher Education sector nationally and internationally, useful also when comparing other principalities with ESDGC high on their agenda. The findings will facilitate in the sharing and collaboration of good practice in achieving sustainability.

Theoretical Perspectives

Definitions

In contextualising the indicators evident for the impact of Higher Education Institutional policies and strategies for ESDGC there are several important theoretical perspectives that it is vital to explore. Defining 'Sustainable Development' causes much debate, but the World Commission on Environment and Development (1987) provided the definition of sustainable development as 'development that meets the needs of the present without compromising the ability of future generations to meet their own needs.' (WCED, 1987, p. 43). The Welsh Assembly Government also uses this definition. Nevertheless, others believe that a degree of ambiguity exists when defining the concept and that this can be positive, 'the sustainability transition is plagued by a clash of interpretations and reactions regarding the purpose of sustainable development' (O'Riordan and Voisey, 1998, p. 24). These inconsistencies will be explored further within the context of society and the Higher Education sector, as Sibbel (2009) argues:

'It is the lack of understanding of the concept of sustainability that lies at the core if society is to become sustainable and for higher education to actualise its potential to contribute to sustainability' (Sibbel, 2009, p. 75).

Therefore, it will be vital to establish a clear understanding of the interpretation of sustainability at individual HEIs, across the whole sector, and the perception at Welsh Assembly Government level.

As for the Global Citizenship aspect, the Welsh Assembly Government emphasises the need for people to understand global forces that exist if they are to participate in decision making that results in an equal and just society. Within the context of sustainability, global citizenship is a much less developed concept. As far as Higher Education is concerned the concept has emerged via International Strategies (developing opportunities and recruitment internationally) and Internationalisation Strategies (attempting to ensure Higher Education incorporates local → national → global, on campuses and in curricula). Many are raising the profile of this aspect of sustainability, including Shiel and McKenzie (2008) where they draw together the relevance of globalization and citizenship and the important role that Higher Education has to play.

Progress

Internationally the profile of Sustainable Development is increasing, notably with the United Nations Decade of Education for Sustainable Development, 2005-2014, being well underway. A major element of the United Nations Program is the emergence of Regional Centres of Expertise and Wales is aiming to submit an application to be acknowledged with such a Regional Centre of Expertise in 2009. The evolution of sustainability within the Higher Education sector has been fairly rapid since the 1990s, with various international declarations being signed. Wright (2004), in Corcoran and Wals, provides a useful synopsis of the increasing number of HEIs signing such declarations. A more detailed examination of these declarations is necessary to understand the sustainability transition that is happening. However, signed agreements do not necessarily reflect changes to policies and actions within an institution. Tilbury and Wortman (2008) explore the implications for such fundamental changes within the Higher Education sector and propose that 'institutions must seek opportunities to engage the entire campus by developing a shared future vision' (Tilbury and Wortman, 2008, p. 10). This 'future vision' will need to incorporate all aspects of Higher Education; from the built environment and management of estates to sustainability and citizenship issues encompassing staff and students within an enlightened curriculum. Again, examples of such successes will be examined: Corcoran and Wals (2004), and Gornitzka, Kogan and Amaral, (2005) present many case studies to show good practice of reform and change in Higher Education.

Policy Implementation

The study of policy implementation and change provides precision to the goals aimed for by HEIs. It is vital to identify the factors that both contribute and hinder the realization of goals and Cerych and Sabatier (1986) developed a framework within which to analyse such policies. It will be possible to incorporate their theory in the early stages to establish the main variables involved and discover the impact each has on successful policy implementation. For example, commitment to objectives, adequate financial resources, interested groups, and social and economic changes (Cerych and Sabatier, 1986, p. 16) all need to be investigated if the impacts of effective policy implementation are to be identified.

The role of HEIs in implementing changes towards a more sustainable future cannot be under estimated and role models are needed to embody ideals totally as:

'the crisis we face is first and foremost one of mind, perception and values; hence, it is a challenge to those institutions presuming to shape minds, perceptions and values…...more of the same kind of education can only make things worse' (Orr, 1994, p. 27).

Supporting this argument, Sterling (2001) advocates a radical transformative paradigm shift in education with a strong emphasis on successful changes emerging from ownership and empowerment of principles and it is imperative that such rhetoric should emerge as reality.

From such ownership, 'deep-seated changes in our mental frames' (Doppelt, 2008, p. 141) will need to permeate and Doppelt provides much to support the processes required to implement strategies, concurring with many of the arguments edited by Corcoran and Wals (2004). The whole policy formation process will perform an important factor in successful policy impacts and it is imperative to identify the key stakeholders involved and whether this has an impact on successful implementation (Jenkins and Healey, 2005).

Progression towards sustainability can be associated with learning stages (Sterling, 2001) and these will be explored and exemplified in the real world to enable case studies and comparisons to be identified. Parallel to this the location of the institutions within models of the transition to sustainability will be established (O'Riordan and Voisey, 1998, p. 16). Specific to HEIs, a four phase model has been proposed (HEFCE, 2008, p. 80). This provides criteria to locate an institution within the following stages towards sustainability:

1. Grass roots enthusiasts,
2. Early adopters,
3. Getting really serious,
4. Full commitment.

It should be possible to clarify where Welsh HEIs are within the model as a result of the data collection and subsequent analysis.

Research Methodology

Data Collection

The data will be collected primarily by reviewing and analysing HEI policy and strategy documents. Such documents will include:

- Strategic Plans,
- Lead Strategy documents,
- Third Mission Strategy,
- Specific policies targeting environmental and sustainability issues; both from a campus stance and within the curriculum.

This will identify targets and actions reflecting institutional ESDGC changes that can be mapped accordingly to the Welsh Assembly Government's ESDGC requirements. It will be possible to apply some statistical analysis to the qualitative data by coding data, categorizing, and theorizing. Potentially applying Computer Assisted Qualitative Data Software Analysis (CADQAS), such as Nvivo (the program facilitates text searches, ideas can be linked; data coded and searched, and models to be drawn) to assist. Alternatively, making reference to STAUNCH as used to complete the curriculum audit. Also, there will be data available specifically concerned with environmental management systems and this will reveal changes over time. For instance, whether raising the profile of sustainability on campus is resulting in a more energy efficient environment.

Questionnaires and small focus groups with students and/or staff will broaden the data collection and provide explanation of some of the policy initiatives, in addition to pertinent case study material for dissemination within the sector. Also, the student and staff expectations, perceptions and demands of the sustainability transformation will emerge. It is appreciated that the good practice study (HEFCW, 2009) collected data via interviews with senior managers, but alongside this it was pointed out that it was not clear what the student demand for ESDGC is, whether it should prevail as a specific optional course or within a cross-cutting context (HEFCW, 2009, p. 28). Also, the importance of publishing good practice was re-emphasised (HEFCW, 2009, p. 52) as well as the potential for exploring developments within the curriculum to embed ESDGC. Corcoran and Wals (2004) offer detailed arguments to support the inclusion of the case study methodology particularly if they are theorized and well documented, which will inevitably be the aim. Both deductive and inductive approaches will emerge; for instance predefined categories used for content analysis of strategies as well as inductively drawing out themes that arise within documents and collected data.

Summary

All HEIs in Wales will be studied to ensure a full evaluation of the condition of ESDGC within the Higher Education sector in the Principality. On completion of the Welsh study it may be relevant to make an international comparison and this would use some of the same methodology to acquire the data, which would allow for an accurate comparison to be completed. Following comprehensive examination and evaluation of the policies and resulting actions it will be possible to make recommendations in relation to good practice within the sector to facilitate a thorough transition to sustainability.

REFERENCES

BATESON, G. 1972. *Steps to an Ecology of Mind*. Chicago: University of Chicago Press.

CERYCH, L., SABATIER, P. 1986. *Great Expectations and Mixed Performance. The Implementation of Higher Education Reforms in Europe*. Stoke on Trent: Trentham Books Ltd.

CORCORAN, P., WALS, A. (eds) 2004. *Higher Education and the Challenges of Sustainability Problematics, Promise and Practice*. Dordrecht: Kluwer Academic Publishers.

DOPPELT, B. 2008. *The Power of Sustainable Thinking*. London: Earthscan

GORNITZKA, A. KOGAN, M., AMARAL, A. (eds) 2005. *Reform and Change in Higher Education*. The Netherlands: Springer.

HEFCE (Higher Education Funding Council for England) 2008. *HEFCE strategic review of sustainable development in higher education in England*. London: Policy Studies Institute.

HEFCE (Higher Education Funding Council for England) 2009. *Sustainable Development in Higher Education, 2008 Update to Strategic Statement and Action Plan*. London: HEFCE.

HEFCW (Higher Education Funding Council for Wales) 2009. *Education for Sustainable Development and Global Citizenship (ESDGC): Analysis of good practice in Welsh Higher Education Institutions*. SQW Consulting.

JENKINS, A., HEALEY, M. 2005. *Institutional Strategies to Link Teaching and Research*. York: The Higher Education Academy.

O'RIORDAN, T., VOISEY, H. 1998. *The Transition to Sustainability: The Politics of Agenda 21 in Europe*. London: Earthscan.

ORR, D. 1994. *Earth in Mind, on Education, Environment, and the Human Prospect*. Washington. D. C. Island Press.

RYAN, A. 2009. 2008 *Review of Education for Sustainable Development (ESD) in Higher Education In Scotland*. York: The Higher Education Academy.

SHIEL, C., MCKENZIE, A. (eds) 2008. *The Global University*. DEA.

SIBBEL, A. 2009. Pathways Towards Sustainability Through Higher Education. *International Journal of Sustainability in Higher Education*, 10 (1), pp. 68-82.

STERLING, S. 2001. *Sustainable Education Revisioning Learning and Change*. Devon: Green Books for the Schumacher Society.

TIBURY, D., WORTMAN, D. 2008. Education for Sustainability in Further and Higher Education. *Planning for Higher Education*, 36 (4), pp. 5-16.

WCED. 1987. *Our Common Future*. Oxford: Oxford University Press.

WRIGHT, T. 2004. The Evolution of Sustainability Declarations in Higher Education. In P. CORCORAN, A. WALS (eds) *Higher Education and the Challenges of Sustainability Problematics, Promise and Practice*. Dordrecht: Kluwer Academic Publishers.

University of Wales, Newport

Prifysgol Cymru, Casnewydd

Linking Research and Teaching in Higher Education
Simon K. Haslett and Hefin Rowlands (eds)
Proceedings of the Newport NEXUS Conference
Centre for Excellence in Learning and Teaching
Special Publication, No. 1, 2009, pp. 59-64
ISBN 978-1-899274-38-3

Working lives experience: narratives of the new researcher.

Caryn E. Cook

Newport Business School, University of Wales, Newport, Allt-yr-yn Campus, Allt-yr-yn Avenue, Newport, NP20 5DA, United Kingdom. Email: Caryn.cook2@newport.ac.uk

Abstract

This paper looks at the background to the formation of the 'Working Lives' team and the initial involvement and reflections of the 'new kid on the block' as an early career researcher. The Welsh Education Research Network (WERN) was funded by the Economic and Social Research Council and the Higher Education Funding Council for Wales for a pilot period between 1st October 2007 and 30th June 2008. The aim of the Network is to develop educational research capacity, by building a collaborative partnership which shares expertise, between all the higher education institutions with the education and related departments in Wales. The 'Working Lives' team links the University of Glamorgan, the University of Wales, Newport, and Cardiff University. The team consist of early and mid career academics and the bursary awarded by WERN enabled the team to collect and analyse data on the work-life experience of lecturers in Higher Education/Further Education contexts via a pilot which consisted of focus groups.

Introduction

The Welsh Assembly Government acknowledged that research is of vital importance to the development of education policy and practice in Wales; however there is evidence of a steady decline in the capacity of most educational institutions in Wales to undertake research. Welsh educational research, in advance of other parts of the United Kingdom (UK), has for the most part been on a trajectory of decline for more than a decade. Rees and Power (2007) provide powerful evidence for this trend in analysis of Research Assessment Exercise (RAE) returns since 1991 that demonstrate an overall decline in capacity and a concentration in fewer institutions. It is felt that there is a decline in "home grown research to inspire, guide and evaluate it". Davies & Salisbury, (2008, in press) have written about working and learning together within the Welsh Education Research Network (WERN) funding initiatives

and the challenges arising from inter institutional collaboration. This paper represents an experiential narrative of working within a funded bursary group on a project about the Working Lives of Further Education (FE) and Higher Education (HE) professionals as an early career researcher.

The WERN bursary funding initiative is aimed at enabling Higher Education institutions to work together to find a solution and this has been acknowledged by the funding provided by the Economic and Social Research Council (ESRC) and the Higher Education Funding Council for Wales (HEFCW) to provide a pilot capacity building network. All ten institutions in Wales with education or related departments are committed to building the collaboration by participating in the leadership and activities of WERN/Rhywdwaith Ymchwil Addysg Cymru (RhYAC).

It was seen as an opportunity to begin to reverse the decline in research capacity within education in Wales and encourage collaborative responses to submit applications to WERN/RhYAC for funding to support the writing of a proposal to a funding organisation. Despite having only a few weeks to find partners and develop these bursary application, it was reported that there was an excellent response with 24 applications received. WERN/RhYAC only had the resources to award eight group bursaries, and these were selected on the basis of academic merit and capacity building potential.

The emails of invitation to participate within the group started just before Christmas 2007, initial reaction of the author (second and third) was *'to ignore it and it would go away, who were these mad people, who gave them my details? Why me?, it's Christmas anyway, it might disappear during the holiday. I was already doing some research for my teaching! don't feel able to take on any more'*

On return in January,

'There was a message from a line manager, they had contacted him, and he thought what a good idea and an opportunity for me!!!!!, So I took the call, and set up the first meeting'

At the first meeting,

'The feeling of inadequacy numbed my brain, here I was faced with all these experienced researchers and academics. The introductions calmed me somewhat, in that they were all at differing levels with their research careers, I was however still the most inexperienced, and then realised that having someone NEW was a requirement of the winning team for the bursary, which really reassured me! NOT!'

The Working Lives study was conceived as one of these pilots, and as such it identified a cluster of FE and Higher Education Institutions (HEIs) in south-east Wales as a target sample population. In studying the experiences of lecturers, the main objectives of the project were to:

- develop an initial thematic review of relevant literature sources to set the theoretical context,

- organise a research event in order to explore and rehearse issues in data collection,
- use qualitative software to analyse results and identify themes,
- build the capacity of the team for the development of future work in the area,
- establish and create a collaborative research framework and network,
- create abstracts, papers, proposals and presentations to disseminate and promote the work.

The WERN Bursary created the opportunity to engage in collective empirical study, with a view to developing this research agenda further – and also for engaging in collaborative cross-disciplinary research. The project brought researchers together from Education and Social Sciences, Human Resource Management and Business Schools – staff working in different institutional settings and in different phases of career and research development.

Working together brought about interesting debates and challenging issues, of building collaborative capacity across sometimes competing institutions and otherwise autonomous disciplines (Sillitoe, 2007). It also involved much reflective thinking and discussion.

The aims from the bursary bid was to develop a small data-set of teacher's working lives narratives and to refine research techniques and models of collaborative inquiry, to share expertise, and explore methods of elicitation, analysis and identify management issues in research methodology building upon existing expertise at the collaborating institutions.

Given the short lead time and timescales, the Working Lives team had to develop a common understanding of the research area very quickly, to build on their collaborative communication tools and capacity within a short space of time, and to identify productive and sustainable research questions (Cook and Gornall, in press). This also required time for those less experienced members to participate, contribute, and learn how to undertake research. *Like Me !!!* This would then enable them to gain and share their experiences within the group. The team were time-poor but well-resourced in experience, so despite constraints, all research issues and processes were agreed through frequent discussions and debate across the three campuses, ensuring that the research skills and 'knowledge capital' of all were fully utilised (Cook and Gornall, in press).

The multi institutional and multi disciplinary aspect brought about challenges for the participants. Collaboration is not simply a treatment which has positive effects on the participants, it is arguably a social structure in which two or more people interact with each other and, in some circumstances, some types of interaction occur that have a positive effect (Dillenbourg *et al.*, 1996).

'Interacting and being part of the discussions and debates, aiding in the design of research, and interpreting data from research within a supportive network was extremely interesting and rewarding in part, however, the perceived differences in status still acted as a barrier'

An important aspect of the process was that of having an experienced mentor as part of the team. Professor Sally Power of Cardiff University made expert interventions at a number of points which, because this was formally structured into the WERN scheme, created access to a resource that improved the work and helped the individuals to 'professionalise' as researchers.

Rationale behind study

The rational behind the study focus was that occupational research in HE and FE is an area of study that it is argued has been neglected, not only in Wales but in the UK generally; it has been neglected in educational research, and in employment research on occupations (Gornall, 1999). As a result, and whilst there have been moves to address this (*e.g.* Musselin, 2007) there is arguably a paucity of data not only on Lecturing staff careers and aspects of professionalism, but on the changing nature of educational and teaching work as employment.

Teaching professionals in post-compulsory education, compared with teachers within other sectors, have been largely left out of the picture (Gerwitz and Mahoney, 2006). There has been some research on transforming learning cultures in FE in England (Gleeson and James, 2007; James *et al.*, 2007), on learning and working in FE colleges in Wales (Jephcote and Salisbury, 2007, 2008) and on academic work in HE (Fulton, 1996; Henkel, 2000; Tight, 2002; Deem, 2003). These contribute to our understanding of lecturer's experience, but it was argued that there is important research still to be done in the context.

A data gathering research day, with participants from HE and FE, was organised for March 2008 in the former ELWa (Education and Learning Wales, now Wales Assembly) Building in Bedwas. A short introduction was given by the team on the purposes of the study. A wide spread of institutions and regions were represented.

Two structured focus group sessions were held, one for FE staff, one for HE, each running simultaneously. The sessions were facilitated and recorded, with observers taking notes. This context also provided an apprenticeship and learning arena for two PhD students, each differently located in their own doctoral trajectories, who assisted in the collection and then later transcription of the data.

The focus groups were the mode of data-gathering preferred, because they comprised of groups of individuals who were selected and assembled by researchers for the purposes of discussion and comment, from their personal experience (Powell and Single, 1996).

'I was put with the FE focus group, which was useful to get a fuller understanding of the 'FE viewpoint' I was lucky here in having Dr. Jane Salisbury as a companion in running this focus group, Jane is an experienced researcher and was extremely competent in this field. All the team were extremely supportive and really treated me as any other researcher, the day was extremely interesting and exhausting, and

produced some very interesting and rich data. The following discussions and meetings following reading and analysis of this data were enlightening, it became apparent that there are so many avenues that the research could take, and that it was impossible to take them all! It was extremely interesting to be part of that process, which at times was quite reflexive and in some ways emotional, as it has to be remembered that we are all part of the system and process that we are investigating'.

Researchers are Learners Too

The existence of the WERN initiative legitimised the formation of a collaborative research team, and if one considers the aspiration of widening research capability it is clearly about learning about research and in many ways, for some of the participants, doing your apprenticeship. There also exists the real issue of learning to work collaboratively which brings about issues of participatory research, action research, collaborative inquiry and experiential research (Solomon *et al.*, 2001).

The concept of shared cognition, which is deeply intertwined with the 'situated cognition' theory (Suchman, 1987; Lave, 1988), argues that the environment is an integral part of the cognitive activity, and not just a set of circumstances, it includes physical context and the social context of the research activity within this collaborative group, which under the influence of sociologists and anthropologists places the focus largely on the social context, not only is there the aspect of the temporary group of collaborators, but the social communities in which these collaborators participate (Dillenbourg *et al.*, 1996).

As a new researcher with a few confidence issues it was bewildering, not without fear of inadequacy yet exciting to be sat for the first time with a group of perceived more experienced researchers. Perception and assumptions took over and imagination of illustrious research portfolios silenced the brain. However, as time and experience passed it became apparent that differing stages of research careers were present.

An important aspect of the process was having an experienced senior academic and 'Mentor' as part of the team.

As illustrated by reaction and feelings, group heterogeneity has to be taken into account if you consider the differences with respect to general intellectual development, social status or domain expertise. If you consider that this group of researchers are at varying levels and stages of their research capability development, and also different hierarchical levels of their respective institutions. The pressure to conform in the presence of someone with higher perceived status is not likely to lead to any genuine cognitive development or change (Dillenbourg *et al.*, 1996). It has also been argued that collaboration does not benefit an individual if he or she is below a certain developmental level (Dillenbourg *et al.*, 1996).

The sharing of work and responsibilities had to be dealt with, it could be argued that there was a need for cooperation and collaboration, and it was assumed that these are synonymous, but it is argued that in cooperation, coordination is only required when assembling partial results, whilst collaboration is "…a coordinated, synchronous activity that is the result of a continued attempt to construct and maintain a shared conception of a problem" (Roschelle and Teasley, 1995, p. 69). It is, therefore, important to understand the meaning of collaboration, in that it is argued to be more of the notion of domain-based "goals".

Real Progress?

Since the beginning of this journey with the 'Working Lives' team there has been outputs and developments as would be expected from a 'bursary funded' project. The objectives of the original WERN that inspired the team was the research capacity building. The research has taken on a life of its own, very much building on the original remit of the WERN bursary, the author has gained in confidence and visible output. The Working Lives team has presented at a Colloquium at Llandrindod Wells, an article to *Welsh Journal of Education* (Cook and Gornall, 2009), various news items within the *Glamorgan Journal*, and papers at the British Education Research Association 2008 (Gornall *et al.*, 2008) and Society for Research into Higher Education 2008 (Daunton *et al.*, 2008) conferences. The author has registered for a Doctorate, albeit in a totally unrelated area, it has had the effect of encouragement and heightened confidence which it is felt was brought about by interacting with others: "… it is above all through interacting with others, coordinating his/her approaches to reality with those of others, that the individual masters new approaches" (Doise, 1990, p. 46). "Individual cognitive development is seen as a result of a spiral of causality: a given level of individual development allows participation in certain social interactions which produce new individual states which, in turn, make possible more sophisticated social interaction, and so on" (Dillenbourg *et al.*, 1996, p. 3).

Conclusion

This has been a journey of discovery which has not been easy both mentally and psychologically. All parties have their own personal goals within human-human collaboration, add to this the presence of institutional goals with regards to research agendas. The experience was worthwhile and rewarding on various levels. As a participant it led to experiences of being the researcher and being a subject *(given the subject area, we could not help but use and refer to our own reflexive moments)* – which the nature of the subject allowed, as weren't we all part of the issue and system being investigated? Also, and very importantly, the opportunity of working with and learning to work collabora-tively with a group of researchers of varying levels of research experiences, within various areas of academia, learning the social and research etiquette, writing of papers, writing of and submitting funding applications, *etc …* It was not however without its difficulties, if you consider a number of individuals who had not worked together before, if you consider Tuckwell's model of team formation, the team clearly went through all the stages of forming,

storming, norming and performing, however, given the time constraints it was of para-mount importance that professionalism came to the fore and the team produced tangible results, and this was achieved, which was not without pain. The journey goes on for now, but what also needs to be taken into account is the eventual exit strategy (Dillenbourg *et al.*, 1996) as it is of paramount importance to maintain the goodwill of this collaborative and professional network of knowledge and experience *(of which I am now part)*.

The Future?

The team are seeking to widen the 'Working Lives' network and to focus the research by (i) building a team of associates through cascading 'capacity building' opportunities and (ii) applying professional development to real data collection and refining our methods of study in collecting sensitive data about work practices and locations. This proposal has led to a successful extension of funding from the WERN 2 extension to pilot 2008-2009. For more information you can contact: knowledge@glam.ac.uk.

ACKNOWLEDGEMENTS

This research was undertaken as part of a WERN Group bursary project (ESRC and Welsh Assembly Government funded initiative). I would like to acknowledge the 'working lives' team without whom this would not have been possible and my colleagues at Newport for their support and encouragement. In addition to the author, the 'Working Lives' Team are:

- Lyn Daunton, University of Glamorgan Business School
- Dr Lynne Gornall, (Project leader), University of Glamorgan
- Professor Sally Power, (Project Mentor), Cardiff University, School of Social Sciences
- Dr Jane Salisbury, Cardiff University, School of Social Sciences
- Dr Brychan Thomas, University of Glamorgan, Business School

REFERENCES

COOK, C., GORNALL, L. in press. The 'working lives' research report on narratives of occupational change in further and higher education in post-devolution Wales. *Welsh Journal of Education*.

DAUNTON, L., GORNALL, L., COOK, C., SALISBURY, J., 2008. *'Starting the day fresh': hidden work and discourse in contemporary academic practice*. Society for Research into Higher Education Annual Conference, Liverpool.

DAVIES, S. M. B. 2008. *Welsh Education Research Network*. Available at www.trinity-cm.ac.uk, (accessed: 24th April, 2009).

DAVIES, S. M. B., SALISBURY, J. 2008. *Researching and learning together: inter-institutional collaboration as a means of capacity building*. Keynote symposium paper presented at the Annual conference of the British Education Research Association, Heriot Watt University.

DAVIES, S. M. B., SALISBURY, J. in press. Building educational research capacity through inter-institutional collaboration: An evaluation of the first year of the Welsh Education Research Network (WERN). *Welsh Journal of Education*.

DEEM, R. 2003. New managerialism in UK universities: manager-academic accounts of change. In: H. EGGINS, H. (ed.), *Globalisation and reform in higher education*. Maidenhead: Open University and McGraw Hill Education.

DILLENBOURG, P., BAKER, M., BLAYE, A., O'MALLEY, C., 1996. The evolution of research on collaborative learning. In: E. SPADA, P. REIMAN (eds), *Learning in Humans and machine: towards an interdisciplinary learning science*. Oxford: Elsevier, pp. 198-211.

DOISE, W. 1990. The development of individual competencies through social interaction. In: H. C. FOOT, M. J. MORGAN, R. H. SHUTE (eds) *Children helping children*. Chichester: J. Wiley & sons, pp. 43-64.

FULTON, O. 1996. Which academic profession are you in? In: R. CUTHBERT (ed.), *Working in higher education*. Buckingham: Society for Research into Higher Education and Open University Press, pp.157-169.

GEWITZ S., MAHONY, P. 2006. *Changing teacher roles, identities and professionalism*. ESRC CTTRIP Seminar Series, King's College, London.

GLEESON, D., JAMES, D. 2007. The paradox of Professionalism in English further Education: a TLC perspective. *Educational Review*, 59 (4), pp. 451-467.

GORNALL, L. 1999. New professionals, change and occupational roles in higher education. *Perspectives, policy and Practice in Higher Education*, 3 (2), pp. 44-49.

GORNALL, L., THOMAS, B, SALISBURY, J. 2008. Working Lives: narratives of occupational change from Further and Higher Education in post-devolution Wales, British Education Research Association Conference.

HENKEL, M. 2000. *Academic identities and Policy Change in Higher Education*. London: Jessica Kingsley.

JAMES, D. HODKINSON, P., BIESTA G. 2007. *Transforming Learning cultures in Further Education*. London: Routledge.

JEPHCOTE, M., SALISBURY, J. 2007. The long shadow of incorporation: the further education sector in devolved Wales. *Welsh Journal of Education*, 14 (1), pp. 100-116.

JEPHCOTE, M., SALISBURY, J. 2008. The wider social contexts of learning: beyond the classroom door. *International Journal of Learning*, 15 (6), pp. 281-288.

LAVE J. 1988. *Cognition in Practice*. Cambridge: Cambridge University Press.

MUSSELIN, C. 2007. The transformation of academic work: facts and analysis. *Research & Occasional Paper Series*, CSHE, 4.07. Berkeley: Centre for Studies in Higher Education, University of California.

POWELL, F. A., SINGLE, H. M. 1996. Focus groups. *International Journal of Quality in Health Care*, 8 (5), pp. 499-504.

REES, G., POWER, S. 2007. Educational research and the restructuring of state: the impacts of parliamentary devolution in Wales, *European Educational Research Journal*, 6 (1), pp. 87-99.

ROSCHELLE, J., TEASLEY, S. D. 1995. The construction of shared knowledge in collaborative problem solving. In: O'MALLEY, C. E., (ed.), *Computer Supported Collaborative Learning*. Heidelberg: Springer-Verlag, pp. 69-97.

SILLITOE, P. 2007. Anthropologists only need apply: challenges of applied anthropology. *Journal of the Royal Anthropological Institute (N.S.)*, 13, pp.147-165.

SOLOMON, N., BOUD, D., LEONTIOS, M., STARON, M., 2001. Researchers are learners too: collaboration in research on workplace learning. *Journal of Workplace Learning*, 13 (7/8), pp. 274-282.

SUCHMAN, L. A. 1987. *Plans and Situated Actions: The problem of human-machine communication*. Cambridge: Cambridge University Press.

TIGHT, M. (ed.) 2002. *Academic work and life: what it is to be an academic; and how this is changing*. Oxford: Elsevier Press.

University
of Wales,
Newport

Prifysgol
Cymru,
Casnewydd

Linking Research and Teaching in Higher Education
Simon K. Haslett and Hefin Rowlands (eds)
Proceedings of the Newport NEXUS Conference
Centre for Excellence in Learning and Teaching
Special Publication, No. 1, 2009, pp. 65-70
ISBN 978-1-899274-38-3

How do I manage my role yet still maintain my values as a lecturer? A personal reflection.

Matthew Gravelle

School of Art, Media and Design, University of Wales, Newport, Lodge Road, Caerleon, South Wales, NP18 3QT, United Kingdom. Email: Matthew.gravelle@newport.ac.uk

Abstract

In this paper the author examines the implications experienced when inadvertently faced with student's personal problems. Believing in providing constructive feedback and a fair grade on their work, the author questions whether he was providing his true honest opinion to certain students due to his unfortunate awareness of their personal circumstances. Spending countless hours dealing with issues surrounding divorce, bullying, family loss, immigration, racism, hate crime, addictions, disabilities and mental illnesses, the author found himself in uncomfortable situations where he was unable to hold a professional distance with his students. Wishing to maintain his values as a lecturer, he searches for a solution to this problem with the aim of discovering an approach where he is capable of managing his role and not being shadowed by issues or swayed in his judgement by personal information when assessing their work.

Before starting my lecturing post I had a very clear idea what my responsibilities would be. Weekly meetings, preparing and delivering lectures and assessing student work I anticipated, and was clearly informed by the university before starting the position. However, I did not expect what became a very common and extremely difficult occurrence to manage – emotionally supporting students. As many of us are aware, entering student life can be a very daunting and difficult experience. Harrison (2001) collated a series of surveys and statistics dating back to 1997. The newspaper reported a study that claimed sixty one percent of first year university students experienced depression, twelve regularly considered suicide while one student attempted suicide. Another investigation stated that between 10 and 20% of students required psychiatric help before graduating. *The Mental Health Foundation* discovered that 50% of university students showed signs of clinical anxiety and more than one in ten suffered from clinical depression. *The Times,* in 2000, disclosed that more than 17% of students entering university felt lonely, suffering from self-doubt and isolation. In fact, feeling isolated was reported by the majority of students, where around one third of all students said their main problem was linked to loneliness, a common reason for leaving university without graduating. According to *The Times,* the most likely students to suffer from isolation whilst at university are:

- overseas students;
- mature students;
- students living in single-sex halls;
- first year students living off campus;
- joint Honours students who felt they did not belong in either of their home de-partments.

Caring for students is one of a university's highest priorities. The university has a very strong policy in keeping its retention figures high. As lecturers we are expected to listen to student needs. If students were to leave due to lack of support it would have repercussions on staff members. Although the university offers student support, seeking advice from a tutor seems to be the most common and comfortable solution for many, regardless of what the issue may be. Since becoming a lecturer, I have inadvertently found myself heavily involved in the personal and pastoral care of students, listening to issues surrounding divorce, family loss, immigration, racism, hate crime, addictions, disabilities and mental illnesses. Despite knowing deep down I was unable to help with these issues, I ended up spending countless hours talking or writing e-mails outside of my contracted hours, counselling students on matters I had very little knowledge or experience with myself. *The British Association of Counselling* (1991, p. 1) claims that:

'counselling is the skilled and principled use of a relationship to facilitate self-knowledge, emotional acceptance and growth, and the optimal development of personal resources. The overall aim is to provide an opportunity to work towards living more satisfyingly and resourcefully.'

As I am not a trained counsellor, my involvement with certain student issues was a constant concern of mine. The cohort of students that I have experienced, unexpectedly revealing personal issues, not only made managing my role very difficult in terms of hours and inexperience, but also caused a serious implication on one of my important values as a lecturer, which is providing constructive criticism and a fair grade for their work. When students were coming to me on a regular basis regarding personal issues of theirs, I sometimes questioned whether I was giving them my true honest opinion due to my personal awareness of the individual:

'If you are ultimately responsible for assessing your learners by determining their grades, then that limits the extent to which an open relationship is possible' (Mortiboys, 2005, p. 16).

What is interesting, before I became a permanent lecturer my grades and feedback were far more critical as a visiting tutor. I recall being told by a member of staff how *'harsh'* I was. Yet my reason for being so judgmental of their work was that I purely assessed it for what it was, without any knowledge of the individual who had produced it. Now as an employed lecturer and being with the students on a more regular basis, I found I was being frequently approached by students with issues unrelated to their studies. From intense conversations to difficult e-mails, I found myself in uncomfortable situations beyond my control at the time, spending a considerable amount of time with each scenario. To highlight my experiences, in December 2006, I received an e-mail from a student who was lacking confidence. Surrounding this issue were mentions of depression, divorce, loneliness and wanting to open a bottle of wine to drown her sorrows. What started as a manageable issue cumulated into a very difficult and uncomfortable read. Despite not being contracted to work on this particular day, I was unable to ignore it, mainly because I was concerned about the individual and did not want to leave it until I was back in work in case the student was waiting for a reply. Spending hours writing and rewriting my response, taking careful consideration of my wording, I concluded suggesting seeing a university councillor. I quickly received a reply from the individual thanking me for my words of encouragement. The individual mentioned not *'been overly impressed'* with councillors and preferred not to see one. The e-mail finished on mentioning a recent family loss. Two weeks later whilst assessing, I passed that particular student giving the lowest possible grade, despite feeling the grade should possibly have been lower.

Although I had tried to change by becoming less approachable, unavailable or simply ignoring e-mails, I found myself not living in the direction of my values (McNiff and Whitehead, 2006, p. 46). In March 2007 I was approached in my office, unexpectedly again, by a student who was clearly distressed about something. This student was, I felt, one of the most talented students we had and showed a great flair for his work. Despite trying my best to get to the bottom of what the problem was, I failed to find what I could do to help him. I was now in the middle of a Postgraduate Certificate in Developing Professional Practice in Higher Education and had started working on an action research cycle report, that forms the basis of this paper. I knew I had to put methods into practice and think of new approaches. When I realised he was not going to tell me what his concerns were, I decided to let him leave the office and not worry about him. A week later he sent an e-mail apologising for his behaviour and said *'I'm fine now ... don't worry about me.'* I felt I should have responded to the e-mail, but actually I did not. The following month, before graduating, the student thanked me for my help and support during his time at university. This reminded me of why I enjoy the work that I do. I was not proud of the way I had dealt with this situation and it made me feel very uncomfortable. Although it ended happily, I regret not being supportive enough with the student when he clearly needed it. I was concerned that my insensitive approach was giving the wrong impression to students. Carson (1996) collected, over a period of twenty six years, responses from past students who had graduated from Rollins College in Orlando. In 1996, she published her findings and discovered that the most effective teachers were the ones who demonstrated a *'love of subject and even more often than enthusiasm in the classroom – was a special attitude toward and relationship with students'* (Carson, 1996, p.14). In my experience, teachers/lecturers who have a passion for what they and their students are doing always were the most effective teachers and managed to get the best work out of everyone. Now as a lecturer myself, my aim has always been to follow their example. However, I needed to find a way of dealing with these matters that were affecting my values as a lecturer, enabling me to judge the situation for myself and deciding on what action I should take.

Alan Mortiboys, lecturer and author of *'Teaching with Emotional Intelligence'* (2005), believes handling your own emotions as well as your students is central to your success as a lecturer (2005, p. 1). This means having the ability to identify mine and students feelings in order to motivate and manage each other (Goleman, 1998, p. 317). Nevertheless, what Mortiboys (2005) and so many others fail to realise, or at least develop, is the consequences of this. To describe someone who is demonstrating his emotional intelligence, Mortiboys uses words such as *'approachable,' 'positive,' 'good listener' 'attentive'* and *'respectful,'* which are all common traits I identify with myself. However, the problem with presenting these qualities to your students is that they can sometimes see you more as a close friend who they can approach at anytime to discuss personal issues. As Mortiboys (2005, p. 80) says:

'I certainly would not suggest that you become a counsellor, ready to deal with the range of feelings an individual has and to assist them with their personal problems. That is not your job and would be inappropriate and damaging behaviour, so be sure to have a clear understanding of your limits in this respect.'

For Mortiboys to state this clearly brings to light his understanding of the potential circumstances that may occur through engaging your emotional intelligence in dealing with students. Unfortunately, he does not delve into this area any further. Therefore, I decided to contact him and query his quote, asking if he had any advice on how I should manage this problem. His reply was extremely useful as it made me question what I was doing. My main problem is that I do not want to come across as being heartless to my students if I decide to not help them in anyway. Mortiboys (2005) believes that advising students on issues I have very little knowledge or experience with is *'irresponsible'* and that I needed to change my approach immediately to benefit the student as well as myself. He felt I needed to identify what my boundaries were so that I can immediately respond to how far I want to listen when these situations occurred. My overall feeling from Mortiboys's (2007) response to my query was that I needed to be clearer with my students regarding what support I am prepared to offer.

I began looking into ways I could communicate how I wished to be perceived by my students. In the 1960's, Eric Berne developed a method of understanding human behaviour through a model which he called Transactional Analysis (Berne, 1961). By analysing the interactions between people when communicating, he identified three ego states to our personality – parent, adult and child. His model enables us to become aware of these components in our individual personality and to understand which ego states we are operating our interactions with, hence explaining our various relationships with different people. The goal is to identify and change our ego states if we wish to achieve a better outcome when communicating with certain people in our lives. My feeling from reading his three ego states was that I possibly behave as a *'nurturing parent'* constantly encouraging and guiding students. Berne (1961) sees a *'nurturing parent'* as someone who is caring and concerned, calming people when they are troubled. Words, I admit, that I identify myself with when faced with distressed students. This is again mainly down to me as a person and my experiences in life with teachers and lecturers. When I was a student, I myself felt more comfortable approaching my tutor regarding a personal issue of mine as it felt to be the safest and most comfortable option from talking to anyone else. We see our lecturers on a weekly basis and connections easily develop without one being aware. Now as a lecturer myself, I have quickly realised how extremely difficult this can be. Berne's (1961) description of the adult ego state includes someone who is rational and talks reasonably and assertively, yet neither tries to control or react. Although an adult to adult approach with all my students seemed the most obvious approach in resolving this issue, there was no general rule as to the effectiveness of any ego state in any given situation. My general feeling was that I need to achieve a balanced approach between the adult and parent ego states, yet be fully aware of where I drew the line in terms of my involvement in the personal and pastoral care of each individual.

Obviously, I did not want to immediately abandon a student if a personal issue was brought to my attention. Therefore, I decided to identify the most common personal problems I have experienced from students, and others that I am likely to experience in the future, and researched what services and support groups were available, including visiting student support and researching organisations outside the university. This allowed me to signpost the student in the right direction if the issue was unrelated to their studies. Since my research, I have experienced several situations where students have unexpectedly emerged with private information. For example, a student was falling behind with her studies for several reasons which she brought to my attention, including a recent family loss, financial difficulties and her current mental health. Her mother was unaware she had failed the previous year, which was causing huge stress for the student. A month later, I was approached by a student who was clearly distressed and anxious about her choice of study. This eventually led to more personal information being revealed explaining her behaviour, including family loss, feeling isolated, and ill health within the family and herself. She told me she had not made many friends since starting the course and was finding it very difficult to settle in. Her confidence and self-esteem was very low and pressure from the family to achieve a degree was causing immense strain to her. Another situation at the same time, involved a mature student breaking down during a one to one discussion on her work. Unwilling to tell me what the problem was, she admitted that the issue was personal. Overall, these experiences were not enjoyable. Clearly I do not wish for anyone to feel alone or unable to talk to anyone. I approached each situation with careful thought and consideration. I made it clear that I was unable to help with their private circumstances, but offered my full support and time in helping them with their work. Personally, I did not feel cold or heartless by not delving into their issues. I actually felt a better person and possibly more responsible by responding in this way. I informed them of the services that were available but left it in their hands to decide if they were going to make use of what the university has to offer.

How do we manage our role as lecturers?

Figure 1. "How do we manage our role as lecturers?" (cartoon by author).

Although this account has been very personal, I feel what I have achieved as a result has been a step in the right direction. As one can never predict when these difficult situations will occur, I feel this research has really helped me decide on an appropriate action to take. Whether it is a knock on the door, e-mail or approached in a corridor, the information I have collated has made me more aware of the support that is available and has helped build my confidence by being better prepared when I am faced with these situations. I feel far more equipped to deal with student concerns and direct them to the appropriate person or agency if I am unable to help. I can now decide if a brief conversation with myself will help the student, or if their need requires more specialist support (locally or nationally). I always ensure that students are aware that I can offer my support in achieving their degree, however, I now feel I am able to *'stand back'* from personal situations when they arise and look at the issue from a lecturers angle, holding a professional distance. This has enabled me to deliver constructive criticism during assessment time, evaluating students work simply for what it is and not being shadowed by issues or being swayed in my judgement by personal information, and I hope my journey will be of use to others.

REFERENCES

BERNE, E. 1961. *Transactional Analysis in Psychotherapy*. New York: Grove Press, Inc.

BRITISH ASSOCIATION FOR COUNSELLING 1991. *Code of Ethics and Practice for Counsellors*. Rugby: B.A.C.

CARSON, B. 1996. Thirty Years of Stories: The Professor's Place in Student Memories. *Change*, 28 (6), pp. 10 – 17.

GOLEMAN, D. 1998. *Working with Emotional Intelligence*. London: Bloomsbury.

HARRISON, M. 2001. *Feeling Lonely or Depressed?* [Online information], p. 1. Available from The University of Warwick at http://www2.warwick.ac.uk/fac/soc/economics/staff/faculty/harrison/advice/depress2/ (accessed 14 July 2007).

MCNIFF, J., WHITEHEAD, J. 2006. *All You Need To Know About Action Research*. London: SAGE Publications Ltd.

MORTIBOYS, A. 2005. *Teaching with Emotional Intelligence*. London: Routledge.

MORTIBOYS, A. 2007. *Advice to author*. Personal correspondence (20 September 2007).

University of Wales, Newport

Prifysgol Cymru, Casnewydd

Linking Research and Teaching in Higher Education
Simon K. Haslett and Hefin Rowlands (eds)
Proceedings of the Newport NEXUS Conference
Centre for Excellence in Learning and Teaching
Special Publication, No. 1, 2009, pp. 71-81
ISBN 978-1-899274-38-3

Issues surrounding the use of social network sites in Higher Education.

Joanna Jones and Ruth Gaffney-Rhys

Newport Business School, University of Wales, Newport, Allt-yr-yn Campus, Allt-yr-yn Avenue, Newport, NP20 5DA, United Kingdom. Email: Joanna.Jones@newport.ac.uk; Ruth.gaffney-rhys@newport.ac.uk

Abstract

This paper presents a summary of the main issues relating to the impact of social networks in Higher Education in the United Kingdom (UK), with particular emphasis upon students' communication and engagement with faculty via social network sites. There is a strong argument that barriers remain that prevents student/lecturer engagement, via social networks, becoming mainstream. For instance, student users' attitudes regarding 'ownership' of the space, the nature of 'friends', pre-entry legal issues and the lecturer-student relationship. Furthermore, particularly in the context of large international student intake, it would be erroneous to assume that a lecturer could create a profile on one social network site (e.g. Facebook) in order to communicate with all students. Whilst UK Higher Education institutions (HEIs) cannot spurn the educational opportunities that social network sites offer, perhaps the minimum role of an educator is to encourage students to understand how the publicly available content on a social network site could be viewed as a direct reflection upon their professionalism both now and in the future. Additionally, UK HEIs need to grapple with the legal and ethical issues relating to monitoring and surveillance of social network sites, particularly with a view to preventing legal proceedings relating to defamation and harassment.

Introduction

A leading researcher in the field of social networks in the United States (US) (boyd, 2007) stated that 'today's teenagers are being socialised into a society complicated by shifts in the public and private. New social technologies have altered the underlying architecture of social interaction and information distribution' (p. 1). Consequently, this paper presents a summary of literature and the main issues relating to the impact of social networks in Higher Education (HE) in the United Kingdom (UK), with particular emphasis upon students' communication and engagement with faculty via social network sites and the legal issues surrounding the use of social network sites. The review will be used at a later date to form a context and catalyst for the collection and analysis of empirical data relating to attitudes and perceptions of both students and faculty at University of Wales, Newport.

Social Network Sites

boyd & Ellison (2007, p. 20) define social network sites as:

"Web based services that allow individuals to 1) construct a public or semi-public profile within a bounded system, 2) articulate a list of other users with whom they share a connection and 3) view and traverse their list of connections and those made by others within the system."

This 'profile' acts as the user's homepage and includes a range of personal information (*e.g.* gender, favourite music) and uploaded content such as photos and video clips. Ofcom (2008) explained that in the UK many peoples' first exposure to social network sites was via media coverage of Friends Reunited. The Ofcom study also confirmed that Facebook is presently the most popular social network site in the UK, followed by MySpace and Bebo. Indeed, the extent to which social network site usage has grown, in a relatively small timeframe, is astounding. In February 2009, Facebook reported having reached 175 million active users worldwide (www.inside facebook.com); whilst in the UK, Ofcom (2008) research indicated that 22% of adult internet users (16+) have set up a profile on at least one social network site, with 49% of 8-17 year olds also having set up profiles. There is evidence to indicate that the use of social network sites in the US is increasing amongst people who were not seen as habitual users, that is over 25 year olds (www.inside facebook.com). Perhaps, the creation of such social network sites as Sagazone is an indication that this trend will be duplicated in the UK. Prior to moving on from the facts and figures relating to social network sites, it is appropriate to comment upon the transient nature of the popularity of specific sites; whilst Facebook presently holds a dominant position in the UK, past evidence would indicate that this may not be maintained. Therefore, if UK HE staff are to embrace social network sites as a communication tool, they will need to change their usage to coincide with current trends. This may well raise a technical barrier for some academics, particularly considering the fact that the ability of some UK academics to engage with ICT was questioned by recent Ipsos Mori research (2008, commissioned by the Joint Information Systems Committee, JISC). For instance, one respondent bemoaned 'it's annoying when they waste their time trying to figure out how to turn the projector on' (p. 25).

Many academics (boyd 2007; Cain 2008; Tufekci 2008) have attributed four properties to social networks that have relevance for educators when considering their response to the use of social networks: persistence; searchability; replicability; invisible audiences. Persistence is significant as users' content *e.g.* uploaded photos, could be stored on servers indefinitely, thus potentially causing embarrassment to users at some time in the future. Searchability can leave users open to searchers using the social network site for unintended uses, such as universities using social networks for applicant screening. Replicability refers to the ease with which content can be copied from one space to another; whilst invisible audiences pertains to the ease with which online expression can be 'overheard' both in real time and as a result of the persistence property, at a later date. These attributes are also relevant when considering liability for defamation, which may be committed via a social network site (see below).

It should be noted that although the array of social network sites can appear bemusing, the definition and properties described above can be generally applied to all such sites. However, that is not to say that the features, privacy settings and atmosphere of each site are not unique. This leads to a conundrum for educators who wish to engage with students via social network sites: on which site should they create a profile?

Usage of Social Network Sites

Hargittai (2007) attempted to find a rationale for use and non-use of various social network sites, including Facebook, MySpace, Xanga, Friendster, Orkut and Bebo. In this study Facebook was by far the most popular site (although it should be noted that the sample were all US college students and the study took place at a time when Facebook was dominated by education groups). Additionally, it was found that students living at home with parents (as opposed to those living with roommates) were less likely to use Facebook. This could have implications for UK HE staff when attempting to utilise social networks sites to strengthen bonds with students who do not live on campus, for example, part-time students or the growing number of full-time students who choose to study at a local university for financial reasons.

Moreover, findings indicated that people from diverse ethnic groups were more likely to use or not use specific social network sites. For example, Hispanic students were significantly more likely to use MySpace than Whites while Asian and Asian American students were significantly less likely to use MySpace. Correspondingly, Asian American students were more likely to use Xanga and Friendster, a practice that the author attributed to the immigrant nature of the sample and the popularity of these services in the Philippines, Singapore and Malaysia. It is important to note that whilst some sites such as Facebook have grown popular worldwide, regional sites catering for non-english speaking populations have also established large user bases (e.g. Cyworld in Korea, Mixi in Japan and QQ in China.) Therefore, the difference in the cultural atmosphere of social network sites cannot be underestimated, particularly in the UK where universities enrol many more international students

Kim & Yun (2007) analysed how the design features of a Korean Social Network Site (Cyworld) mirrored Korea's collectivist culture. In essence, the researchers were assessing 'to what degree and how are Korean cultural principles about interpersonal relationships realised in the use of Cyworld' (p. 5). An interesting finding related to the almost unique use of Cyworld for self reflection; indeed users seemed to have dual motivations for using the site (cying) that is maintaining their social networks and reflecting upon themselves. This is yet another example of how the usage and cultural atmosphere of social network sites can differ. Interestingly, Ofcom (2008) research identified that in the UK there were also socio-economic variations regarding social network site preference, with for example ABC1s being more likely to have a profile upon Facebook than C2DEs (who would be more likely to have a profile on MySpace). However, it could be argued that this differential could also be explained by the ethnic make-up of these socio-economic groups.

US research (Lampe *et al.*, 2008) seemed to indicate that student users predominantly tended to utilise Facebook to connect with and maintain relationships with people in an existing social network rather than to seek out new friends and acquaintances. The term 'social searching' was coined to describe the use of Facebook to find out more about people they have either met or have become aware of off-line. (*e.g.* attending the same lecture). Similarly, the term 'social browsing' was used to describe a secondary motivation of using the site to meet someone with the view of arranging a later offline meeting. One of the few UK based studies (Joinson, 2008) further developed this theme of motives and uses of Facebook and confirmed that users (the sample was not limited to students) utilised the network not only to connect with existing contacts but also to surf social networks and to carry out surveillance.

The Ofcom (2008) research utilised somewhat quirky categories to describe the behaviour and motivations of social network users. These are pertinent as they describe UK users and the data are derived from a wide sample not only linked to student populations.

- Alpha socialisers relate to a minority of users who use sites in short bursts to flirt, meet new people and be entertained. This could be seen as being broadly equivalent to elements of 'social browsing' (Lampe *et al.*, 2008; Joinson, 2008).

- Attention seekers relate to some people who crave attention and comments from others, often by posting photos and customising their profiles. This corresponds with Tufekci's (2008) notion relating to the fact that 'kids want to be seen' (p. 20).

- Followers are described as the majority who join sites to keep up with what their peers are doing, and Faithfuls the many who tend to use social networks to rekindle old friendships. This could be seen as broadly equivalent to elements of 'social searching' (Lampe *et al.*, 2008; Joinson, 2008).

- Finally, the Ofcom research categorised a minority of users as 'Functionals' that is, users who tended to be single minded in using sites for a specific purpose.

Friends and Audiences in Social Networks

Regardless of the social network site being explored or the users' motivations, a key concept is the notion of online connections, that is, 'friends'. It has already been established that many users utilise social network sites to maintain existing offline relationships, so in this context the meaning of 'friend' is uncontroversial. However, there is a nascent academic disagreement regarding the concept of off-line and online 'friends'. For example, boyd & Ellison (2007) argue that friends on social networks are not the same as friends in the traditional, everyday sense. Whilst Beer (2008, p. 520) counters that 'we cannot think of friendship on social network sites as entirely different and disconnected from our actual friends and notions of friendship, particularly as young people grow up and are informed by the connections they make on social network sites.' A practice that reinforces boyd and Ellisons' viewpoints is that some users appear to directly equate the size of a contact/friend list to popularity (Tufekci, 2008). However, it should be remembered that various research projects have confirmed that keeping in touch with existing connections (offline friends) is by far the most prevalent use of social network sites (Lampe et al., 2008; Joinson, 2008).

The term 'friend' is significant when considering possible interaction between student and faculty via social network sites. It could be seen as an emotive word that does not convey the nature of the relationship between students and faculty. Hewitt & Forte (2006) investigated student/faculty relationships at a US college and found that a large minority of the students surveyed (particularly females) were not positive regarding engaging with faculty via social network sites. Concerns expressed included fear of monitoring and the erosion of a professional tutor/student relationship. Interestingly, some

respondents stated that 'it's a social network for students' and 'if they poke me, I might find it strange' (p. 2). In 2008, Ipsos Mori published the results of a comprehensive UK study, commissioned by JISC, which assessed how universities are meeting students' expectations regarding the use of ICT. This study confirms that some students 'can feel uncomfortable when teachers relate to them in a flat, non-hierarchical structure (e.g. via Facebook)' (p. 14). Generally, there was a wide range of opinion relating to whether students wished to engage with faculty using social networks; however, in this study females were found to be more receptive to the idea than males. Nevertheless, the educational value of self formed Facebook study groups should not be underestimated. The Ipsos Mori research indicated that all students who have used social network sites as a collaborative learning tool found it useful, but this generally related to informal student initiated discussions. Nonetheless, it is interesting to note that 91% of respondents declared e-mail to be their preferred method of communication with tutors.

A common theme in social networks research is that many students consider the space to be theirs (Hewitt & Forte, 2006; Cain, 2007; Tufekci, 2008). In the Lampe et al. (2008) study, student users' perceptions of who used and viewed the sites were seen to be unrealistic. Indeed, student users believed that their Facebook profiles were viewed only by peers and close online connections. 'Non peers such as faculty, law enforcement and employers were seldom thought to have viewed profiles' (p. 729). This example illustrates that student users are unmindful regarding the threat of the 'invisible audience' (boyd, 2007) despite the fact that they may well themselves utilise social network sites for surveillance activity (see discussion below on the law of privacy). However, it should be noted that these perceptions may not be as relevant in the UK context because, in the US, initial Facebook usage was confined to education establishments (users requiring a valid college e-mail address); therefore, students' perceptions may have been influenced by this fact. Whereas in the UK, by the time Facebook gained meaningful penetration, it was already open to non-academic users. This peculiarity of initial Facebook usage in the US (that is, the networks that were built were based upon offline geographical groups, *e.g.* campus) may mean that some of the early research could now lack resonance in the UK context and that some of the monitoring activities undertaken by US education establishments may not spread to the UK.

Nevertheless, the ease with which educators can carry out surveillance activity upon social networks opens up ethical debates for UK HE staff. For instance, Cain (2008) reported occasions when students have been expelled from respective universities for threats of crime; others disciplined for alcohol violations and Facebook has been used to track down the instigators of campus brawls. At George Washington University (US) college students, knowing that their Facebook activity was being monitored by campus officials deliberately advertised a beer party (legal drinking age being 21). When the campus officials raided the party all they found was cake and cookies with the word 'beer' emblazoned (Hass, 2006).

Privacy and e-Professionalism

Whilst it is not the purpose of this paper to dwell upon the complexities of privacy and trust in the social network environment, it is important to note that understanding audiences and privacy is essential for an educator. Firstly, this understanding is imperative if UK HE staff are going to utilise social networks to communicate with students and, secondly, appreciation is essential if educators are to advise students regarding the possible repercussions of inappropriate social network usage. Acquisti and Gross (2006) found that 30% of their respondents (US College students) were unaware that they could change the default privacy settings offered by Facebook. Furthermore, Joinson (2008) found that users who wished to use social network sites to meet new people found privacy settings to be too stringent. Similarly, Lampe *et al.* (2007)

found that only 19% of the profiles surveyed were set as "friends only" (thus limiting the audience who could view the content of the profile) and an alarming number of these profiles contained information relating to political view, romantic status, sexual orientation, religion, phone number and address. The issue is further complicated by the fact that each social network site has differing search arrangements and privacy settings. For example, on some sites (*e.g.* Facebook) an academic can protect themselves from friends revealing information or uploading images which the academic may not wish students to see, whilst on other sites (*e.g.* Friendster) this protection is more difficult to achieve. In addition to trying to educate students regarding the obvious immediate dangers associated with divulging to much personal information; perhaps one of the roles of an educator is to encourage students to understand how the publicly available content on a social network site could be viewed as a direct reflection upon their professionalism both now and in the future. For instance, Ferdig *et al.* (2008) investigated medical students' use of social network sites and concluded that educators need to better understand how such environments work so that they are better placed to teach about e-professionalism. Perhaps such education would prevent the type of incident described in the *Times Higher Education Supplement* (2008) where the title of a Facebook student group left little doubt about what some University of Bradford undergraduates thought of one of their lectures! Using social network sites to abuse lecturers (or indeed other students) is a legal issue that HEIs need to consider carefully. The remainder of this paper discusses the law that impacts upon the use of social network sites in detail.

Legal Issues Surrounding the Use of Social Network Sites

The use of social network sites by HEIs falls into two broad categories. Prior to enrolment, universities will utilise social network sites to provide pre-entry support for individuals who have been accepted on a course. Post-enrolment, such sites will be used to communicate with groups of students and as a learning and teaching tool. These separate uses raise quite different legal issues, which need to be carefully considered in order to avoid complaints being made to the Office of the Independent Adjudicator for Higher Education (OIA) and ultimately litigation.

Since 2001 (when the Student Room was launched), UK social network sites have been employed to provide prospective students with information and advice. The Student Room, which was previously known as UK Learning, was initially used to locate teaching materials but has since become a place for young people to find information about careers, university courses and studying at higher education institutions. The popularity of the Student Room and the importance of providing pre-entry support have been recognised by many UK HEIs. As a consequence, several universities have set up their own social network site to support applicants prior to enrolment or have established a group on existing networks, such as Facebook, for the same purpose. Given that current students and a wide range of university staff will communicate with applicants via the site, problems can arise if the advice provided is inaccurate or inconsistent. Indeed, action could potentially be taken for breach of contract because the relationship between a student and his or her HEI is based on a contract (see Clarke v University of Lincolnshire and Humberside, 2000). A legally binding agreement is formed when an offer made by an HEI, is accepted by the applicant (Moran v University College Salford, No. 2, 1994). Although the contract between an applicant and a university is usually formed in writing (by letter), it is not legally necessary to present the contractual terms in a written document. As a result, the terms of the relationship are not always clear. The OIA has confirmed that promises made by an HEI in its prospectus or on its website may take effect as contractual terms (OIA, 2007, p. 10). It thus follows that information provided on an official university social network site or a group set up on an existing social network

site by the university can potentially constitute terms of the contract. Some statements made via social network sites will not be considered 'terms of the contract' because they are too vague or because they do not define the parties' rights and responsibilities. Even if these statements are not technically terms of the contract, action can be brought for misrepresentation if an applicant accepts an offer made by an HEI based on a false statement of fact (but not a mere opinion). Furthermore, the HEI is contractually bound to provide adequate teaching and facilities. Information contained on an official social network site can affect whether the teaching and facilities are deemed to be adequate (see Buckingham v Rycotewood College, 26/3/2002).

The university can be held responsible for the contents of its social network site or official Facebook group, if the information was posted by a member of staff because an employer is vicariously liable for the acts of its employees that occur in the course of employment. An HEI will be held accountable for advice provided by university staff even if the latter contravened express instructions, because an employee has apparent authority to act on behalf of the university. The terms of conditions of a university social network site may exclude liability for breach of contract or misrepresentation, but these disclaimers are subject to the Unfair Contract Terms Act 1977 and the Unfair Terms in Consumer Contracts Regulations 1999, and consequently may be rendered unenforceable on the basis of unreasonableness and unfairness respectively. Moreover, if a student has taken a complaint to the Office of the Independent Adjudicator decisions are based on 'what is fair and reasonable in the circumstances' (OIA, 2007, p. 11). A disclaimer or exclusion clause could, therefore, be ignored by the OIA on the ground that it is unfair. In contrast, if an HEI establishes a group on an existing social network site, it may not be able to determine its own terms and conditions and may not, therefore, be able to exclude liability for its contents.

At the University of Wales, Newport, student mentors post information on

'NewSpace', the university's social network site. As student mentors are employees, the university is vicariously liable for their actions and, thus, needs to take great care when appointing them and when training them to use NewSpace. Several HEIs allow any existing student to communicate with applicants via their social network site. Given that the site officially belongs to the university, the latter is arguably responsible for its contents. However, most students will be stating their views on the university, its staff, its facilities or a particular course. A mere opinion does not constitute a term of the contract and cannot give rise to liability for misrepresentation. The same can be said for opinions cited by students on a Facebook group set up by the university. From a contractual perspective, information posted by students is not, therefore, problematic, but it can potentially infringe the law relating to harassment and defamation (see below) and should therefore be monitored.

Post-Enrolment Legal Issues

As explained above, social network sites are also used post-enrolment as a learning and teaching tool and to communicate with current students. Post-entry use of social network sites can contravene the law of Harassment, Defamation and Privacy and may have Intellectual Property implications. It is beyond the scope of this paper to discuss these complex legal issues in any detail; however, it is crucial to raise awareness of them.

Social network sites can potentially be utilised by students and staff to bully or harass each other. This can violate the university's code of conduct and the various Equality Regulations that prohibit harassment on the grounds of sex, race, religion, age, disability and sexual orientation. Comments allegedly made on a Cardiff University Facebook group about a lecturer being gay (Thompson, 2009) could thus breach the Employment Equality Sexual Orientation Regulations 2003. In extreme cases, if the victim of harassment feels threatened in some way, criminal liability can be incurred under the Protection from Harassment Act 1997. Staff and students that engage in e-harassment can thus face internal disciplinary action, legal action for damages or an injunction in the civil courts or even criminal proceedings which can ultimately result in a fine, community punishment or prison sentence. An institution will be vicariously liable for civil wrongs committed by its employees in the course of employment and could, therefore, be required to compensate the victim of harassment. However, an employer is not vicariously liable for crimes committed by employees and as a consequence a university would not face criminal proceedings. If a student (who is not an employee of the university) uses a social network site to bully or harass a fellow student or member of university staff, the liability of the HEI will arguably depend upon the control that the HEI has over the site and whether it failed to take reasonable steps to prevent or put an end to the harassment. As explained earlier, a university that sets up its own social network site is responsible for its contents. It is, therefore, essential to appoint a member of staff to monitor the information posted on the site and to promptly remove harmful information in order to minimise or avoid liability. Furthermore, the university should establish a code of conduct which makes it clear that such behaviour is unacceptable and should discipline students and staff who contravene the code (for example, see the Guidelines produced by Birmingham University entitled 'Social Networking Sites and Students Issues' 2008). If the HEI has set up a group on an existing social network site the position is less certain as the group may be open, closed or secret and as a result the control that the university has over the site varies considerably. If a Facebook group is completely open (as the Cardiff University group is) any Facebook user can post information on the discussion site or wall. Although the administrator would be able to remove offending material he or she may be unable to do so quickly, given the large numbers of people who can potentially contribute to the site. It can be argued that the HEI should only be liable for the information if it failed to explain to staff and students that certain behaviour is unacceptable, if it failed to monitor the content of the site and failed to remove harmful material as soon as possible.

If staff or students post incorrect information about another person on a social network site the tort of defamation could be committed. Defamation occurs if one person publishes an untrue statement about another that harms the latter's reputation. Contrary to popular belief, a statement does not have to be published in a national newspaper or magazine or spoken on television or radio to be actionable. An individual can sue for defamation provided that the statement has been communicated to someone other than the claimant him or herself and the defendant's spouse. Information posted on a secret site that has few members can legally constitute defamation. Although the level of damages awarded in such cases would be nominal, the defendant could be compelled to remove offending material and prevented from publishing defamatory information in the future. Given that anything posted on a social network site can be retained indefinitely on a server or as a printed copy, a defamatory posting constitutes libel (the permanent form of defamation) rather than slander (the transitory form).

The individual does not need to be expressly named on the site for defamation to occur. Provided that a reasonable person could work out that the statement refers to the claimant, the latter can initiate legal proceedings. The person who posted the information will incur personal liability and could, therefore, be sued in the civil courts for damages. In addition, the university will be vicariously liable for the acts of employees and may be responsible for information posted by students if it has not taken reasonable care to monitor the content of the site and to remove defamatory information (see above on harassment).

Articles that have appeared in the press demonstrate that students are surprised and aggrieved by the fact that social network sites are being monitored and that the information that they post can potentially give rise to disciplinary action and legal liability. This is because there is a common misconception that individuals have an absolute right to freedom of speech and to privacy (see Thompson, 2009). Indeed, at Keele University, students have responded to an email warning them about inappropriate use of Facebook by establishing groups entitled 'Freedom of Thought at Keele' and 'Freedom of Speech' (Thompson, 2009). It is therefore essential to clarify the human rights position regarding the use and surveillance of social network sites. Privacy and freedom of expression are rights provided by the European Convention on the Protection of Human Rights and Fundamental Freedoms 1953, which was incorporated into UK law by the Human Rights Act 1998. Article 10 (1) of the Convention states that 'everyone has the right to freedom of expression', however, article 10 (2) goes on to explain that freedom of expression 'comes with duties and responsibilities' and is subject to laws that are necessary in a democratic society to 'prevent crime' and 'protect the reputation of others'. The right to freedom of expression is, thus, subject to the law on harassment and defamation and is subordinate to the right of individuals not to be harassed or defamed. Article 8 (1) of the Convention provides individuals with a right to 'respect for his private and family life'. Although it is unlawful for public authorities (such as universities) to act in a way that is incompatible with a Convention right (due to section 6 of the Human Rights Act 1998), it is difficult to accept that monitoring information on social network sites infringes the right to privacy, given that individuals are voluntarily posting material on a public site that the university itself has established. Furthermore, article 8 (2) enables public authorities to interfere with the right to private life in order to 'prevent a crime' or to 'protect the rights and freedoms of others'. Monitoring posts on a social network site can, thus, be justified under the Act in order to protect the rights of others (*e.g.* staff and other students). Indeed, it may be essential if the university is to protect itself from incurring liability for harassment and defamation committed by its staff or students. In contrast, several universities have allegedly checked social network sites in order to discover whether applicants have engaged in inappropriate behaviour, before deciding whether to accept them. As explained earlier, it is difficult to argue that an individual's right to privacy has been violated. However, this form of surveillance is clearly unethical.

Finally, the use of social network sites may raise issues regarding intellectual property because lecturers may post notes and research papers on the site for students to read and discuss. If the HEI has its own social network site no intellectual property issues arise. However, if the university has set up a Facebook group, the terms and conditions provide that 'all content on the Site and available through the Service, including designs, text, graphics, pictures, video, information, applications, software, music, sound and other files, and their selection and arrangement are the proprietary property of the company' (www.facebook.com/terms. php?ref+pf). Using a Facebook group as a learning and teaching tool is, thus, problematic, as a lecturer will lose the intellectual property to his or her work.

It is thus clear that pre- and post-enrolment use of social network sites by Higher Education Institutions impacts upon several complex areas of law, which must be carefully considered when making decisions such as which type of site to employ, who should be able to post information on the site and whether to monitor student usage. In addition, the university should draft a code of conduct for staff and students in order to make it clear that harassment and defamation are prohibited and those that engage in such behaviour will be disciplined.

Conclusion

This paper has explored some of the issues surrounding the interaction of students and UK HE staff through the medium of social network sites. There is a strong argument that barriers remain that prevents this type of communication becoming mainstream. For instance, student users' attitudes regarding 'ownership' of the space, the nature of 'friends', pre-entry legal issues and the lecturer-student relationship. Furthermore, particularly in the context of large international student intake, it would be erroneous to assume that a lecturer could create a profile on one social network site (*e.g.* Facebook) in order to communicate with all students. Moreover, the seemingly ephemeral nature of specific social network site dominance, could well require lecturers to continually change their usage; a factor that could be seen as a technical barrier.

Whilst UK HEIs cannot spurn the educational opportunities that social network sites offer, perhaps the minimum role of an educator is to encourage students to understand how the publicly available content on a social network site could be viewed as a direct reflection upon their professionalism both now and in the future. That is, how can we help young people in the navigation of the 'murky waters' (boyd, 2007, p. 1) that are social network sites? Students and staff also need to understand that posting inappropriate material on a social network site can result in disciplinary action and even legal proceedings. Given that an HEI can be held accountable for the content of its social network site, it seems that some sort of monitoring is essential. UK institutions, therefore, need to grapple with this ethical and legal issue. These issues and other emerging dilemmas will be investigated via quantitative and qualitative research in the next stage of the project.

REFERENCES

ACQUISTI, A., GROSS, R. 2006. *Imagined communities' awareness, information sharing and privacy on Facebook.* Privacy Enhancing Technologies Workshop (PET). Available at www.heinz.cmu.edu/~acquisti/papers/acquisti-gross-facebook-privacy-PET-final.pdf (accessed 2/4/2009).

BEER, D. 2008. Social network(ing) sites … revisiting the story so far: a response to danah boyd and Nicole Ellison. *Journal of Computer Mediated Communication*, 13, pp. 516-529.

BIRMINGHAM UNIVERSITY 2008. Social networking sites (Facebook, Myspace etc) and student issues. Guidelines. January. Available at www.as.bham.ac.uk/study/support/ sca.

BOYD, D. 2007. Social network sites: public, private, or what?' *Knowledge Tree*, 13, pp. 1-7.

BOYD, D., ELLISON, N. B. 2007. Social network sites: definition, history and scholarship. *Journal of Computer Mediated Communication*, 13 (1), article 11.

CAIN, J. 2008. Online social networking issues within academia and pharmacy education. *American Journal of Pharmaceutical Education*, 72 (1), pp. 1-7.

DWYER, C., HILTZ, S. R, PASSERINI, K. 2007. Trust and privacy concern within social networking sites: a comparison of Facebook and MySpace. In *Proceedings of the Americas Conference on Information Systems* (Keystone, Colorado, USA, August).

FACEBOOK 2009. www.insidefacebook.com/2009/02/14/facebook-surpasses-175-million-users-continuing-to-grow-by-600k-usersday/ (accessed 2/4/2009).

FERDIG, R. E., DAWSON, K., BLACK, E. W., BLACK, N. M., THOMPSON, L. A. 2008. Medical students' and residents' use of online social networking tools: implications for teaching professionalism in medical education. *First Monday*, 13 (9), pp. 1-9.

FERREL, G. 2008. Exploiting the potential of blogs and social networks. *ARIADNE*, 54 www.ariadne.ac.uk/issue54/social-networking-rpt/ (accessed 2/4/2009).

HEWITT, A., FORTE, A. 2006. Crossing boundaries: identity management and student/faculty relationships on Facebook. Available at www.cc.gatech.edu/~aforte/HewittForteCSCW Poster2006.pdf (accessed 2/4/2009).

GILL, J. 2009. You know what I really hate ... ? *Times Higher Education Supplement*, 15th January.

GILLHOOLEY, G. 2009. Accessing social-networking sites at work – a note of caution ... ? *Times Higher Education Supplement*, 1st April.

HARGITTAI, E. 2007. Whose space? Differences among users and non-users of social network sites. *Journal of Computer Mediated Communication*, 13 (1), article 14.

HASS, N. 2006. In your Facebook.com. *New York Times*, 8th January.

IPSOS MORI (for JISC) 2008. *Great expectations of ICT - how Higher Education Institutions are measuring up*. Available at: www.jisc.ac.uk/media/documents/publications/jiscgreatexpectationsfinalreportjune08.pdf (accessed 2/4/2009).

JISC 2008. Great expectations of ICT findings from second phase of research. Available at www.jisc.ac.uk/media/documents/publication

s/bpstudentexpectationsphase2v1.pdf (accessed 2/4/2009).

JOINSON, A. N. 2008. Changes in use and perception of Facebook. In *Proceedings of the ACM 2008 Conference on Computer Supported Cooperative Work* (San Diego, CA, USA, November 08 - 12).

KIM, K., YUN, H. 2007. Cying for me, Cying for us: relational dialectics in a Korean social network site. *Journal of Computer Mediated Communication*, 13 (1), article 15.

LAMPE, C., ELLISON, N. B., STEINFIELD, C. 2008. Changes in use and perception of facebook'. In *Proceedings of the ACM 2008 Conference on Computer Supported Cooperative Work* (San Diego, CA, USA, November 08-12).

MITRANO, T. 2006. Thoughts on Facebook. *Cornell Information Technologies* Available at www2.cit.cornell.edu/policy/memos/facebook.html (accessed 2/4/2009).

OFCOM 2008. Social networking – a quantitative and qualitative research report into attitudes, behaviours and use. Available at www.ofcom.org.uk/advice/media_liteacy/medlitpub/medlitpubrss/socialnetworking/ (accessed 2/4/2009).

OFFICE OF THE INDEPENDENT ADJUDICATOR FOR HIGHER EDUCATION 2007. *Resolving student complaints*. Annual Report. www.oiahe.org.uk.

SMITH, D. 2009. MySpace shrinks as Facebook, Twitter and Bebo grab its users. *The Observer*, 29th March.

SWAIN, H. 2007. Networking sites: Professors – keep out. *The Independent*, 18th October.

THELWALL, M. 2008. MySpace, Facebook, Bebo: social networking students. *Association for Learning Technology Newsletter*. Available at newsletter.alt.ac.uk/e_article000993849.cfm (accessed 2/4/2009).

THOMPSON, H. 2009. Universities to take disciplinary action against Facebook students. *Gair Rhydd*. Available at www.gairrhydd.com/news/846/university-to-take-disciplinary-action-against-facebook-students.

TUFEKCI, Z. 2008. Can you see me now? Audience and Disclosure Regulation in Online Social Network Sites. *Bulletin of Science, Technology and Society*, 28 (1), pp. 20-36.

CASES

Clarke v University of Lincolnshire and Humberside [2000]

Moran v University College Salford (No. 2) [1994]

Buckingham v Rycotewood College 26/3/2002.

LEGISLATION

The Employment Equality Sexual Orientation Regulations 2003

The European Convention on the Protection of Human Rights and Fundamental Freedoms 1953

The Human Rights Act 1998

The Protection from Harassment Act 1997

The Unfair Contract Terms Act 1977

The Unfair Terms in Consumer Contracts Regulations 1999

University of Wales, Newport

Prifysgol Cymru, Casnewydd

Linking Research and Teaching in Higher Education
Simon K. Haslett and Hefin Rowlands (eds)
Proceedings of the Newport NEXUS Conference
Centre for Excellence in Learning and Teaching
Special Publication, No. 1, 2009, pp. 83-91
ISBN 978-1-899274-38-3

Learning the Law: Stage II.

Alexandra M. Dobson and Teresa A. Marsh

Newport Business School, University of Wales Newport, Allt-Yr-Yn Avenue, Newport, NP20 5DA.
Email: Alexandra.dobson@newport.ac.uk; Teresa.marsh@newport.ac.uk

Abstract

This paper will consider the second stage in a cross-disciplinary research project at Newport Business School. The study looks at the challenges facing accountancy students who are required to study law as part of their professional accreditation programme. There is a sizeable body of literature that points to non-law students feeling disengaged with subject matter that they feel is only an adjunct to the main purpose of their studies. The empirical study has utilised questionnaires and focus groups as a method of gaining an insight into the student experience. Current students and those who have completed the module have been canvassed as part of the research. Interventions in the form of vodcasts have also been used to help facilitate student participation, and the cohort have been asked to comment on the usefulness or otherwise of this approach. The researchers, one from accountancy and the other from a law background are hopeful that in the long-term the fruits of the study will assist in enhancing the student experience.

Introduction

This paper charts the progress of the research project - Learning the Law. The project is concerned with examining central pedagogic issues that arise in teaching law to non-law students in a higher education setting. The purpose of the research is to attempt to better understand the needs of students and by doing so facilitate learning. It is being conducted by an inter-disciplinary partnership drawn from two lecturers with different academic backgrounds, one in accountancy and the other in law. It is evolutionary in nature, arising from an initial conversation between the authors and gradually blossoming into what it is hoped will prove to be a project that will add to pedagogic understanding and debate. Following an introductory paper (Dobson and Marsh, 2008) that looked at the reasons for carrying out the research; provided a brief overview of some of the literature in the area, and discussed the early stages of the empirical research, the

authors are now in a position to discuss some of the latest findings.

Before considering the most recent research, a brief resume of the results of the first stage is necessary. The initial stage looked specifically at the teaching of law on a professional accountancy programme. The learners, part-time students attending the University for one day each week follow a course of study which leads them to a qualification as Chartered Certified Accountants. It was clear prior to the 'Learning the Law' study, from the comments of external examiners, and the wider dissemination of information from the Association of Chartered Certified Accountants (ACCA) that students were more comfortable with the study of numerically based material.

The cohort under discussion was made up of some 90 students of who 82 replied to the first questionnaire, giving a response rate of 84%. The questionnaire asked for a response to five questions. In order to explore the early responses to learning, the group were asked about their views on learning material for the law and tax paper. The purpose of the questions was to elicit initial responses to learning law and tax which would form the basis of more in-depth analysis as the academic year progressed. The assumption that students studying an accounting qualification would have a preference for numerical subjects was borne out by the results of the survey in which more than three-quarters indicated a preference for such subjects. Only 7% preferred discursive subjects with 15% being comfortable with both numerical and discursive subjects.

Learning the Law - Stage II.

The next stage, which forms the subject of this paper, aims to add depth to the initial findings. The same cohort (as in the first stage of the study), were asked to fill in an identical questionnaire to that used at the beginning of the year in order to elicit views as the learners progressed. Importantly in the second stage data was also collected from focus groups. This allowed the researchers to explore the feelings, attitudes and ideas of the learners in relation to the study of law and tax. An intervention in the form of a vodcast was used to gauge students' reaction to alternative methods of teaching. The results of the questionnaire reviewing the responses to the vodcast is not included in this paper but will be used to add to the completed study in the future.

As well as charting the responses of the part-time accountancy students, a small scale comparative study sought to consider the views of full-time undergraduates studying criminal law and to place this against those of the accountants. The authors are aware that this additional material needs to be treated with caution; the groups are not easily comparable with each having distinct characteristics, most obviously one cohort consists of part-time professional students, with the second made up of full-time undergraduates. The undergraduates study law as part of their business degree and it is likely that in future this aspect of the study will be extended to consider other groups

learning law outside the parameters of the traditional law degree. However the findings do reveal some interesting differences in attitude and perception.

Why Use Focus Groups?

As a method of academic research the focus group provides the opportunity to allow for the 'thick description' which enriches any study (Suter, 2000). The first stage had gathered data through the use of question-naires and the authors felt that it was necessary to use qualitative methodology to delve further. Much has been written about the usefulness of the focus group as a mechanism for investigation. As Kitzinger (1995) has pointed out, the face-to-face interaction typical of the focus group allows the opportunity for participants to talk to one another by exchanging experience and sharing knowledge. While the initial questionnaire revealed some interesting early data, it was limited. Direct questions do not allow the participant to enlarge upon, reflect and share anecdotes which can provide insights into attitudes and perceptions. In one sense the assembly of a focus group appears simple as Powell *et al.* (1996, p. 499) comment 'a focus group is a group of individuals selected and assembled by the researchers to discuss and comment on, from personal experience, the topic that is the subject of research'.

While the authors were fortunate in that both the student accountants and the undergraduates were prepared to participate in the focus groups and the University provided appropriate accommodation they were mindful that although group sessions provide useful data, there are pitfalls. There are limitations and difficulties to be overcome. For instance, a particularly vociferous participant may dominant proceedings if allowed to go unchecked. The use of a skilled facilitator is vital to ensure both, that all of the participants take part, guarding against an individual or individuals unbalancing the group, and by contrast that the group identity does not subdue the individual voice. The facilitators were aware of the need to guide and to assist the flow of 'conversation' but not to dominate or lead the discussion. There are also issues in relation to protecting confidentiality and the researchers were careful to protect the anonymity of the participants. Further the data that is collected requires careful analysis; the sessions were transcribed and then coding was used to develop systematic methods for identifying key themes.

The focus groups fell into three sets, the first carried out by a facilitator working with the second year accountancy students who are studying law for the first time. The second group with a different facilitator involved gauging the views of students who had successfully navigated Year Two, passing through the tax and law modules and who were engaged in the third year of their studies. The final group using the same facilitator (Year Two accountants) involved a focus group held to elicit the views of criminal law students who were studying law as a part of their business degree. All of the focus groups were carried out in Semester Two. It is important to point out that further analysis of the data will be undertaken in the future and that what is presented here forms an initial stage only in the analysis. The authors intend to use triangulation to further refine their findings. In this paper verbatim commentary is provided from the discussions in the focus group carried out with students in the third year who had already studied law. In relation to the two other focus groups, the results are not available at the time of writing but the circulated questionnaires have been analysed and are provided.

Focus Group Findings – Third Year Student Accountants

The third year accountancy students presented a useful resource in terms of the research. They had passed through the tax and law modules and have the advantage of being able to reflect on their experience. What follows is an overview of some of the commentary that came from the discussions, one area in which the majority of the participants agreed was in relation to the relevancy of the material studied as part of the law module. However what follows presents a snapshot only of the findings, and it is intended that the material will be subjected to further scrutiny. The facilitator guided the groups through a range of questions closely linked to the questionnaire. In order to preserve the subject's anonymity, the respondents are referred to alphabetically.

Facilitator. Did you feel positive or negative about the study of law? Responses indicate that more students feel positive about the study of tax than law. Why do you think that is?

Participants.
A) Neither. Its part of the course requirement and it's got to be done.
B) I didn't expect law in an accounting course as I missed the induction and when I found out I said 'Law what's that about?' Whereas tax I'd studied previously as part of AAT. On ACCA we did tax quite heavily but you can relate it more to real life.
C) I certainly felt positive about both of them because I hadn't studied law before so I was quite looking forward to that because obviously I didn't know what to expect. And we covered tax on AAT but only the personal taxes and I really enjoyed that.
D) I was negative for law and positive for tax because law I didn't see the relevance of it to the qualification I was doing. I thoroughly enjoyed tax. I hadn't studied law before. I just couldn't get it in my head that it was really relevant

Facilitator. Give your reasons for studying law and studying tax? Responses indicate that the reason for studying these papers is that you have to but do you think it is useful to study these papers?

Participants.
A) As the previous comments its part of the course requirement.
B) If law had been optional I probably wouldn't have done it.

C) Oh I don't know, out the three papers we studied it was the easiest one. If we get down to passing the exams, law was easier than tax. So if I was given the choice I would do law.

Facilitator. So what do you think about the relevance? You said you could understand why you were studying tax. You all said your reasons for studying law were because you all said you had to. None of you have said because you want to or you feel it's relevant or you feel it's important to becoming an accountant to have that knowledge?

Participants.

B) I think that's the bit that three of us agree on. Perhaps it's being taught by a law professor that when I would think of law I would think of covering your backside when you're doing a set of accounts and knowing the penalties that exist and that's why you need to know the International Standards and the penalties for not using them. I don't recall we ever did that. I don't recall any reference to any financial accounting. Insider trading was the closest we ever came to doing something that you would think well actually I need to know that. If you were doing something in retail or something like that, a lot of the cases were relevant, if you were looking at contract and consumer law. As an accountant you wouldn't really get involved in the contract law.

C) If I'd wanted to learn about contract and offer and acceptance then I would have done contract law. We came here to learn to be accountants and sometimes when it's dry and boring and mundane you revert back to why am I doing this? I think with tax, whether you love it, hate it or are indifferent to it, if you're going to be an accountant you have to aware of tax and that's just the long and the short of it. Whereas law, I'll never do anything with law again'.

D) "I would have thought in law, especially now with the global emphasis that it would be the perfect opportunity to spend however many weeks going through Arthur Anderson, going through Enron, Worldcom, however many more they mention. Real life, current cases rather than something from 1840 involving two horses"

E) I found law boring, if anything. I worked very hard at doing a lot of things crammed into one subject. Before I studied law, it was more consumer law. It was quite interesting but this law I found hard to relate to real life so I found it quite boring. I do like tax.

Facilitator. Give your reasons for studying law and studying tax? Responses indicate that the reason for studying these papers is that you have to but do you think it is useful to study these papers?

Participants.

A) Although I was very positive about the course, not having studied law before I thought it would be the law aspects relating to accounts. So I thought we would go over lots of scenarios relating to corporations, so I found it really interesting that we were covering all the different aspects of law. This year now, things that you covered last year are much far more relevant to the course this year. So it shows on how a year builds on the year before.

What is presented in the section above forms only a small part of the transcription from the focus group but is presented here to provide a 'flavour' of the participants views.

Second Year Accountancy Students

In this section the results of the questionnaires that were completed by the second year accountancy students are presented in Tables 1-15 and Figures 1-3.

(+)	(-)	Neutral
71%	25%	4%

yes	no
67%	33%

Table 1. Law Questions: Positive, Negative or Neutral about the Study of Law (total number of respondents = 24).

Table 2. Law Questions: Have you ever studied law before? (total number of respondents = 24).

Part of Course
100%

Table 3. Law Questions: Reasons for studying Law (total number of respondents = 24).

(a) Dry & Boring	(b) Lots of Reading	(c) Memoris-ing	(d) Dy-namic/Stimulatin g	(e) Real Life
8%	42%	38%	0%	13%

Table 4. Law Questions: What do you think the study of law will be? (total number of respondents = 24).

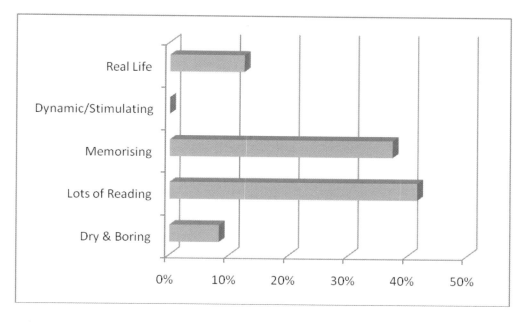

Figure 1. Law Questions: What do you think the study of Law will be? (total number of respondents = 24).

Numerical	Discursive	Equal
75%	0%	25%

Table 5. Law Questions: More comfortable with Numerical or Discursive? (total number of respondents = 24).

yes	no
38%	63%

Table 7. Tax Questions Have you ever studied tax before? (total number of respondents = 24).

(+)	(-)	Neutral
92%	4%	4%

Table 6. Tax Questions: Positive, Negative or Neutral about the Study of Tax (total number of respondents = 24).

Part of Course	Career
92%	8%

Table 8. Tax Questions Reasons for studying tax (total number of respondents = 24).

(a) Dry & Boring	(b) Lots of Reading	(c) Memorising	(d) Dynamic/Stimulating	(e) Real Life
5%	10%	41%	13%	31%

Table 9. Tax Questions What do you think the study of tax will be? (total number of respondents = 24).

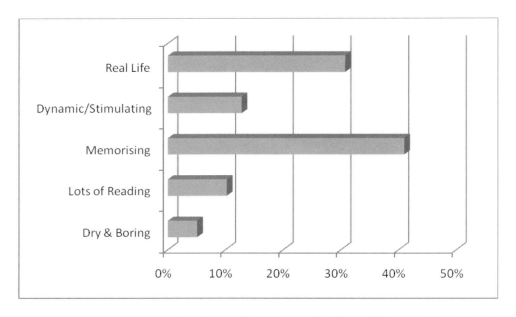

Figure 2. Tax Questions What do you think the study of tax will be? (total number of respondents = 24).

Numerical	Discursive	Equal
75%	0%	25%

yes	no
50%	50%

Table 10. Tax Questions: Comfortable with Numerical or Discursive? (total number of respondents = 24).

Table 12. Undergraduate Questions Have you ever studied law before? (total number of respondents = 8).

The Undergraduate Responses are presented in Tables 11-15 and Figure 3. The questionnaire was modified for the criminal law students. The questions on tax were removed as they were not considered applicable.

Interest	Career
75%	25%

Table1 3. Undergraduate Questions Reasons for studying Law. (total number of respondents = 8).

(+)
100%

Table 11. Undergraduate Questions: Positive, Negative or Neutral about the Study of Law. (total number of respondents = 8).

(a) Dry & Boring	(b) Lots of Reading	(c) Memoris-ing	(d) Dy-namic/Stimulating	(e) Real Life
0%	29%	29%	17%	25%

Table 14. Undergraduate Questions What do you think the study of law will be? (total number of respondents = 8).

Numerical	Discursive	Equal
25%	50%	25%

Table15. Undergraduate Questions: More comfortable with Numerical or Discursive? (total number of respondents = 8).

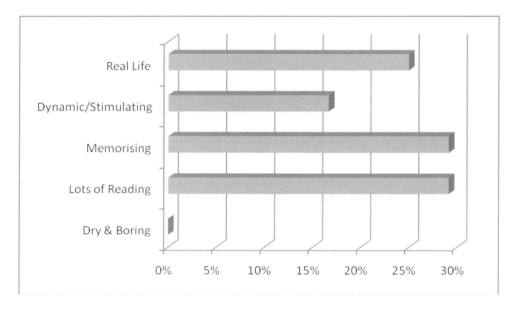

Figure 3. Undergraduate Questions: What do you think the study of Law will be? (total number of respondents = 8).

Findings

The findings contained within this paper are at a preliminary stage and will be subjected to further scrutiny. Further not all of the research that has been carried out is contained within the paper. But what is interesting at this stage is to listen to the 'voices' of the participants in order to start to better refine strategies to facilitate learning. The 'snapshot' of voices presented in verbatim form from the third year focus groups provides some interesting material in relation the relevancy of the material offered on the law module. The syllabus is prescribed externally and the range of subject matter is broad but the authors are already considering new strategies in an attempt to address the views of those who took part.

In relation to the findings of the questionnaires completed by the second year accountants, it is clear that the students remain more comfortable with numerical subjects and this is in line with the results of the early research carried out at the beginning of the year. In comparison the undergraduate students appear much more comfortable with discursive subjects and their responses reveal a more positive attitude to the study of law.

The next stage is to further refine the results and to add in the results of the 'intervention' which will assist with considering ways to improve the learning experience for the ACCA students. The project is still at a preliminary stage and in the authors view it is vital to approach the project incrementally, building and adding to the research which will inform the next stage.

Conclusion

This paper has presented an overview of some of the latest fruits of the on-going study, 'Learning the Law'. At the time of writing not all of the material that has been collated from this first academic year has been analysed fully and consequentially what has been presented must be treated with caution. However the authors consider that the body of research already presented begins to add a useful contribution to the pedagogic knowledge in this area. As Kokakulah *et al.* (2009) point out 'knowledge of the law is important to those who conduct business and especially to those professionals who conduct business in the form of a public accounting practice. Accountants are similar to other business professionals in that they must be able to identify important legal issues as they arise so as to reduce their exposure to legal liability' (p. 137). Finding ways to further facilitate 'learning the law' is important for the students who form the basis of this study, but there are also wider issues in relation to learning generally. The authors are grateful for the opportunity to provide a small addition to the research in this field.

REFERENCES

DOBSON, A. M., MARSH, T. 2008. Learning the law: a pilot study examining challenges facing non-law students studying law. *Newport CELT Journal,* 1, pp. 23-28.

KITZINGER, J. 1995. *British Medical Journal*, 29 (311), C70001: 299-302.

KOCAKULAH, M., AUSTILL, D., LONG, B. 2009. The Present State of the Business Law Education of Accounting Students. *The Business Law Professor's Perspective*, 26 (1), pp. 137–183.

POWELL, R. A., SINGLE, H. M. 1996. Focus groups. *International Journal of Quality in Health Care*, 8 (5), pp. 499-504.

SUTER, E. A., 2000. Focus groups in ethnography of communication: expanding topics of inquiry beyond participant observation. *The Qualitative Report*, 5 (1/2) (available at http://www.nova.edu/ssss/QR/QR5-1/suter.html).

University of Wales, Newport

Prifysgol Cymru, Casnewydd

Linking Research and Teaching in Higher Education
Simon K. Haslett and Hefin Rowlands (eds)
Proceedings of the Newport NEXUS Conference
Centre for Excellence in Learning and Teaching
Special Publication, No. 1, 2009, pp. 93-99
ISBN 978-1-899274-38-3

The self regulated community of learning and its impact on learning in 3D virtual learning environments.

Joe Wàn[1] and Mike Reddy[2]

[1]Centre for Excellence in Learning and Teaching, University of Wales, Newport, Lodge Road, Caerleon, South Wales, NP18 3QT, United Kingdom. Email: Joe.wan@newport.ac.uk

[2]Department of Computing, Newport Business School, University of Wales, Newport, Allt-yr-yn Campus, Newport, South Wales, NP20 5XR, United Kingdom. Email: Mike.reddy@newport.ac.uk

Abstract

This paper investigates Self Regulated Learning in 3D Virtual Learning Environments (3D VLEs). The theory of the Self Regulated Community of Learning (SRCL) proposed in this paper is within the paradigm of cognitive theory and social constructivist conceptual framework. The theoretical research in this paper is two-fold, taking both ecological (*i.e.* animal behaviourism) and pedagogical perspectives (*i.e.* cognitive psychology and constructivism) into consideration and suggests that, similar to the division of labour within ant society, Multi-user Online Role Play (MUORP) is a mechanism behind SRCL within 3D VLEs. SRCL leads to an optimum state of VLEs and, in turn, maximises learning enhancement. Two different aspects of 3D virtual worlds, *i.e.* Second Life and EVE Online, will be explored. The intended research outcome is to disclose the interrelatedness between SRCL and 3D VLEs and the impact of SRCL on Learning. New insights in distance learning and on-campus e-learning pedagogy are expected to be gained via a multidisciplinary study at University of Wales, Newport, in the next two years. This research project will involve the School of Health and Social Science, the Newport Business School and the Centre for Excellence in Learning and Teaching.

Introduction

Virtual Learning Environments (VLEs) facilitate the shift from traditional teaching and learning to modern settings. Simply put, from knowledge transfer to collaborative learning. The recent development of 3D Multi-user Virtual Environments (3D MUVEs) (*e.g.* Second Life, Wonderland) has further advanced this transition which leads to student-led learning.

The proposed theory of SRCL in this paper is derived from "Self Regulated Society" (Arcaute *et al.*, 2007) in the study of ant behaviour, and will be tested fully via a multidisciplinary study at University of Wales, Newport, over the next two years. The 3D MUVEs employed at the initial phase of the research include Second Life (SL) and EVE Online (a Massively Multi-player Online Role-Playing Game - MMORPG) which will be discussed further in this paper. The second phase of the research involves new project implementation which will be based on the findings from initial live case studies in terms of platform selection, learning outcomes and other cost and rewards indicators.

Like all instructional technologies 3-dimensional virtual worlds for learning are only as effective as the vision and the pedagogy that guide them (Bronack *et al.*, 2006). Besides the proposed theory of SRCL, new insights into distance learning and on-campus e-learning pedagogy are expected to be gained via the aforementioned multidisciplinary practice, because not only can technology aided learning help tutors be more creative in teaching, but also encourage students to grapple the opportunities with improved learning capabilities.

Theoretical Background

SRCL and SRL

The concept of Self Regulated Learning (SRL) has been introduced and developed over decades and its root can be traced back to 1964 (Bandura and Kupers, 1964) or even earlier. SRL recognizes that each individual is balancing her/his learning needs, all the learning needs of the society with other commitments s/he has. However, their learning is being controlled and regulated by the environment which may or may not be the learning environment they are working in. SRL is defined as "students personally initiate and direct their own efforts to acquire knowledge and skill rather than relying on teachers, parents, or other agents of instruction" (Zimmerman, 1989). It includes three elements: "students' self-regulated learning strategies, self-efficacy perceptions of performance skill, and commitment to academic goals" (Zimmerman, 1989).

Contrary to Zimmerman's approach, which only tends to be individually focused, this paper considers the metaphor of the community being dominant and the people's roles within it being mitigated by the community. A SRCL is egalitarian by nature. Rather than being seen as suppressing and subordinating the experience of the individual in favorite state, it is being seen as the key element within the learning process and is actually a positive thing. It's not like a terrible imposing state or educational communism; instead it's about the individual creating something with other people. Existing research suggests that a learner "first becomes able to subordinate her behaviour to rules in group play and only later does voluntary self-regulation of behaviour arise as an internal function" (Vygotsky, 1978, p. 90).

SRCL in collaborative and social learning

The social aspect is a principle focus in the existing literature regarding learning in virtual environments (*e.g.* Bronack *et al.*, 2006; Zimmerman, 1981; Paris and Byrnes, 1989; Minocha and Roberts, 2008), because "'learning occurs first on the social level (interpsychological level) and next on the individual one (intrapsychological level) (Vygotsky, 1978)" (Bronack *et al.*, 2006) and "knowledge construction is achieved by the interaction that takes place within oneself through reflective thinking and by the interaction that occurs in communications and collaboration with other people (Vygotsky 1978)" (Minocha and Roberts, 2008, p. 184). Whilst following the same theoretical line and the theory of SRCL, this paper develops these ideas further within the paradigm of cognitive theory and social constructivist conceptual framework.

Theoretical research paper approaches pedagogical perspectives taking cognitive psychology and constructivism psychology into consideration (*e.g.* Zimmerman, 1981; Paris and Byrnes, 1989; Bandura and Cervone, 1986; Pressley *et al.*, 1987). However, this research project wants to contrast that with animal behaviorism where the division of labour serves as a self-regulatory mechanism, which previously has not been used in a pedagogical context. Therefore, this project will look at animal behaviour, SRCL and social roles within the community.

Although the existing literature acknowledges the presence of SRL within Virtual Learning Communities (VLCs) (Delfino *et al.*, 2008), matters such as the form of it, and the mechanism behind it, have not been explored in great detail. Also, the importance of role-play in SRL has not been examined within synchronous contexts (*e.g.* 3D MUVEs). Thus, the real impact of MUORP on the learning in 3D VLEs remains unclear.

The similarities between insect (*e.g.* ants and wasps) behaviour in the real world and human behaviour in VLEs have emerged from comparative literature review. "In the ant colony system, the relevant "optimum" state is when division of labour is achieved" because the "resilience and robustness" of ant society is dependent upon a "self-regulatory mechanism", and "division of labour is one such mechanism giving rise to self-regulation in nature" (Arcaute *et al.*, 2007, pp. 2, 11, 12). The division of labour within ant society could be a close analogy to MUORP featured in 3D MUVEs, and is manifested via the 3D objects such as avatars which resemble the generic relationship between ants (*e.g.* proximity and anonymity). Hence, the hypothesis here is that MUORP is essential to the establishment and development of SRCL in 3D VLEs.

Furthermore, Arcaute *et al.* (2007) suggest that within wasp society, "the elites" do most of the work. The similar kind of behaviour also exists among learners in a classroom setting as well as in asynchronous VLEs though in different forms. However, the social distance and psychological distance between "the elites" and other learners are expected to be reduced via the adoption of 3D Multi-user Virtual Learning Environments (3D MUVLEs)[1], through SRCL evolved in the learning process because within such communities, it is more natural, spontaneous and convenient to communicate. In turn, the "shared sense of belonging, trust, expectation of learning, and commitment to participate" (Minocha and Roberts, 2008, p. 182) will help learners achieve both individual and communal benefits. This finding has further advanced Zimmerman's claim (1995), not only is self-referential system the core to explain the failure of self regulation at the individual level, but also at the community level.

As a result, the earlier hypothesis can be amended as the following:

MUORP is essential to the establishment and development of SRCL in 3D MUVEs. Learning can be achieved via SRCL by speeding up the transition from interaction to collaboration within a broad online social context. In turn, it contributes to the sustainability of VLCs in terms of both individual and communal benefits.

---

[1] The acronyms - 3D MUVLEs, 3D MUVEs, 3D IVWs and 3D IMUVLEs will be used interchangeably throughout this paper, because these are distinctions without difference.

Discussion

SRCL in modern learning settings

Due to the pedagogical shift in modern learning settings, the top-down instructional approach has been gradually losing its prominence, and is being replaced by the bottom-up, student-led (or student- centred) approach. As a result, the role of educator will be shifted from instructor to facilitator and this is the major difference between pedagogical learning and andragogical learning. "Andragogy assumes that the point at which an individual achieves a self-concept of essential self-direction is the point at which he psychologically becomes adult" (Knowles, 1976, p. 56). However, Self Directed Learning (SDL) is fundamentally different from SRL, the former is about what to learn, the latter is about when and how quickly to learn.

The pedagogical shift in modern learning settings is accompanied by technological development, because the "growing interest in social dimensions of learning has led to institutions adopting Virtual Learning Environments (VLEs)" (Minocha and Roberts, 2008, p. 181). The ubiquitous nature of internet and web 2.0 technologies (*e.g.* wikis, blogs, video online, social networks) have given prevalence to distance learning in particular. However, current distance education "has more in common with traditional classroom-based instruction than it does with what distance education can become" (Bronack *et al.*, 2006, p. 221). The most recent technological development in 3D VLEs has started to challenge the status quo. As Taylor and Chyung suggest (2008), the structure and function of the 3D graphic interface are rather significant to studies in the andragogical use of virtual reality, though the term, virtual reality, has already been dated.

In order to understand how 3D VLEs enable learners to break down the traditional pedagogical steps "from minimal or no knowledge to being a master of a certain set of information in a context" (Wasley, 2008, p. 2), the comparison between modern learning and traditional learning settings is essential.

The adoption of the latest technologies beg the following questions: What elements of our traditional experiences should be preserved online, which should be modified and what are the impacts of the tools (platforms) we use on our abilities to achieve all of the above (Holmes, 2007)? Has socialisation been fully integrated with all the collaborative activities within a learning community (Minocha and Roberts, 2008)? How do 3D VLEs facilitate SRCL in modern learning settings?

SRCL in modern learning settings is largely dependent upon the degree of social presence. Social presence is vital to stimulate intellectual productivity in VLEs (Oravec, 1996), which is influenced by factors such as learner experiences, virtual proximity (immediacy) and anonymity (privacy) (Minocha and Roberts, 2008).

Research suggests that "ants increase their "keenness" to perform a task if they did it before" (Arcaute et al., 2007, p. 11) and individualized learning is achieved via group activities. Delfino et al. (2008) take user heterogeneity into consideration and reckon that individual learning experiences do matter a great deal in the process of SRL. As a result, learner experiences can be deemed as both a cognitive/metacognitive indicator and an emotional indicator in the study of the intertwined relationship between SRCL and the learning in 3D VLEs. Furthermore, as suggested by Boekaerts et al. (2000) "a lack of social learning experiences is the first important source of self-regulatory dysfunctions" (Delfino et al., 2008, p. 195). In other words, social learning experiences indicate the inseparable nature of cognitive theory and social constructivist theory, because not only can collective knowledge be constructed, but also the individual learner's "intellectual sense of the materials on their own" (Minocha and Roberts, 2008, p. 182). Thus, Felix (2005) suggests having a synthetic view of the cognitive and social constructivist approaches (Minocha and Roberts, 2008).

In 3D VLEs, immediacy (proxy for realism) engendered from virtual proximity, is almost equivalent to real classroom setting, but not available in asynchronous learning. Contrary to Castronova's (2005) point of view, the social environment that emerged from 3D VLEs is different from other social environments, because of the employment of 3D objects such as avatars in Immersive Virtual Worlds (IVWs). Avatars create anonymity, which also tends to reduce the gap between "the elites" and other learners and will have a positive impact on building SRCL within VLEs. It is worth noting that "the elites" are not necessarily bad things under different circumstances and the egalitarian nature of IVWs doesn't promote educational communism as discussed earlier.

The existing literature of VLEs overwhelmingly concentrates on distance learning; the impact of virtual worlds on physical classroom learning has been somewhat overlooked. The potential cost and rewards from the integration of virtual world and classroom learning shall be explored further.

SRCL in mixed virtual world and classroom setting

Some existing practices in higher education are keen to apply the latest development of 3D VLEs to distance learning exclusively. In other words, the potential impact of SRCL on learning has been partially ignored because what higher education can become and the necessity of integrating 3D VLEs within classroom learning have not been fully realized.

In higher education settings, the orthodox formal learning is dominated by classroom learning. Virtual learning may either be a form of informal learning or serve as an experiential playground for both on-campus and off-campus students. 3D VLEs are complementary to classroom learning (*i.e.* didactic tutor-led learning), facilitating all learning activities, and informal learning in particular. This has made Zimmerman's (1998) three-phase SRL activities model (*i.e.* planning, monitoring and evaluation) partially obsolete because it is purely based on the planning school. It fits in with formal classroom learning but has discounted the fact that "co-ordination of work in distributed teams is accomplished through spontaneous informal communication" (Minocha and

Roberts, 2008, p. 186). Informal networks evolve from informal learning. Not only can informal networks facilitate learning, but also contribute to the sustainability of VLC. As suggested by Delfino *et al.* (2007), there is a need for informal networks within members of the community to emerge for the sake of VLC regeneration.

"Informal learning can be a valuable component of the educational process, but it is hard to facilitate. Organized informal learning is an oxymoron" (Pence, 2007-2008, p. 175). This indicates the importance of SRL in 3D VLEs. Thus, this finding has broadened the hypothesis in the earlier section to place the concept of SRCL in a wider social context *i.e.* SRCL exists in fluid learning communities rather than simply established groups (De Lucia *et al.*, 2009). However, it has also raised the question 'are fluid learning communities capable of self regulating'?

One researcher suggests that he has learned many things about his real life by reflecting on his virtual world experiences (Antonacci and Modaress, 2008); however, this is only half of the spectrum. In order to have a holistic view of Technology Enhanced Learning (TEL), the reciprocation between real world (classroom learning) and virtual world experiences needs to be investigated further *i.e.* how does classroom learning experience affect virtual learning and how does virtual world learning experience benefit the classroom learning?

Although 3D VLEs harness collaborative learning via hybrid (*i.e.* linear and non-linear) interactions among learners and tutors "when the content warrants it [for instance], a class within the virtual world may be as linear and as structured as any" (Bronack *et al.*, 2006, p. 230). Thus, a model can be constructed as the following: linear approach in general and non-linear approach at different stages of the development of SRCL, facilitated by techno-logical development.

Way Forward

New learning and teaching activities foster SRCL

The latest technological developments in 3D VLEs have made new learning and teaching activities possible in virtual worlds. 3D VLE's enable both learners and tutors to think creatively, rather than simply replicating real-world classrooms in 3D virtual worlds (Minocha and Roberts, 2008). However, it is worth noting that real-life classrooms are not inherently negative. Guided by cognitive theory and a social constructivist conceptual framework, the two different aspects of virtual worlds are being explored *i.e.* open ended MUVEs (*e.g.* SL) and gated MUVEs (*e.g.* EVE Online), which both feature synchronous interactions and collaboration among users.

SL will become the focal point for both distance learning and on-campus e-learning in this paper, because research shows that SL supports almost all the web features and the "social interaction is comparable to class-rooms" (Atkinson, 2008, p. 18). However, the following questions need to be answered prior to the implementation of SL: what are the differences between traditional learning and virtual learning? How does SL facilitate learners breaking down the traditional pedagogical steps (Wasley, 2008)? How does SL foster SRCL?

Although online games "often support the creation of communities that actively develop and maintain themselves" (Bronack *et al.*, 2006, p. 220), the effectiveness of existing MMORPGs (*e.g.* EVE Online) on the learning in higher education have not been given enough recognition yet.

From a software design point of view, SL and EVE Online have the same root in games and both feature role plays and simulations. However, SL is not a game and has real-life impact. Research suggests that as an active social experience, learners cannot be inactive in a game or simulation (Antonacci and Modaress, 2008). The actions of other people make the game or simulation open-ended and "add complexity and unpredictability" (Antonacci and Modaress, 2008, p. 117). This echoes the earlier suggestion in this paper that MUORP is the mechanism behind SRCL. Furthermore, not only can 3D IVWs facilitate learning, but unlearning, in order to achieve the acquisition of learner specialisation and adaptability (Arcaute *et al.*, 2007) for the purpose of knowledge construction and knowledge base replenishment. If each *ad hoc* group evolved within the specialisation and adaptability process they can be deemed as an activity centre, and then the above statements can be interpreted as similar to the emerging behaviour of ants *e.g.* when repairing damage to nest; other activity centres within the Self Regulated Society are stimulated. However, it is worth noting that the ant colony system is not open-ended, rather, it is predictable to a certain extent.

3D VLEs promote SRCL. Not only do 3D VLEs break down the traditional power hierarchy, but also impose minimal rules to regulate the learning environment as a fence to prevent SRCL from being eroded by other external factors. 3D VLEs are to provide students the resources to build the educational environment themselves, rather than being completely controlled by a tutor or being in complete isolation.

Both SL and EVE Online have their advantages and drawbacks. For example, it is not the time to abandon the existing web-based VLEs (2D VLEs) yet, because although 3D IVWs (*e.g.* SL) provide "strong support for synchronous interactions and collaboration, and immersive environments for experiential and constructionist learning" (Livingstone *et al.*, 2008, p. 140), many elements for supporting learning and teaching are still absent, in particular the support for asynchronous collaboration, because most of the 3D IVWs are not designed for educational purposes though it facilitates "a high degree of interactivity and participation" (Kearsley, 2000, p. 78). As a result, it is important to integrate 3D IVWs with existing web-based (2D) VLEs (*e.g.* Moodle) and transform 2D MUVLEs into graphic rich 3D Immersive Multiuser Virtual Learning Environments (3D IMUVLEs). This gives rise to Sloodle (*i.e.* the deployment of SL via Moodle) to form a blended VLE. Under this approach, both social and technological benefits of the 2D and 3D VLEs will be examined further. In addition, EVE Online is a thematic MMORPG, thus its usage for higher education will be limited.

We expect Sloodle, an open-source project, will lead learners to focus on learning rather than technology and make effective use of the virtual world (Livingstone *et al.*, 2008). We also expect to be able to better understand changes and challenges, student preferences, expectations and the "effective use of tools in ways unintended by the developer" (Livingstone *et al.*, 2008, p. 147). Also, to better understand the difference between co-dependency and interdependency of individual learners in both virtual world and classroom settings, understand the three main factors (*i.e.* cost, quality and speed) of successful implementation of the 3D VLEs, and what can or cannot be compromised during the practice.

Through empirical research and real practice, an attempt to disclose the interrelatedness between SRCL and 3D VLEs and the impact of SRCL on learning will be made. New insights in distance learning and on-campus e-learning pedagogy are expected to be gained via a multidisciplinary practice at University of Wales, Newport, in the next two years. There will be a three-case approach in this research. The first two are parallel to each other, exploring two different aspects of the 3D virtual world *i.e.* the deployment of Second Life via Moodle for the first year undergraduate students in the School of Health and Social Sciences and EVE Online for the Newport Business School where students will set up virtual organisations. The third case, the Centre for Excellence in Learning and Teaching led university-wide Postgraduate Certificate in Developing Professional Practice in Higher Education programme, will be developed and executed online and informed by the findings from the two aforementioned live case studies in terms of platform selection, learning outcomes and other cost and rewards indicators.

ACKNOWLEDGEMENTS

The authors are grateful for discussion with David Longman (School of Education, University of Wales, Newport) on aspects of this research.

REFERENCES

ANTONACCI, D. M., MODARESS, N. 2008, Envisioning the educational possibilities of user-created virtual worlds. *AACE Journal,* 16 (2), pp. 115-126.

ARCAUTE, E., CHRISTENSEN, K., SENDOVA-FRANKS, A., DAHL, T., ESPINOSA, A., JENSEN, H. J. 2007. *Division of labour in ant colonies in terms of attractive fields*, Unpublished Paper.

ATKINSON, T. 2008. Inside Linden Lab. *TechTrends: Linking Research & Practice to Improve Learning,* 52 (3), pp. 16-18.

BANDURA, A., CERVONE, D. 1986. Differential engagement of self-reactive influences in cognitive motivation. *Organizational Behaviors and Human Decision Processes,* 38, pp. 92-113.

BANDURA, A., KUPERS, C. J. 1964. The transmission of patterns of self-reinforcement through modeling. *Journal of Abnormal and Social Psychology,* 69, pp. 1-9.

BOEKAERTS, M., PINTRICH, P. R., ZEIDNER, M. 2000. *Handbook of self-regulation.* San Diego, CA: Academic Press.

BRONACK, S., RIEDL, R., TASHNER, J. 2006. Learning in the zone: a social constructivist framework for distance education in a 3-dimensional virtual world. *Interactive Learning Environments,* 14 (3), pp. 219-232.

DE LUCIA, A., FRANCESE, R., PASSERO, I., TORTORA, G. 2009. Development and evaluation of a virtual campus on Second Life: the case of SecondDMI. *Computers & Education,* 52 (1), pp. 220-233.

DELFINO, M., DETTORI, G., PERSICO, D. 2008. Self-regulated learning in virtual communities. *Technology, Pedagogy and Education,* 17 (3), pp. 195-205.

FELIX, U. 2005. E-learning pedagogy in the Third Millennium: the need for combining social and cognitive. *ReCALL,* 17 (1), pp. 85-100.

HOLMES, J. 2007. Designing agents to support learning by explaining. *Computers & Education,* 48 (4), pp. 523-547.

KEARSLEY, G. 2000. *Online education: learning and teaching in Cyberspace.* Toronto: Wadsworth.

KNOWLES, M.S. 1976. *The adult learner: a neglected species.* Houston, TX: Gulf.

LIVINGSTONE, D., KEMP, J., EDGAR, E. 2008. From multi-user virtual environment to 3D virtual learning environment. *ALT-J: Research in Learning Technology,* 16 (3), pp. 139-150.

MINOCHA, S., ROBERTS, D. 2008. Laying the groundwork for socialisation and knowledge construction within 3D virtual worlds. *ALT-J: Research in Learning Technology,* 16 (3), pp. 181-196.

ORAVEC, J. A. 1996. *Virtual individuals, virtual groups: human dimensions of groupware and computer networking.* New York: Cambridge University Press.

PARIS, S. G., BYRNES, J. P. 1989. The constructivist approach to self-regulation and learning in the classroom. In: B. J. ZIMMERMAN, D. H. SCHUNK (eds) *Self-regulated learning and academic achievement: theory, research, and practice.* New York: Springer, pp. 169-200.

PENCE, H. E. 2007-2008. The homeless professor in Second Life. *Journal of Educational Technology Systems,* 36 (2), pp. 171-177.

PRESSLEY, M., BORKOWSKI, J. G., SCHNEIDER, W. 1987. Cognitive strategies: good strategy users coordinate metacognition and knowledge. In: R. VASTA, G. WHITEHURST (eds) *Annals of child development.* Greenwich, CT: JAI Press, pp. 89-129.

TAYLOR, K. C., CHYUNG, S. Y. 2008. Would you adopt Second Life as a training and development tool? *Performance Improvement,* 47 (8), pp. 17. Available from: http://www3. inter-science.wiley.com/journal/121391229.

VYGOTSKY, L. S. 1978. *Mind in society: the development of higher psychological processes.* Cambridge, MA: Harvard University Press.

WASLEY, P. 2008. U. of Phoenix lets students find answers virtually. *Chronicle of Higher Education,* 54 (48), pp. A1-A10.

ZIMMERMAN, B. J. 1981. Social learning theory and cognitive constructivism. In: I. E. SIGEL, D. M. BRODZINSKY, R. M. GOLINKOFF (eds) *New directions in Piagetian Theory and practice.* Hillsdale, NJ: Erlbaum, pp. 39-49.

ZIMMERMAN, B. J. 1989. A social cognitive view of self-regulated academic learning. *Journal of Educational Psychology,* 81 (3), pp. 329-339.

ZIMMERMAN, B. J. 1995. Self-regulation involves more than metacognition: a social cognitive perspective. *Educational Psychologist*, 30 (4), p. 217.

ZIMMERMAN, B. J. 1998. Developing self-fulfilling cycles of academic regulation: an analysis of exemplary instructional models. In: D. H. SCHUNK, B. J. ZIMMERMAN (eds) *Self-regulated learning: from teaching to reflective practice.* New York: Guildford Press, pp. 1-19.

Linking Research and Teaching in Higher Education
Simon K. Haslett and Hefin Rowlands (eds)
Proceedings of the Newport NEXUS Conference
Centre for Excellence in Learning and Teaching
Special Publication, No. 1, 2009, pp. 101-115
ISBN 978-1-899274-38-3

University of Wales, Newport

Prifysgol Cymru, Casnewydd

NEWPORTDIGITAL: community empowerment through digital inclusion study.

Matt Chilcott and Johana Hartwig

Institute of Digital Learning, University of Wales, Newport, Allt-yr-yn Campus, Allt-yr-yn Avenue, Newport, NP20 5DA, United Kingdom. Email: matthew.chilcott@newport.ac.uk; Johana.hartwig@newport.ac.uk

Abstract

Despite considerable quantitative research undertaken into digital inclusion in the United Kingdom (UK) there remains considerable gaps in academic understanding of effective digital engagement strategies and their impact on individuals and communities. There is also a need for a greater qualitative evidence base of successful practice in this field in Wales and the wider UK. This study offers qualitative evidence on the personal and social impact of community empowerment enabled through a joint digital and social inclusion programme. The findings also provide new insight into the forms of internet use by new adopters in the core non-participating digitally excluded age group of society, those aged 75 and over, and provides new evidence in relation to the beneficial use of utilising the social applications of the internet with these groups. This study increases understanding of the key role played by social enterprise in addressing the digital exclusion of communities. It also highlights the need for fresh consideration of digital infrastructure planning and third sector network engagement in future urban regeneration initiatives to ensure greater opportunity for individuals to enhance their contribution to their community, the local and wider digital economy, and to enhance the quality of life available within that community.

Introduction

In 2008, a Communities First funded project in the Gaer community, Newport (South East Wales) successfully addressed the social exclusion of elder citizens through their engagement with digital technologies. The project helped to rebuild and empower the Gaer community, which had been affected by an urban renewal programme that relocated the former residents of prefabricated housing stock into replacement new build bungalows on the same land.

An action research programme led by the University of Wales, Newport's, Institute of Digital Learning investigated the most effective uses of digital technology in regenerating and empowering communities.

This research programme also explored in parallel the philosophy, practice and operating environment of social enterprise as an enabler of digital inclusion and community empowerment. The research attempted to respond to the UK Online Centre's (2007) *Understanding digital inclusion* research paper's call for further research into the soft impacts and the social benefits of digital inclusion and the HM Government's Communities and Local Government's (2008) *Understanding Digital Inclusion* research paper's call for new investigation into motivational engagement approaches with digital technology and the identification of wider benefits and uses of digital technologies.

The research also builds on the *E-Inclusion*

Recycling C.I.C: Bridging the Digital Divide in the UK's Greenest City (2008) case study (available from http://idl.newport.ac.uk/einclusion and has been driven by the Institute of Digital Learning's continued dialogue and collaboration with members of Welsh and wider UK Digital Inclusion and Social Enterprise champions and practitioner communities.

This research paper includes a joint component in the form of a multimedia case study resource that is available from http://idl.newport.ac.uk/newportdigital. The multimedia publication was designed to share access to personalised accounts of the impact of the 'Gaer community empowerment through digital inclusion' programme had and to offer reflections on the experiences of digital and community engagement.

Core research themes for the action study examine:

1. Effective applications of digital technology in empowering communities
2. The social impact of addressing the digital exclusion of elder citizens
3. The role and function of social enterprise in enabling digital inclusion.

This paper, firstly, explores the digital and social inclusion methodologies deployed in the programme in consideration of wider academic perspectives on the domestication and demystification of technology. Thereafter, the paper evaluates qualitative feedback from new adopters from the core non participating group, focusing on their utilisation of the internet, the social impact of this activity and evidence of learning aspirations arising. The paper then considers the role of social entrepreneurship in enabling effective digital engagement of the most digitally excluded members of our society independent to traditional market forces. The paper then reveals the medium term impact of the Gaer inclusion programme and offers conclusions aimed at policy makers preparing future urban renewal activity.

Research Methodology

The study employed a small scale investiga-

tive action research approach seeking to facilitate knowledge accumulation and transfer in relation to the three core research themes.

The approach to the study was open, in as much as the researchers made no attempt to disguise their role. The nature of researcher engagement with members of the community was through introductions and it was clarified that the researcher role in interviewing Gaer residents was for investigative purposes. The research was primarily, but not exclusively, qualitative. The evaluation of the materials obtained drew on ethnographic approaches in seeking to provide meaning to people's narrative in interpreting an understanding of both their individual and social lives.

This approach was clarified with participating Gaer residents and it was understood that their qualitative responses and testimony formed the core material for the investigation. Supplementary video capture of the Gaer programme's instigator and the E-Inclusion team as programme enablers focused on the other research themes for the project. As some video interviews lasted over thirty minutes it was decided to professionally edit the video capture to emphasize key messages from respondents. Whilst this approach was deemed useful for the media dimension of the publication, the researchers endeavored to create a full critique of the Gaer programme in the written dimension of the study.

The E-Inclusion team who developed the social programme were known to the researchers. To ensure a lack of bias regular moments were taken out of the programme to ensure a level of independence for the researchers. It was agreed that all dialogue with the E-Inclusion team would be open and frank so dialogue could help inform a true picture of the Gaer empowerment programme.

All interviews reviewing the digital engagement and social impact on the programmes' beneficiaries were undertaken in the Gaer community and predominately in residents' homes. This enabled full investigation into the impact of new adopters of digital technology in a domestic context, allowing the harvesting of more accurate data due to residents sense of ease in their own homes. This also enabled the recording of participants' real time computer usage.

With the emphasis on the social impact of digital inclusion activities, the publication adopted a research methodology that utilised multimedia content to offer direct access to individual accounts from beneficiaries. In publishing the media dimension of this study the researchers were influenced by their interest in interactive journalism publication practice. As a consequence the qualitative video materials were presented in such a manner as to provide a narrative of the programme investigated with the focus on the first hand accounts of beneficiaries.

Upon completion of the media publication dimension of this study the researchers accepted an invitation from the Gaer community to present the video based dimensions of the study at the Gaer community centre in March 2009. This event provided the research team with the community's endorsement of the accuracy and authenticity of the publication.

Effective Methods to Empower Communities with the Application of Digital Technologies

The approaches undertaken in the Gaer community empowerment through digital inclusion programme operated in three principal phases. These responded to identified need through the delivery of the programme and remained responsive to wider opportunities for social and digital inclusion arising as a 'by-product' of an empowered beneficiary group. The methodology implemented was tailored specifically to meet the needs of the Gaer community on behalf of the commissioning agents and the spectrum of support needs of community residents. The phased approaches are summarised in the Appendix of this publication and presented diagrammatically in Figure 1.

Warschauer's (2003) consideration of the role of technology in facilitating social inclusion identifies that 'ability' or 'digital literacy' is an essential dimension of enabling social inclusion with technology. He summaries this view point as follows:

A central premise is that, in today's society, the ability to access, adapt, and create knowledge using information and communication technologies is critical to social inclusion. This focus on social inclusion shifts the discussion of the "digital divide" from gaps to be overcome by providing equipment to social development challenges to be addressed through the effective integration of technology into communities, institutions, and societies. What is most important is not so much the physical availability of computers and the Internet but rather people's ability to make use of those technologies to engage in meaningful social practices.

The investigation into the community empowerment through digital inclusion programme methodology deployed in the Gaer concludes that the E-Inclusion team effectively enabled an 'ability' or 'digital literacy' of a community that had little or no prior engagement with computers and the internet. This was achieved in a short period time and delivered through a targeted empowerment approach that maximised the ability of individuals and the community as a whole to overcome their own social isolations, access to services and low level of digital literacy. The emphasis on the social application or practices of the computer in the home appears to have been a key ingredient in the success of the programme. Building on Warschauer's perspective the skills of digital literacy were enabled by creating the perception of computers as domestic tools that enabled greater engagement with other members of the community and wider institutions and agencies. The ability to utilise the new domestic tool effectively offered enhancement in quality of life through digital engagement to meet personal aspirations relating to the application of the technology provided.

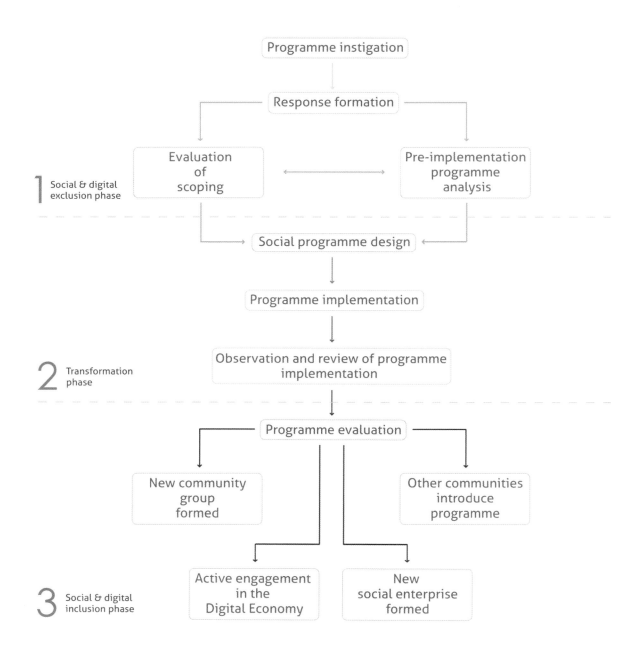

Figure 1. Community Empowerment through digital inclusion dynamics.

The success of the Gaer social programme supports this premise and also reveals the focus of the programme design in managing relationships and aspirations of both the *individual* and the *group*. Personalised development programmes that responded to the spectrum of individual empowerment or creativity/skills development needs served as the enablers or engagement drivers in utilising digital technology. The hands on personalised, 'one to one', 'always there' delivery approach also appears to have reduced anxiety and fear levels of programme beneficiaries. The focus of enabling people's digital engagement from their own homes was a further key dimension for this programme. This approach accords with Boeltzig and Pilling's (2007) study which investigated successful digital inclusion initiatives in the United States and the United Kingdom. In seeking to offer recommendation to future policy development and digital engagement methodologies they proposed that:

(Digital Inclusion) Projects should take into account people's needs for long term computer and Internet access if new users' interest and use is to be sustained. The full benefits of Internet access cannot be realized without home access, and this is particularly the case for older people and people with disabilities.

The methodology reviewed in this study helps to reveal a practical interpretation of Bharat and Merkel (2004) consideration that in order for the internet to play a more substantial role in facilitating social and personal empowerment a greater or deeper understanding of the everyday life of individuals from minority and marginalised communities needs to take place. The methodology's use of personalised development plans with a nurtured community impact has proved successful from this perspective. Figure 2 summaries key community resident instigation drivers. The

need for personal empowerment, increased communication and socialisation and in other instances greater stimulation were enabled through the programme. Emphasis on different approaches tailored to individual needs and personal development aspirations took precedence in engaging participants with computers and the internet. The use of social applications of the internet underpinned all of the responses to the key instigation drivers.

The 'demystification' approach also appears to have been pivotal in the success of the programme, which involved beneficiaries visiting the E-Inclusion Recycling facility to recognise the effort made in providing beneficiaries with 'their own' computer. The beneficiaries first hand experience of seeing a computer being broken down into its component parts, refurbished, and then brought into their homes appears to have eliminated many of the initial barriers to technology and created a sense of ownership in advance of engagement with the application side of the digital tools. The study supports Williams and Stewart (2005) considerations of the appropriation and 'normalisation' of technology in which they identify the need for approaches to encompass informal social and cultural processes in achieving familiarity with computer based technologies for marginalised groups in offering opportunity in addressing social exclusion. The demystification method also offers a transferable approach that responds to the OFCOM (2006) study of older people and communication technology. In consideration of barriers to digital engagement and considerations of skills and abilities, this study identified that the vast majority of non users of computers or the internet lacked exposure to these technologies, which raised personal doubts in older people about their ability to cope with learning this form of technology.

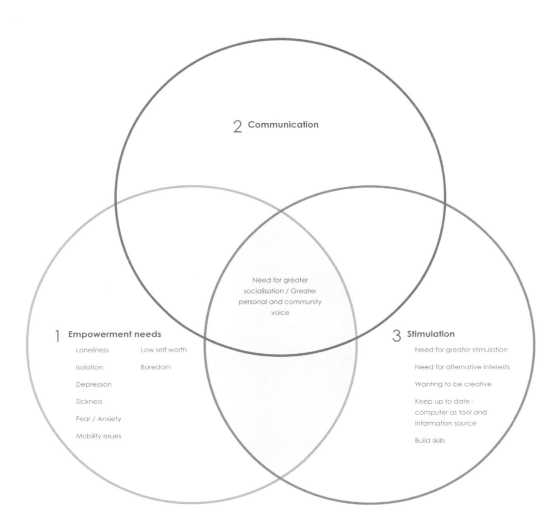

Figure 2. Community Resident Instigation drivers.

The home instillation support component of the programme appears also to be a further crucial dimension of the programme's design. In particular the E-Inclusion engineer's role in configuring both the computers and broadband in each beneficiaries home addressed a major engagement barrier for residents. Investigation revealed that the additional financial cost of broadband access in the home for most residents on the programme was negligible. This was because residents were already subscribers to digital television packages (predominately Sky and Virgin Media) that also provided broadband within their purchased package. The programme provided residents with an opportunity to access the broadband facility of these packages that they had not otherwise been able to do. This therefore served as a further motivational driver for engaging in the programme.

It was also revealed through questioning of the programme enablers that the start up instillation and support phase evolved into a longer term more informal support approach where, for example, if a web camera or mouse no longer worked they were replaced by the E-Inclusion team at no cost to the programme beneficiaries. This continued care support approach clearly sits outside of traditional market force approaches to computer support and it was acknowledged that the Computer Recycling social enterprise facility was a crucial element in enabling the ability to 're-supply' users with hardware over a longer period than the programme time-frame.

The longer term sustainability of this approach, beyond very effectively channelled altruism, would be a useful focus for further exploration. This experience accords with Williams and Stewart (2005) argument that the abilities or competencies 'beyond start up' in addressing technical problems experienced by new adopters are not widely available. It is apparent that the Gaer computer club had enabled a growing independence within the community in addressing problems collaboratively as a group and a community led independence to care for one another in both a social and digital context.

The Gaer programme's focus of 'home based' digital inclusion also accords with Berker *et al.* (2006) in their consideration of the successful 'domestication of technology', when perception of technology in a domestic context move from a negative to positive position and technologies are considered 'comfortable', 'functional', 'reliable' and 'trustworthy'. At a symbolic level the invited technology becomes part of the family. It is evident that the Gaer programme methodology enabled this with computers providing new domestic tools that somewhat 'pet like' offered company and access to family and community networks in new ways. In a number of interviews with Gaer residents it was apparent that the computer was a welcome new tool, in the way that it both enabled new forms of community based communication, but also engaged communication with family members living abroad or at a significant distance. In particular the use of 'Skype' was regularly noted as a positive tool and in a number of instances was considered to serve as a replacement for the telephone in a number of households.

It became evident to the researchers that this social programme methodology supports the recommendations made in Boeltzig and Pilling's (2007) study which reviewed successful digital inclusion initiatives in the United States and the United Kingdom. They identified that methods seeking to increase digital inclusion of targeted groups would need to involve the provision of free computers and internet access, the provision of long term support to organisations seeking to reach groups and effective partnership working to share resources and expertise. The Gaer programme's focus on the 'needs or concerns of target groups in ensuring purposeful engagement with the internet' also supports Boeltzig and Pilling's perspective.

The Social Impact of Addressing the Digital Exclusion of Elder Citizens

The HM Government's (2008) *Delivering Digital Inclusion Action Plan for Consultation* publication identified an estimated 17 million people over the age of 15 were not using computers or the internet. The Action Plan also revealed that 15% of the UK population - more than six million adults - are both socially and digitally excluded. Only 37% of over 65's have internet access at home against an all-adult average of 67% and dropping to 22% for those aged 75 or older. The focus Gaer inclusion study was on this core non-participating age group categorised from these statistics as the most digitally excluded.

The mean average age of programme beneficiaries involved in this study was 76.5 years of age with a mean average engage-ment with computers at the time of the research interviews of 1.29 years. It was clear that the sample beneficiaries could be considered as 'new adopters' of digital technology in regard of both the use of computers and accessing and utilising the internet. As a consequence the Gaer study provides insight into the latest uses of computers and the internet by this age group.

As Figure 1 of the Gaer programme meth-odology identified, one of the impacts of the Gaer inclusion programme was a new active engagement in the digital economy. Within a short period of time it had become a social normality for the programme beneficiaries to undertake a range of transactions in an online context. These engagements concentrated on shopping in the context of online clothing, household goods and media products retail, grocery shopping, holiday 'research' and in supporting the purchase of niche products in the form of materials for craft-based hobbies. Such activity required effective use of online search engines and navigation around commercial websites. The ability to undertake online banking for managing household accounting, payment of bills and financial planning was also identified as a valued new skill.

The beneficiaries' new abilities to engage with the digital economy in these ways were noticeably celebrated as a new literacy that offered enhancement to the quality of the programme beneficiaries lives. The action research identified that there was some identifiable individual excitement, shared cultural merriment in the community and

personal development planning identified in relation to eBay and the ability to engage effectively with the eBay website in order to 'eBay' as an 'action'. This was a next step for this group's advancement in a journey of digital literacy.

A further common internet activity for the Gaer residents was the use of internet search engines to locate information and research topics of interest. These interest topics ranged from holidays, recipes, geography and history information to craft-based interests. The motivational drivers of the quest for new knowledge and information had been apparently successfully enabled through the E-Inclusion teams' approach. The researchers had anticipated that current affairs may also have been an identified web quest for beneficiaries but this did not materialise with the sample group.

With the exception of the animated use of Skype and email as the principal internet use for the community members (and an identified lack of use of the internet for examining current affairs) these findings are in accordance with the Oxford Internet Survey's 2007 findings of what activities people across the UK undertake online. The stronger emphasis on the use of social networking through Skype and email is identifiable as a key method in maximising the social impact of the Gaer resident's digital inclusion. In all cases respondents identified 'Skyping' as new skill and digital literacy that was adding value to their engagements online and within the community.

Investigation revealed a preference for Skype over email amongst most sample beneficiaries on account of Skype's ease of use and the video dimension bringing family and friends directly into their homes for real time visual communication. The social impact of this social application appeared striking. On one level Skype became a social engagement and communication tool to facilitate networking across the Gaer community and to access the support and guidance of the E-Inclusion team. On the other level the social impact and enhancement of quality of life offered from Skype's live video feed engagement with family and friends, located at a distance and often internationally, was shared extensively across the sample group. The research also identified that there remained nervousness amongst some Gaer residents that using email could highlight poor written English skills with their peers in the community.

The ability to engage more effectively with family and friends through the internet was identified as a major turning factor in the enhancement of quality of life for the Gaer residents. Within the context of family, greater intergenerational engagement with other family members and grandchildren was referred to by the sample group. Respondents were interested in the ease with which young people engaged 'quickly' and 'naturally' with computers. This appeared to have served as a further motivational driver to learn more about computers and the internet to offer new discussion topics and activities with grandchildren. In several instances new digital literacy was being put to use to provide digital engagement with family businesses, for example the development of small business marketing flyers through desktop publishing applications. Evidence of active citizenship in the form of new social entrepreneurship was reported to the research team and the Gaer Community Network were confirmed to be offering support to community residents in forming new Gardening, DIY and Laundry social businesses.

The qualitative responses in regard to the social application of the internet are in contrast to predominately quantitative findings from Helsper (2008) Oxford Internet Institute's study that analysed 'Social Disadvantage and the Information Society' as part of the HM Government's Digital Inclusion Action plan for Consultation. In seeking to explain digitally excluded group's engagement with digital resources the report identified:

… being elderly (and more likely to be isolated, with constrained social networks) reduces the likelihood of benefiting from social applications of the internet.

It is apparent that the methodology used in this study focused on the use of social communication applications enabled through the internet as the principle tools of digital and social engagement in the Gaer. The addressing of experiences of social isolation was supported through the use of Skype and email as key tools in facilitating the development of a joint real world and online social network. Through personal development support the Gaer residents became comfortable and subsequent regular users of Skype and email communication tools. These approaches are supportive of the European Parliament's (2007) consideration of 'Ageing well in the community' where staying socially active and creative through Information Communication Technology solutions for social networking offer opportunity for improving quality of life and reducing social isolation.

The Gaer study supports the findings of Helsper's (2008) work in relation to the extension of home access as a key barrier to tackling the digital inclusion of the most disadvantaged and also confirms the low aspiration levels to access government services in an online context. This was emphasised through the investigation of the Gaer residents' willingness to make use of the internet to vote online for local and national elections. It was apparent that in most instances residents preferred the socialisation and ritual of physically visiting the polling station to tender their vote. However, the access of localised care services and the ability to engage with carers and social workers using Skype was desired by a number of residents. In particular the ability to contact these professionals directly through the medium of Skype was particularly desired.

Boeltzig and Pilling's (2007) transnational study identified that:

In both the United States and the United Kingdom, considerable emphasis has been placed on government information and services being online, and increasingly on the possibility of carrying out online transactions (e-government). The intention has been to deliver better quality, more convenient services to individuals, and also to increase efficiency and cut costs. While both countries are well on the way to Internet delivery of government services, this does not necessarily mean that all citizens are equally able to access them. In both countries, those who have most to gain from e-government may have least access to it—people on low incomes, older people, people with disabilities—thus providing evidence of a continuing digital divide.

The qualitative evidence from the Gaer inclusion programme study indicates that social care and potentially wider health care services do offer opportunity for increased internet service delivery. Dialogue has taken place between the E-Inclusion team and Newport City Council in regard of the feedback from programme beneficiaries and their desire to engage with their care workers through Skype. The extent to which social care practitioners are equipped with suitable digital skills sets and access to appropriate technologies to achieve these aims offers an opportunity for further investigation.

The evaluation of qualitative responses identified that the programme appeared to have initiated a sense of reinvigorated desire for new forms of lifelong learning classes in relation to the new digital literacy enabled by the project. Mainstream offering of Microsoft Office training had been undertaken by a number of the residents alongside 'Computing for the Terrified' classes. The interview process identified that the main internet access for lifelong learning had centred around more informal learning and the enrichment of interests and hobbies including online shopping, model boat building, history, geography, craft, cooking and puzzles. Digital photography was also identified as a popular lifelong learning subject in the community. It was identified that the Digital photography group offered residents additional social contact opportunity alongside the development of further digital literacy skills.

The action research programme identified that a number of the empowered Gaer residents had self initiated their own social forums outside of the programme's planning and implementation approaches. The group developed a monthly computer club and a separate monthly coffee morning both held at the Community Centre to offer a face to face dimension to the social network of the Gaer community otherwise supported by online communication (in addition to their meeting at computer classes). A number of other programme beneficiaries self initiated their own creative group focused on making art works from non-hazardous electronic waste that could not be recycled by the E-Inclusion team. Also a number of residents had received support from the Gaer community network to undertake mentor training to develop their skills in active citizenship in supporting other community members to make use of computers and extend social aspiration activities.

These findings offer support to the policy call from Help the Aged's 2008 *Learning for Living policy* document that focused on the need for citizenship and ICT literacy. In consideration of the Government's Take Part, 'the national learning framework for active learning for active citizenship' Help the Aged identify that:

There is no commitment to offer this type of learning: the Take Part framework simply provides a manual for learning providers to 'enable' them to develop programmes of citizenship learning to help adults gain the knowledge, skills and confidence they need to become empowered as members of their communities. In the current climate of reduced funding for informal learning and adult learning in general, it seems unlikely that these initiatives will be taken forward.

The Gaer findings support the arguments put forward by Slack and Williams (2000) who considered that social learning approaches were required in regard to the social uses of Information Communication Technology in communities and the manner in which these need to focus on a complex web of interactions, articulations and understandings that constitute a technology as it is currently active and utilised in society.

The social programme approaches taken in the Gaer appear to have strong parallels to the Age Concern digital inclusion project active in the Neath and Port Talbot area of South Wales (funded through the Communities @ One initiative). Future research could focus on comparative study of the 'Go for IT' project methodology and the approaches employed by the E-Inclusion team in the Gaer community.

Reference was made during the action research programme to the Community's interest in engaging with Second Life as an additional form of social networking and exploration of the internet. Any additional study on the longer term impact of the Gaer residents' digital engagement may wish to explore the outcomes of this interest in relation to ease of new adopters' engagement with emerging internet based technologies and activities.

The Role and Function of Social Enterprise in Enabling Digital Inclusion

The social business approach that underpinned the Gaer programme accords with Chell's (2007) work into defining 'Social Enterprise and Entrepreneurship' models in the early part of the twenty first century. Chell argued that:

Social entrepreneurs have the intellectual capacity, the thought processes and the imagination to recognise opportunity based on their technical and/or professional experience; they have the social and personal networks that add non-material human and social capital resources; and they have the personal ability to make judgements about appropriate courses of action that will result in the pursuit of an opportunity of socio-economic value based on the realisation of a competitive advantage. All businesses involve customer choice. Competitive advantage confers rarity or some other socio-economic value that social entrepreneurs can create. In these ways social and community enterprises can become self-sustainable; indeed they can create social and economic change

through the development of a vibrant form of doing business.

The Gaer programme study clearly identifies that the E-Inclusion Recycling social business consultancy model operated without grant aid and in so doing enabled a greater entrepreneurial approach in the pursuit of social and digital inclusion for the E-Inclusion team operating outside of perceived targeted grant aid restrictions. The business exerts competitive advantage in offering consultancy services to communities seeking to address their own social and digital exclusion. The ability to create income generation activity that creates surplus for the company enables the opportunity for increased social and economic impact by expanding business activity that seeks to help increased numbers of people and maximise the impact of the company's mission. The lead programme enabler for the E-Inclusion team identified simply that:

The standard business is focused on making money and there is absolutely nothing wrong with that. A social enterprise is wired on making money to help people. So therefore the more money you make the more people you can help. The more money you make the less you rely on funding which leaves social entrepreneurs to be creative. They can be entrepreneurial in the way that we have been to address a social issue.

Wessel's (2008) in evaluating approaches that enable digital inclusion on a regional scale identified:

Strategies to overcome a digital divide are not simply about access to ICT but involve the development of skills, improving literacy including digital literacy, generating relevant e-services to encourage use, and fostering capacity in developing participation in various Internet related communication, activity, and knowledge-generation. To foster eInclusion therefore involves providing training and supporting participation in ICT related activities, whether at work, in education, in political participation, in culture and in everyday life. Everyday life is an important dimension in fostering inclusion because situations of exclusion are experienced and managed in everyday life and the take up and use of ICT is negotiated in everyday life.

It is clear that the Gaer programme has identified the social enterprise goal of enabling a positive social impact from their business activity has enabled this 'fostering' or facilitation role for social and digital inclusion. The focus on both social aspects of exclusion and the use of digital technologies as tools to enable greater social inclusion has enabled digital inclusion as a 'by-product'. This by-product has developed new literacy in the use of digital technology and, in so doing, served also as an engine of greater individual and community capacity building. The fostering and nurturing of these new human relationships and sense of comfort with computers was encapsulated in the 'e-service' approach embedded in the programme. This approach, in working freely of traditional market forces, appears to have enabled and encouraged the helping of others as a consequence of the social enterprise philosophy in practice. The essence of which appears to be the focus on enabling positive relationship outcomes with other people and with technology.

This is supportive of Newholm *et als* (2008) study which considered an effective strategy to engage computers and the internet and the manner in which excluded groups were unlikely to utilise formal sources of technical help in acquiring key knowledge attributes as novices. They identified that those excluded from the knowledge society required a range of support measures from hardware, software and internet start up through to a network of 'friends'. In this instance the social enterprise team were considered informal in their approach to the Gaer residents and also informed and friendly in their personalised support approaches for the residents.

The social entrepreneurial approach as the cornerstone for the programme responds to the issues identified in the European Parliament's (2007) *Action plan on Information Communication Technologies and Ageing* which identified:

Access, accessibility and user-friendliness of devices and services are prerequisites for the inclusive delivery of advanced services for the ageing society. Mainstream ICT products and services rarely address the needs of the older population. Currently the market is not investing sufficiently in innovation for meaningful and affordable solutions for older users. There is a need to break the vicious cycle of insufficient adequate solutions, awareness, economies of scale of standards and sustainable business models, which leads again to insufficient investment in research and innovative solutions.

Whilst the European Parliament do not point to social enterprise as an enabler of the innovative solutions it is clear that the impact revealed in this study provides policy makers with an insight into the role of the Third Sector in effective community engagement and delivering a sustainable business approach focused on enabling the digital inclusion of excluded citizens. The extent to which the partnership approach between social enterprise and the grant funded community development sector enabled a community's social regeneration in partnership with technology serves as a potential new focus for future study.

HM Government's *Digital Britain* Interim report (2009), in consideration of effective strategy necessary to enable digital inclusion and the potential that digital technology can offer to enhance quality of life for all UK citizens in the digital age, identifies that:

The necessary education, skills and media literacy programmes to allow everyone in society to benefit from the digital revolution will be a central part of the Digital Britain work and key to our success. We must ensure that being digital is within the grasp of everyone. If we do not, we risk leaving significant parts of our society disenfranchised and permanently behind the mainstream. In so doing, we would fail to secure the full potential of these technologies for our country.

It is evident that the Gaer programme offers an insight into the type of approaches offered by social enterprises, approaches that differ from main stream, private and public technology providers and that offers a vital contribution to the strategic mix required to enable much greater digital engagement of excluded groups.

Summary of the Medium Term Impact of the Gaer Programme and Reflections on Future Research Opportunities

Since the completion of the social programme for the Gaer community in April 2009, it is worthy of note that the self-generated monthly community events continue at the Gaer community centre with 'self help' and 'peer mentoring' continuing independently of the now concluded empowerment programme. A number of the social programme's beneficiaries have undertaken mentoring training to help strengthen this interest in supporting others. Other beneficiaries have formed a creative group who visit the E-Inclusion Computer Recycling premises in Pill to create art works from non recyclable electronic waste. The E-Inclusion team continue to support residents when asked for advice or home IT maintenance support. This is undertaken at no cost to the Gaer residents as part of their social contribution ethos and is in part enabled by the nature of the host social enterprise as a Computer Recycling facility that IT hardware (such as a mouse or monitor) can be changed promptly with negligible impact on operational costs for the business.

Learning from the success of the programme in the Gaer, other Communities First wards of Newport in Stow Hill and Ringland have now commissioned the E-Inclusion team to undertake the same programme for their communities. In these communities the empowerment drivers will be different to the Gaer experience of long established community networks experiencing major change through an urban renewal programme. It is recommended that further research be made into the resident empowerment drivers of these wards and their social and individual goals from engaging with the programme.

In addition to these new Communities First commissions Newport City Council's Lighthouse project has engaged the E-Inclusion team to offer the same social programme to a number of their clients. The Lighthouse project, offered in partnership with Taff Housing Association and Cefnogi-pobl (Supporting People), seeks to provide low level housing related support to people in their own homes; to encourage independence skills and confidence in living successfully in their own homes and to reduce loneliness and increase engagement with their local community. In this instance the programme beneficiaries are distributed across the City of Newport and the support offered is therefore not community ward centric. It is recommended that further study be undertaken into the modifications required to the existing social programme's delivery methodology and the social impact of these digital inclusion related approaches in enabling the establishment of new Pan-Newport social networks for recognised isolated groups.

In response to the public service delivery opportunities identified in this research a further complimentary research theme could be connected to the Lighthouse project to consider barriers and enabling approaches for Newport City Councils' Social Services Directorate to empower Social workers and other Care professionals in using digital approaches to enhance the service they offer their clients (such as Skype communication and email electronic calendars reminder functions).

This research programme has identified the successful use of Skype as a common digital tool of contact and facilitation of community for the beneficiaries of this social programme. Future researchers that seek to build on this body of work may wish to consider using this tool for qualitative interviews with a broader spectrum of programme beneficiaries on future projects.

Finally, future comparative studies could also investigate the ability of other Cities and rural communities' to undertake the same social programme approaches without the underpinning E-Inclusion Computer Recycling social enterprise. Beyond the philosophy of social entrepreneurship the Recycling facility appears to be an integral cornerstone resource dimension of the programmes design. A study of this nature would then test the full transferability of the E-Inclusion social programme approach to wider community empowerment contexts where such resource community owned Computer Recycling is not currently offered.

Conclusions

In the context of the Gaer project explored in this study it is evident that digital technology can serve as an effective tool in a set of wider social inclusion approaches that enables both personal and community empowerment. The positive social impact is evident and was enabled by a focus on 'relationship building' both in the context of community relationships and in relation to human computer interface approaches. In the context of the Gaer community's experiences of urban renewal, beyond the usual reach of digital inclusion research, it is evident that the opportunity for future urban regeneration programmes to consider the digital context of the new community infrastructure needs to take a higher precedence. The need for new methods of developing new community networks through online engagements requires effective infrastructural planning alongside targeted digital engagement activity. In responding to the Digital Britain interim report this need was articulated effectively by Dodson *et al.* (2009) on behalf of the DC10 Plus Network:

We propose that all Cities and places are mandated to produce digital master plans that will guide their digital future over the coming years... The opportunity now is to build new digital infrastructures and services which provide the foundation for new jobs and skills, new ways of working and a new quality of life that will serve the locality and its people and businesses well for decades to come. All homes and businesses need to be connected so that the

local 'offer' will be second to none, properly future proofed and sustainable.

Arguably policy makers and planners when instigating regeneration that accounts for community networks and online engagements should also undertake mapping of Third Sector organisation partnership opportunities to engage these 'community assets' in enabling the digital literacy of excluded members of that community. Increased digital literacy levels will be required to ensure a realisation of the benefits from the new digital infrastructures and in so doing provide new opportunity for individuals to enhance their contribution to their community, the local and wider digital economy and improve their quality of life within that community.

The HM Government's focus on the use of digital technology as a tool for tackle social exclusion is supported by this study. In particular, the addressing of elder citizen's social isolation in part by utilising social applications of the internet accords with Government thinking on digital inclusion. It is also apparent that the application of digital technology for these ends needs careful planning and clearly identified social goals (beyond the digital inclusion of citizens) to prove most effective. Both personal and community empowerment of elder citizens enabled through social entrepreneurship and philanthropy has been paramount in the achievements of the Gaer community inclusion programme. The role of community owned Computer Recycling social businesses as a further cornerstone in underpinning the achievement of digital inclusion, outside of traditional market forces in excluded communities is also considered of relevance to policy makers and community bodies when exploring strategic and operational digital engagement and electronic waste management planning.

REFERENCES

AGE CONCERN NEATH & PORT TALBOT *Go for IT project*. Available at www.ageconcernneath-porttalbot.org.uk/index.cfm?id=1280.

BERKER, T., HARTMANN, Y., PUNIE, Y., WARD, K. 2006. *Domestication of Media and Technology* Maidenhead: Open University Press.

BHARAT, M., MERKEL, C., PETERSON BISHOP, A. 2004. The internet for empowerment of minority and marginalized users. Journal of New Media and Society, 6 (6), pp. 781-802

BOELTZIG, H., PILLING, D. 2007. *Bridging the Digital Divide for Hard to Reach Groups* IBM Centre for Business and Government – eGovernment Series. Available at http://www.businessofgovernment.org/pdfs/BoeltzigPillingReport.pdf.

CHELL, E. 2007. Social Enterprise and Entrepreneurship – Towards a Convergent Theory of the Entrepreneurial Process. *International Small Business Journal*, 25 (1), pp. 5-26.

CHILCOTT, M. 2008. *Bridging the Digital Divide in the UK's Greenest City* Association of Learning Technology News Feature article. Available at http://newsletter.alt.ac.uk/e_article001151711.cfm?x=b11,0,w.

CHILCOTT, M., TRAYNOR, J. 2008. Social Enterprise and *ReGENeration in the Digital Age* ppts – International Regeneration and Learning Conference – Communities, Continuity and Change Conference: Newport, October. Available at http://idl.newport.ac.uk/presentations/R&L%20Conference_files/frame.htm.

COMMUNITIES @ ONE 2008. *Digital Inclusion Wales Conference Report* Cardiff. Available at http://www.com munitiesatone.org

DODSON, S., CARTER, D., JONES, M., SUMNER, V., STONELEY, E. 2009. *DC10plus Network response to the interim Digital Britain report* UK: DC10 Plus Network. Available at http://www.dc10plus.net/resources/dc10plusnetworkresponsetotheinterimdigitalbirtainr.

EPRACTICE EU 2008. *Leicestershire Care Online.* Available at www.epractice.eu/cases/LCOL.

EUROPEAN PARLIAMENT 2007. *Ageing Well in the Information Society: Action Plan on Information and Communication Technologies and Ageing.* EUROPA. Available at http://europa.eu/scadplus/leg/en/ lvb/l24292.htm.

EYNON, R. 2008. *Internet Use in Britain: Adult Learning and the Digital Divide (Oxford Internet Survey) ppts.* NIACE Digital Inclusion Conference: How do we ensure that all citizens, especially the disadvantaged, benefit from new technologies? Nottingham, November.

HELP THE AGED 2008. *Learning for living – Helping to prevent social exclusion amongst older people* London: http://policy.helptheaged.org.uk/NR/rdonlyres/781C82C1-B30A-4975-A1A9-BA15048944FD/5554/learningforliving.pdf

HM GOVERNMENT DEPARTMENT FOR COMMUNITIES AND LOCAL GOVERNMENT 2008. *Digital Inclusion: An analysis of Social Disadvantage and the Information Society.* Oxford Internet Institute Queen's Printers.

HM GOVERNMENT DEPARTMENT FOR COMMUNITIES AND LOCAL GOVERNMENT 2008. *Understanding Digital Inclusion research report –* FRESHMINDS London: Crown.

HM GOVERNMENT DEPARTMENT FOR CULTURE, MEDIA AND SPORT AND DEPARTMENT FOR BUSINESS, ENTERPRISE AND REGULATORY REFORM 2009. *Digital Britain – Interim Report* London: Crown.

NEWHOLM, T., KEELING, K., McGOLDRICK, P., MACAULAY, L. 2008. The digital divide and the theory of optimal slack. *Journal of New Media and Society,* 10 (2), pp. 295-319.

NEWPORT CITY COUNCIL 2008. *Lighthouse Project-support for people at home.* Available at www.newport.gov.uk/stellent/groups/public/documents/leaflets_and_brochures/cont288736.pdf.

OFCOM CONSUMER PANEL 2006. *Older People and communication technology, an attitudinal survey into older people and their engagement with communications technology* . Available at http://www.ofcomconsumerpanle.org.uk.

SLACK, R., WILLIAMS, R. 2000. The dialetics of place and space – On community in the Information Age. *Journal of New Media and Society,* 2 (3), pp. 313-334.

SOLUTIONS FOR EXCLUSION 2009. Available at http://www.esd.org.uk/Solutions4Inclusion/Default.aspx.

TUROW, J., TSUI, L. 2008. *The Hyperlinked Society: Questioning Connections in the Digital Age.* Chicago: The University of Michigan Press.

UK ONLINE CENTRES 2007. *Understanding digital inclusion – a research summary* FRESHMINDS UFI Ltd.

WARSCAUER, M. 2003. *Technology and Social Inclusion – Rethinking the Digital Divide.* Boston, MA: MIT Press.

WESSELL, B. 2008. Creating a regional agency to foster eInclusion: the case of South Yorkshire, UK European. J*ournal of ePractice*, 5 (3), available at http://.www.epracticejournal.eu.

WILLIAMS, R., STEWART, J., SLACK, R. 2005. *Social Learning in Technology Innovation – Experimenting with Information and Communication Technologies.* Cheltenham : Edward Elgar.

| University of Wales, Newport | Prifysgol Cymru, Casnewydd |

Linking Research and Teaching in Higher Education
Simon K. Haslett and Hefin Rowlands (eds)
Proceedings of the Newport NEXUS Conference
Centre for Excellence in Learning and Teaching
Special Publication, No. 1, 2009, pp. 117-123
ISBN 978-1-899274-38-3

Podagogy: can podcasting enhance the quality of learning and teaching in Higher Education?

Nicola J. Woods and Simon Phillips

School of Education, University of Wales, Newport, Lodge Road, Caerleon, South Wales, NP18 3QT, United Kingdom. Email: Nicola.woods@newport.ac.uk; Simon.phillips@newport.ac.uk

Abstract

"Podagogy" is defined as the "art or science of using podcasts for educational purposes" (IMPALA Project, 2006). A growing literature reports on the many and various ways in which this new discipline is developing: including, for example, podcasts for encouraging reflective learning; podcasts as a new medium for presenting tutor feedback; and, perhaps most prolific in current publications, the potential of podcasts to provide "portable education". This paper presents a review of a selection of publications in podagogy and, in doing so, raises important questions about how podcasting can best be used to enhance the quality of students' learning experiences. The paper includes a critical analysis of the concept 'Digital Native' and argues that any attempt to introduce new technological tools into pedagogy must be empirically informed: specifically, research needs to be undertaken to investigate which technological tools are important for students, how and why students use various aspects of technology and, most importantly, the hopes, ideals and expectations that students have for using technology (for study, work and leisure) in their future lives.

Introduction

Podcasting, the use of pre-recorded personalised on-demand audio (and video) content to subscribers, was first introduced in early in the 21st century and has since seen an exponential growth in use in many and various contexts. Dubbed *word-of-the-year* by the New Oxford American Dictionary in 2005, the term originally derived from a compound of broadcasting and iPOD but is now frequently interpreted as an acronym for "personal on-demand" (Frydenberg, 2006, p. 2).

Following its inception in the media, the educational potential of podcasting was soon recognised. From the practical advantages for teaching that such a 'moveable' device offers (according to Austin, 2007, podcasting makes Higher Education (HE) as "portable as a pop song"), through pragmatic benefits of (re) engaging students who may be "impatient" with other forms of learning (Chan and Lee, 2005) to opportunities for enhancing education through the promotion of critical learning (Reynolds and Bennett, 2008), few have doubted the potential of podcasting to change the way we communicate with our students and organise contexts for learning and teaching.

The use and implementation of podcasting in HE can be traced to the year 2004 when the Duke University, USA distributed to new students over 1,600 iPODS already equipped with induction schedules, academic calendars and podcasts. Other universities were quick to follow[1] and, as many reviewers of podagogy have remarked, there has since been a swift

---

[1] Arizona state University, University of Denver and North Carolina A&T State University were all early adopters of podcasting technology (Lum, 2006, pp. 34-35).

growth in the use of podcasting in universities across the world. According to Udell (2005), the reasons for the rapid rise of podcasting include: the popularity of the internet, broadband connectivity, the accessibility of the multimedia personal computer, blurring of the distinction between streaming and downloading media content and, not least, the proliferation of MP3 playback equipment.

However, despite such rapid development, not all are convinced of the educational merit of podcasts. While some bemoan the lack of pedagogical research into the value of podcasting (Guertin *et al.*, 2007), others report only "marginal" improvement to students' learning experiences following the introduction of podcasting as a method of teaching (Malan, 2007, p. 393). Reflecting such research results, Hargis *et al.* conclude that there are "no examples which clearly indicate proven foundational pedagogical uses and outcomes for podcasts" (2005).

Podcasting and Pedagogy

It is true that the first attempts to incorporate podcasts into HE pedagogy were woefully inadequate. Tales of students tuning in (and swiftly turning off) to long, complex and monotonic podcasts are rife. Frydenberg's (2006) experiences are typical, revealing how the number of students using podcasts (on an introductory technology course) rapidly declined after the initial "novelty period" had worn off. Others have observed little positive influence of podcasting on educational outcomes or achievement (Malan, 2007), while the mismatch between modern educational theory and the learning experience provided by tutor-produced podcasts has also been the subject of considerable critical comment. Reynolds and Bennett (2008) observe, for example, how the passive listening task required by tutor-generated podcasts fails to provide opportunities for communal interaction that a social constructivist approach to education considers vital to successful learning (see Brown *et al.*, 1989, for an exposition of this theory which, in simple terms, centres on the premise that meaningful learning takes place

in situated interactions between learners and not in the minds of individual learners engaging with abstract content).

It is perhaps for these reasons that Malan (2007) argues that the real benefit of podcasting is "not necessarily to educate better, but to educate further" (p. 390) and, by the same token, that the portability of podcasts provides educational opportunities for those for whom traditional enrolment and attendance is not feasible. Mellow (2005) agrees that it is the "flexible learning" opportunity offered by podcasts which is most valuable and, following this line of argument, Campbell asks us to picture the following scene:

"Imagine a busy commuting student preparing both emotionally and intellectually for class by listening to a podcast on the drive to school, then reinforcing the day's learning by listening to another podcast, or perhaps the same podcast on the drive back home" (p. 34).

An obvious corollary to this prospect is that the incorporation of podcasts as an aspect of pedagogy offers the potential for lifelong learning beyond the confines of the classroom. Consequently, the use of podcasts provides opportunities to engage a range of diverse learners and to promote inclusivity[2].

While the importance of facilitating access to (higher) education is indisputable (and the idea that students might access educa-

---

[2] Though it is important to acknowledge that the use of podcasts may discriminate against certain members of diverse student populations: *e.g.* audio pods are clearly inappropriate for students with hearing impairments and may also be less than ideal for students whose learning styles are highly visual. Furthermore, not all are convinced that inclusivity will be enhanced by the simple introduction of technologies into teaching: a British Telecom survey undertaken in 2001 revealed that 85% of school teachers believed that the government's ICT-focused curriculum was likely to put pupils from less privileged backgrounds at a disadvantage. The importance of taking measures to lessen the 'digital divide' are, therefore, considered crucial (reported by Rebecca Smithers in *The Guardian*, Thursday 18 October 2001).

tional content from any geographical location is captivating), the question remains as to whether this is the sole advantage of incorporating podcasting technology into pedagogy. Is podcasting only useful for increasing the *quantity* of education through improving accessibility or, in contrast to Malan's (2007) view, can podcasting be used to enrich the *quality* of learning in HE? This is a key question for the present research and one which, where investigated, has had mixed results.

Reynolds and Bennett (2008) aim to assess the educational value of podcasting by investigating the impact on students' learning experiences. Acknowledging the importance of engaging students beyond the level of passive listening, Reynolds and Bennett distributed gapped handouts for students to complete whilst listening to podcasts. Results of the research were ambiguous: while students appeared to retain more information when the material was presented in audio as opposed to textual form, there was no significant difference in students' understanding or application of the material presented. Notably, a subsequent survey revealed students' negative evaluations of the use of gapped handouts. While Reynolds and Bennett report that they found this criticism "unexpected", it perhaps not altogether surprising since gapped handouts are a particularly traditional method of assessing students' engagement with new technologies.

Nevertheless, the research of Reynolds and Bennett clearly points to the importance of encouraging student activity (especially associated cognitive activity) with podcasts. As Brittain *et al.* (2006) argue, it is vital to "actively involve the client": this can be achieved by (i) engaging students in the design and production of podcasts; and (ii) ensuring that students have a voice in providing formative evaluation of podcasting projects. In the following sections, we consider these two forms of student engagement in greater detail, turning first to a consideration of students as producers of podcasts.

Student Producers of Podcasts

Advocating a method that will be employed in the present research, Frydenberg (2006) invited students to design and create their own podcasts. A key positive consequence of this student-focussed approach is that it shifts the function of podcasts from merely providing a channel for *imparting* information (from tutor to student) to a means of encouraging *collaborative* work in student groups. Podcasting is, therefore, elevated to a pedagogical position in which it has the potential to foster team work and, as a consequence, to create and sustain learning communities - communities in which students are "empowered to express themselves creatively" (p. 6).

It is significant that observed benefits of podcasting are not limited to the HE context. Piecka *et al.* report on a project in which podcasts were developed "by students for students" in a 7th grade science classroom (2008, p. 203). Amongst several positive outcomes, Piecka *et al.* observe that:

"One important reason that podcasts aid in learning is because they provide students with the tools and skills to build and present their own knowledge. Because students actively create and listen to podcasts they develop their research and technical skills and acquire an understanding of the content" (2008, p. 215).

In support of this observation, Lee *et al.* (2008) show how student endeavour facilitates "collective learning, as well as supporting social processes of perspective-taking and negotiation of meaning that underpin knowledge creation" (p. 501). Aiming specifically to develop students' skills in digital literacy as well as to enhance abilities relating to problem solving, conceptualisation, expression and teamwork, Lee *et al.* were particularly interested in the manner in which podcasts can be used to facilitate the social construction of meaning and knowledge. Using a pedagogy aimed at encouraging student ownership of the learning experience, students scripted and produced podcasts in which they engaged in discussion of important issues relating to their IT course and, in some cases, invited lecturers and other experts to give their views on particular topics.

Results reveal that producing podcasts encouraged students to engage with "idea generation, collective problem solving and reciprocal dialogue, as well as in the exchange and revision of ideas" (Lee *et al.*, 2008, p. 513). Outcomes such as these are far removed from the limited impact of tutor-produced, didactic podcasts. Indeed, the types of activities in which students engage in designing and producing their own podcasts (including active and independent learning, team skills and reciprocity) are precisely those which would be promoted by modern collaborative learning theories and constructivist epistemology in which, as noted above, learning is seen as an essentially social activity and process.

The positive impact on learning that results from student engagement with podcast production is confirmed by research in which students have been encouraged to play a key role in evaluating their own (podcast promoted) learning and development.

Student Evaluation of Podcasting

The value of eliciting student evaluations of teaching practices is irrefutable, especially in cases in which new content is being delivered or where the method of teaching is innovative. However, in many cases, student evaluations are used only to review and revise aspects of teaching (be it the content of the curriculum or the methods in which the curriculum is communicated). In this respect, the value for students who provide evaluative feedback can sometimes be neglected and opportunities for students to consider, reflect and deliberate on their own learning experiences are, therefore, missed.

In relation to podcasting, there are a few studies which avoid this trap and, often by use of student-centred focus groups, do attempt to encourage students to learn from their evaluations. In the research of Lee *et al.* (2008), for example, focus group discussions with students reveal how the experience of producing podcasts promoted team building and collaborative construction of meaning. One of the student participants comments that producing podcasts "gives you another angle, and shares other ideas" (sic), while another notes that "I'm trying to encourage other people and hopefully they can criticise me in return". It is interesting to note how the terms 'encourage' and 'criticise' are used synonymously in this last statement. The interpretation that 'criticism' (like encouragement) is something to be welcomed is surely significant in the light of the collaborative nature of podcast production in which the reporting student had engaged.

In her paper 'Confessions of a Podcast Junkie', Windham (2007) provides an engaging account of the growth of podcasting in HE from a student perspective. Supporting the statements of Mellow (2005), Campbell (2005), Dale (2007) and others (see above), Windham highlights the advantages of podcasts as "portable education", pointing specifically to the benefits of podcasted material for students who, perhaps because of family commitments or full-time paid work, have to fit education around their lifestyle rather than their lifestyle around education. Windham (2007) describes students' attitudes towards podcasting and lists the following "tips" for tutors who are intending to introduce podcasting into their teaching practice:

- *Don't assume:* just because a student owns an iPOD "doesn't mean that the student is podcast-savvy".
- *Keep it simple:* podcasts should be concise and engaging.
- *Quality counts:* ensure quality in recording.
- *Make it relevant:* make sure that podcast content is relevant to the rest of the course "otherwise, it's just cool technology to have".
- *Offer something more:* e.g. podcasted material should be additional to, not a replacement for, information provided in

lectures and other learning and teaching contexts.

- *Don't limit imagination:* e.g. when encouraging student production of podcasts, ensure that students are given open license to use their inventiveness and ingenuity and that they are not constrained by lists of criteria such as content and length of podcasts.
- *Encourage exploration:* related to the point above, encourage students to "think outside the box" and support their creativity.

It is worth expanding on just a couple of Windham's (2007) words of advice here. First of all, the importance of her initial recommendation – *Don't assume* – cannot be overestimated. If the introduction of new technologies into learning and teaching is to be successful, it is imperative that students' experiences are used as the focal point for development. As Wyndham points out, it is not justifiable to presume that all students are digitally literate: just because a student may have been born in the digital age, this does not mean that he or she is competent in dealing with digital technologies.

Indeed, there is growing criticism of the construct 'Digital Native': a term coined by Prensky (2001) to refer to individuals who "think and process information fundamentally differently" because they have lived their lives in a culture saturated with "computers, videogames, digital music players, video cams, cell phones, and all the other toys and tools of the digital age" (p. 1). In a study of first year students at the University of Melbourne, for example, Kennedy *et al.* (2008) observe that, outside of the use of well-established digital tools, there is a great deal of variation in students' experience of other technological activities (*e.g.* creating/maintaining a blog, using RSS feeds and, perhaps most surprising, engaging with social networking software). Consequently, Kennedy *et al.*, issue the important warning that students who belong to the 'Net Generation' will not necessarily understand "how to use technology based tools strategically to optimise learning experiences in university settings" (p. 116).

Defining the nature of digital literacies and investigating how we can best help students to develop them is a key aspect of the current research. Ethnographic work will facilitate insights into students' access to technological tools, students' competencies in various technological activities and, not least, students' own ambitions and expectations of technology (for study, leisure and career opportunities, for example). Only once this information has been collected and analysed, will attempts be made to introduce podcasting into pedagogy.

Following Windham (2007), relevancy is another key theme to be addressed and methods of making the content of podcasts relevant has been central in research undertaken with students in the School of Computing, Engineering and Information Sciences at Northumbria University. Having been given the opportunity to provide evaluation and feedback, students point to the importance of "embedding" podcasts into module material in a way that allows for the "migration of learning" – moving from lecture (introduction/explanation) to podcast (preparation/ reflection), for example (Laing *et al.*, 2006, p. 516).

However, while embedding podcasting into pedagogy is clearly crucial, it is interesting to note that student evaluations of podcasting projects reveal aspects of development that go far beyond subject-specific curriculum content. For example, both Windham (2007) and Lee *et al.* (2008) point to the manner in which producing podcasts can support and enhance a range of (transferable) skills, especially language and communication skills: one student podcaster interviewed by Windham reports that, in order to produce successful pods "you have to learn how to gather your thoughts properly, speak properly." (2007, p. 7), while Lee *et al.* (2008) also report the significant influence of podcasting on linguistic skills:

"You want to get your words right. Like your sentence structure, the way you put things together"

"We stumble over words, they don't make sense, or we just can't get the words out! we re-wrote half of our parts, because we just couldn't get it to make sense to us'" (Lee *et al.,* 2008, p. 515).

Many other important skills for study and employability have also been noted as an incidental result of student engagement with podcasting - team working, time management, problem solving and critical thinking, to name but a few (see, for example, Huann and Thong, 2006; Cane and Cashmore, 2008).

Perhaps we should not find these positive outcomes to be too surprising. In 2005, Campell (2005) considered how students have been "blogging, shooting and editing video, creating Flash animations, manipulating photographs, and recording digital audio for many years". Describing how these are the tools of young peoples' "native expressiveness", Campell proposes the convincing argument that, with the right guidance, these tools can be used by students to "create powerful analytical and synthetic work" (2005, p. 36). By incorporating such tools into pedagogy, we recognise that "podcasting, unlike any other medium presently available, allows students to develop a voice of their own to share with the class and the world" (Piecka *et al.,* 2008, p. 215).

Conclusion

Few would dispute the importance of encouraging students to develop a 'voice of their own'. We would only reemphasise that, in order to achieve this most important of aims, it is crucial that the introduction of new technologies (and podcasting in particular) build on students' own experience, knowledge and understanding. By means of ethnographic work with diverse groups of learners from many different walks of life, the current research aims to elicit students' thoughts, values, ideals and expectations about using technology. In the light of this collaborative work, we will then proceed to engage with students to find out precisely how podcasting can be used to develop key competencies in, for example, collaborative learning, communication, literacy and IT.

Generic skills which, somewhat paradoxically, are most successfully taught and learned when embedded into the specific subject areas studied by students. Is podcasting a way forward for embedding skills into the curriculum and developing abilities that are necessary for successful employment, career development and, not least, lifelong learning? Only by building on students own experiences and working together to encourage them to design, develop, produce and evaluate podcasts will we be able provide answers to these important questions. In this way, the potential for podcasting to improve the quality (not merely the quantity) of learning in HE will be revealed.

REFERENCES

AUSTIN, J. 2007. The next class fits in your pocket. *Star-Telegram.com*, 12 February 2007, Fort Worth. http://www.star-telegram.com [accessed on 2nd May 2009]

BRITTAIN, S., GLOWACKI, P., VAN ITTERSUM, J., JOHNSON, L. 2006. Podcasting Lectures. *Educause Quarterly*, 3, pp. 24-31

BROWN, J. S., COLLINS, A., DUGUID, P. 1989. Situated Cognition and the Culture of Learning. *Educational Researcher*, 18 (1), pp. 32-42.

CAMPBELL, G. 2005. There's Something in the Air: Podcasting in Education. *Educause Review*, 40 (6), pp. 33-46.

CANE, C., CASHMORE, A. 2008. Student-Produced Podcasts as Learning Tools. http://www.heacademy.ac.uk/assets/York/documents/events/conference/2008/Chris_Cane.doc [accessed on 4th May 2009]

CHAN, A., LEE, M. 2005. An MP3 a Day Keeps the Worries Away: Exploring the Use of Pod casting to Address Preconceptions and Alleviate Pre-Class Anxiety Amongst Undergraduate Information Technology Students. In: D. H. R. SPENNEMANN, L. BURR (eds) *Good Practice in Practice. Proceedings of the Student Experience Conference*, Student experience conference, Charles Stuart University, Sept. 5-7.

DALE, C. 2007. Strategies for Using Podcasting to Support Student Learning. *Journal of Hospitality, Leisure, Sport & Toursim*, 6 (1), pp. 49-57.

FRYDENBERG, M. 2006. Principles and Pedagogy: the Two P's of Podcasting in the Information Technology *Classroom. Information Systems Educational Journal*, 6 (6). http://isedj.org/6/6/ISEDJ.6(6).Frydenberg.pdf [accessed on 4th May 2009]

GUERTIN, L. A., BODEK, M. J., ZAPPE, S. E., KIM, H., 2007. Questioning the Student Use of and Desire for Lecture Podcasts. *Journal of Online Learning and Teaching*, 3 (2), pp. 133-141.

HARGIS, J., SCHOFIELD, K., WILSON, D. 2005. Fishing for Learning with a Pod casting Net. *iManagers Journal of Educational Technology*, Volume 1.

HUANN, T. Y., THONG, M. K. 2006. Audioblogging and Podcasting in Education. http://edublog.net/astinus/mt/files/docs/Liter ature%20Review%20on%20audioblogging%2 0and%20podcasting.pdf [accessed 4th May 2009].

IMPALA (Informal Mobile Podcasting and Learning Adaptation) Project 2006. Available at http://www.le.ac.uk/impala/projects/Podagog y.html [accessed at 2nd May 2009].

KENNEDY, G., JUDD, T., CHURCHWARD, A., GRAY, K., KRAUSE, K. 2008. First year students' experiences with technology: are they really digital natives? *Australian Journal of Educational Technology*, 24 (1), pp. 108-122.

LAING, C., WOOTON, A., IRONS, A. 2006. iPod! uLearn? http://www.formatex.org/micte2 006/Downloadable-files/oral/iPod.pdf [accessed on 8th November 2008].

LEE, M., CHAN, A., MCLOUGHLIN, C. 2006. Educational Podcasting Using the Charles Sturt University Flexible Publishing Platform. In: T. REEVES, S. YAMASHITA (eds) *Proceedings of World Conference on E-Learning in Corporate, Government, Healthcare, and Higher Education 2006*. Chesapeake, VA: AACE.

LEE, M., MCLOUGHLIN, C., CHAN, A. 2008. Talk the Talk: Learner-generated Podcasts as Catalysts for Knowledge Creation. *British Journal of Educational Technology*, 39 (3), pp. 501-521,

LUM, L. 2006. The Power of Podcasting. *Diverse Issues in Higher Education*, 23 (2), pp. 32-35.

MALAN, D. J. 2007. Pod casting Computer Science E-1. In *Proceedings of the 38th SIGCSE Technical Symposium on Computer Science Education*, pp. 389-393.

MELLOW, P. 2005. The Media Generation: Maximize Learning by Getting Mobile. *Proceedings of Ascilite 2005, Balance, Fidelity, Mobility: Maintaining the Momentum?* http://ascilite.org.au/ conferences/brisbane05/blogs/proceedings/ 53_Mellow.pdf

PIECKA, D., STUDNICKI, E., ZUCKERMAN-PARKER, M. 2008. A proposal for ozone science podcasting in a middle science classroom, *Association for the Advancement of Computing in Education Journal*, 16 (2), pp. 203-233.

PRENSKY, M. 2001. Digital Natives, Digital Immigrants. *On the Horizon*, 9 (5), http://www.marcprensky.com/writing/Prensky %20%20Digital%20Natives,%20Digital%20Im migrants%20-%20Part1.pdf [accessed 4th May 2009].

REYNOLDS, C., BENNETT, L. 2008. A Social Constructivist Approach to the use of Podcasts. *Association for learning Technology Newsletter*, Issue 13. http://newsletter.alt. ac.uk/e-article001142653.cfm [accessed on 8th November 2008].

UDELL, J. 2005. Hypermedia: why now? O'Reilly Network, March 18. Available at http://oreillynet.com/pub/a/network/2005/03/ 18/primetime.html (accessed on 21 May 2009).

WINDHAM, C. 2007. Confessions of a Podcast Junkie: a Student Perspective. *Educause Review*, 42 (3), pp. 50-65.

University of Wales, Newport

Prifysgol Cymru, Casnewydd

Linking Research and Teaching in Higher Education
Simon K. Haslett and Hefin Rowlands (eds)
Proceedings of the Newport NEXUS Conference
Centre for Excellence in Learning and Teaching
Special Publication, No. 1, 2009, pp. 125-130
ISBN 978-1-899274-38-3

Team-based international study visits: an education visit to the Czech Republic.

Alan Rowse[1] and Andre-Dina Pana[2]

[1]School of Education, University of Wales, Newport, Lodge Road, Caerleon, South Wales, NP18 3QT, United Kingdom. Email: Alan.rowse@newport.ac.uk

[2]Inspectoratul Scolar Teleorman, Alexandria, Romania. Email: ghadarod@yahoo.com

Abstract

The main objective of this study visit was to investigate the link between theory and practice taking place in the Czech Republic vocational education system. The European Centre for the Development of Vocational Training (CEDEFOP) funding supports the setting up of these visits and encourages dissemination of good practice throughout Europe. This particular visit lasted seven days (8th to 14th Feb 2009) which consisted of two days travel (Newport – Heathrow – Prague – Ostrava – Frydek-Mistek and back). The five day visit programme was a packed schedule of visits to a number of vocational schools, meetings with local dignitaries, participation in a variety of discussion forums, and evening social programmes. The study group was made up of four head teachers (two French & two German), a Spanish educational inspector, a Romanian academic plus three educationalists from the United Kingdom. The intense mix of educational, cultural and social learning opportunities was very powerful and is to be recommended as a vehicle for the spread of good practice.

Introduction

This paper is based on a final report produced for the European Centre for the Development of Vocational Training (CEDEFOP). The paper describes visits made by an international team of educationalists to the following institutions in the Czech Republic over seven days (8th to 14th Feb 2009):

1. The Secondary School of Clothing and Business, Frydek-Mistek
2. The Secondary School of Electronics and Woodworking, Frydek-Mistek
3. The Secondary Vocational School of Clothing, Strážnice
4. The Secondary Vocational School of Engineering and Transport in Frýdek-Místek
5. The Business School, Ostrava, plc.

The final group report, on which this paper is based, was created by the team using a continuous process of meetings, discussions and inputs mostly gathered and agreed on during the evening leisure time.

The study visit team of nine people was drawn from five different countries. One of the strengths of the team was its diversity. Members represented diverse phases and types of education which included secondary level, tertiary, and vocational schools catering for the ages 11 to 19. There was also representation from educational administration at local level, from an inspector and secondary initial teacher training.

In setting out this paper we have used the template recommended by the transversal study visits team and collate team responses to set questions:

1) Summary of impressions
2) Objectives of the study visit
3) Lifelong learning
   a) Common approaches
   b) Common challenges
   c) Effective solutions
   d) Policies and practice
4) Creating networks

Summary of impressions

It was apparent at the first meeting that all participants were passionate about the ethos, importance and challenges evident in secondary vocational education. The participants came together at the Hotel Silesia which is located in the picturesque town of Frydek- Mistek nestling in the foothills of the Beskydy Mountains. The study visit team consisted of secondary education experts from around Europe (see Figure 1).

The group were given a full programme which began with an introductory session at the host school, 'Stredni skola odevni a

obchodne podnikatelska'. This session explained the educational system currently operating in the Czech Republic and the position of the vocational school.

The main focus for the visits was textiles and engineering vocational schools *i.e.* how they operate, pedagogic strategies used and the curriculum.

Summarising your impressions, please describe what in your opinion are the most important things that you have learned during the visit.

- There are both similarities and differences between the education systems of the countries we represent;
- The absenteeism rate in different countries is significantly variable;
- The age when the compulsory education starts and ends;
- The strict differentiation between vocational schools and theoretical (academic) school;

Figure 1. The study visit team. From left to right: Wilhelm Bredthauer (Headteacher, Germany), Andra-Dina Pana (teacher trainer, Romania), Francis Beltrane (Headteacher, France), Andre Becherand (Headteacher, France), Rainer Lipczinsky (Headteacher, Germany), Alan Rowse (Senior Lecturer, Wales), Irtiza Qureshi (Local Authority/ Schools for the Future, UK), David Parr (English Teacher, UK) and Vladimiro Cubas Garcia (inspector, Univ. Spain).

- It seems common to a number of countries in the European Union to differentiate between vocational and academic education by type of school. The United Kingdom (UK) is an exception to this, as the differentiation is by qualification and not type of school;
- A key difference is the compulsory school age for young people in Czech Republic, starting age is 6 and they can leave at the age of 15.
- Practical education in companies ranges from 10 days (UK) to 3 months (Spain) a year. In Germany, the pupils in vocational education spend 50% of their time in companies whilst in the 11th grade;
- Adults can use the school premises to learn skills in the Czech Republic, Romania, UK, Germany, Spain, France;
- There are Second Chance schools in Romania and Spain.

Objectives of the Study Visit

One of the objectives of the study visits programmes is exchange of good practices among the hosts and participants. CEDEFOP will select examples of good practices and disseminate them among former participants and wider public, including potential partners for future projects (see Table 1).

Lifelong learning

The study visits programme aims to promote and support policy development and cooperation in the field of lifelong learning. That is why it is important to know what is learnt about such policies and their implementation during the visit. The team were invited to describe their findings concerning the questions set out in the following sections.

Common approaches, if any, that are met in all or some countries (both host and participants') regarding the theme of the visit

- It seems common to a number of countries in the EU to differentiate between vocational and academic educa-

tion by type of school. The UK is an exception to this, as the differentiation is by qualification and not type of school.
- A key difference is the compulsory school age for young people in Czech Republic, they can leave at the age of 15, but in the UK, France, Germany and Romania they are able to leave at 16 but few students choose this option.
- Practical education in companies ranges from 10 days (UK) to 3 months (Spain) a year. In Germany, the pupils in vocationa education spend 50% of their time in companies whilst in the 11th grade.
- Adults can use the school premises to learn skills in the Czech Republic, Romania, UK, Germany, Spain, and France.
- There are Second Chance schools in Romania and Spain.

Figure 2. Day 1 visits to the a) host school (textiles and business focus) and b) vocational school (engineering, plumbing, electronics and working with wood).

title of the pro-ject/programme/initiative/	name of the institution that implements it (website)	contact person (if possible), who presented the programme to the group	whom the project/ programme/ initiative addresses	what features of the project/programme/initiative make it an example of good practice
School-industry links, communica-tion with industrial companies	Secondary School of Electronics and Woodworking, Frydek-Mistek	Ing. Antonin Susovski	Pupils, Vocational schools, industry	Workplace Jobs Sponsorships Equipment, resources Theory and practice in the same building
Presenting the school products to the local community	The Secondary School of Clothing and Business in , Frydek-Mistek and Straznice	Ing.Petra Schwarzova Ing.Petra Fialova	Local community	Cooperation and exposing the school to local community
European Funds for equipment	Secondary School of Electronics and Woodworking, Frydek-Mistek	Ing. Antonin Susovski	Vocational Schools	Utilising the EU funding for the school and for the local community
Adult learning on school premises	The Secondary School of Clothing and Business & The Secondary School of Electronics and Woodworking, Frydek-Mistek	Ing.Petra Schwarzova Ing.Petra Fialova	Adults	Adults learn skills in the evening which generates income plus some textiles items are sold through a shop outlet
Change in the curriculum in response to social command	The Secondary School of Clothing and Business in , Frydek-Mistek and Straznice	Ing.Petra Schwarzova Ing.Petra Fialova	Pupils	The school added new branches to train pupils according to jobs required by local economy
Eurocamps	The Municipality of Frydek-Mistek	Mayor Ing.Eva Richtrova	Secondary schools pupils	Cultural exchange between youth in different European countries

Table 1. Examples of good practice.

Common challenges that are faced by all or some countries (both host and participants') in their effort to implement policies related to the theme of the visit

- Vocational education seems to hold lower esteem in the majority of EU countries, with the exception of Germany and some Scandinavian countries;

- To provide good quality vocational education is far more expensive than the provision for academic qualifications;

- There is a lack of work related placements and strong industry links in order to provide vocational learning for pupils;

- Good practical work, old equipment and only basic theoretical education. The students observed have good discipline.
- Motivating students' families to be active in school life is a challenge for most countries represented in the group with the exception of Germany.
- The starting salary for teachers is considered to be below the national average whilst in Germany it is better paid.

Effective and innovative solutions you have identified that the countries (both host and participants') apply to meet the identified challenges

- The vocational schools seem to have developed good sponsorship links with industry.
- Utilising EU funding to provide equipment, programmes and training resources.
- German pupils receive, in part, high level qualifications in vocational education equivalent to someone who graduates from a theoretical school.
- In addition, high quality equipment and work related learning is afforded to the pupils which all helps raise self esteem and perception of value of vocational education.
- With reference to high absence figures (20 – 30%) in the Czech Republic. In Germany (less than 5%), the problem of the lack of parents' motivation is solved due to the Parents' Day in school and the strict laws which makes pupils responsible for themselves. There is also close cooperation with parents and the work placement companies. In France, there is tough action, via social workers, which can lead to the suspension of family allowance.

Policies and practices that can be further explored and possibly transferred to other countries

- Sponsorship, academy links between

industry and education should be increased in all countries represented.
- Partnership between industry and education is critical to successful vocational education provision.
- Transfer of EU funding programme to a larger number of countries will help equality of access to vocational provision.
- Children are allowed to choose what vocational school they attend. If they want another job, they can transfer to other school.

Creating Networks

Creating networks of experts, building partnerships for future projects is another important objective of the study visit programme

- The participants are interested in starting school cooperation under the Life Long Learning frame (Comenius, Youth in Action, Eurocamps).

The study visit team have extensive experience of European projects and the sharing of knowledge during social and programme hours was found to extremely valuable to all concerned *e.g.* the host school are exploring a link with the Lycee Le Castel in Dijon via Comenius funding.

The vocational schools which were visited all managed to give very good examples of student's work which included two highly professional fashion shows, practical exhibits of items made from wood and metal objects created using CNC machines (see Figure 3).

Suggestions for Future Study Visits

- To provide a coherent picture of the educational system in the Czech Republic which indicates all aspects e.g. school accountability to local authority or central government, school budgets, student statistics i.e. assume no prior knowledge of the system at an early stage.
- Facilitate discussion between the study group members and students, parents

and teachers in the schools rather than official guided tours.

Figure 3. Examples of student work at vocational schools, a) fashion show, and b) wood and metal objects.

- Promote short but focused visits to a range of schools which include levels above and below secondary level.
- When visiting school industrial partners, focus more on the student experience rather than the company profile.
- When meeting politicians and decision makers, to focus on the education system and the issues involved *e.g.* funding, buildings, strategies for the future.
- To structure the school visits so that they have a logical thread with regard to educational outcomes *e.g.* maybe visit an elementary school, then a number of vocational schools and finally a college, university or a place of work where previous students have been employed.
- To give examples of how theory and practice are linked in vocational schools.
- To revisit the original objectives and make sure that they are addressed in sufficient detail *i.e.* a number of original objectives were not considered to be met by the group.

On reflection, the rich learning experiences gained from this study visit, in no particular order, were:

- The variety of approaches and range of pedagogies used in vocational teaching are very narrow, but maybe that is good?
- The links from vocational courses *i.e.* 14-19, to Higher Education are not clearly signposted in the UK. How can this be improved?
- A significant number of our trainee teachers would be ideally suited to 14-19 education. Is it possible to vary teaching placements to include FE style placements?
- Study visits are an ideal vehicle to promote research informed teaching although in this case most of the knowledge used in lectures has been drawn from northern European countries *i.e.* France and Germany. What are the political reasons for maintaining a system that is currently not producing what we need as a country in the UK?
- The Czech Republic has a strong vocational educational system but it is geared toward consumerism, what happens next?

ACKNOWLEDGEMENTS

Our warmest thanks are due to the teachers, head and deputy head teachers, administrators and politicians of Frydeck-Mistek and surrounding area, who made us so welcome and who were so generous with their time in order to make the study visit successful. We would particularly like to thank Petra Schwarzova (organiser), Olga (English teacher and interpereter), Roman (photographer) for making our stay so productive and enjoyable. Thanks also to the transversal study visit programme for making the visit possible.

University
of Wales,
Newport

Prifysgol
Cymru,
Casnewydd

Linking Research and Teaching in Higher Education
Simon K. Haslett and Hefin Rowlands (eds)
Proceedings of the Newport NEXUS Conference
Centre for Excellence in Learning and Teaching
Special Publication, No. 1, 2009, pp. 131-136
ISBN 978-1-899274-38-3

European Union Intensive Programme in smart clothes and wearable technology.

Jane McCann[1], Sirpa Morsky[2] and Marion Ellwanger[3]

[1]School of Art, Media and Design, University of Wales, Newport, Lodge Road, Caerleon, South Wales, NP18 3QT, United Kingdom. Email: Jane.mccann@newport.ac.uk

[2]HAMK University of Applied Sciences, Visamäentie 35, P.O.Box 230, FIN-13101 Hämeenlinna, Finland. Email: Sirpa.morsky@hamk.fi

[3]Swedish School of Textiles, University of Borås, Bryggaregatan 17, SE-501 90 Borås, Sweden. Email: Marion.Ellwanger@hb.se

Abstract

This European Union Intensive Programme (IP) has enhanced the capacity for a specialist design led programme, within Europe, through the collaborative development of unique training in the emerging hybrid design area: smart clothes and wearable technology. This programme has helped to prepare students to engage effectively in the new revolution in the merging of the technical textiles, clothing and electronics related industries. It has targeted the needs of students from study backgrounds such as textile design and technology, garment design, electronics and computing in providing an introduction to the knowledge and skills required for participation in the multidisciplinary design team of the future. The aim of the project has been to implement the development of a new shared language that merges science, technology and design in addressing a breadth of needs of society. Teaching and learning modules have been informed by a user-needs driven design methodology for the application of generic smart technologies that may be incorporated in technical textiles within a 'clothing system' for categories such as functional sportswear, corporate wear and inclusive design. The shared expertise of partner institutions was enhanced through collaboration with local, regional and international trade partners keen to engage in this emerging hybrid industry.

Context and Rationale

Context

This European Union Intensive Programme (IP) took place at the University of Wales, Newport, in January 2008, over a three week period, based in the School of Art, Media and Design. The IP was built on preparatory visits and/or established links through the Erasmus/Socrates teacher and student exchange programme. It was intended to strengthen links between HAMK University, Finland, and the University of Wales, Newport, in clothing and footwear design, in introducing the innovative topic of smart textiles and wearable technology. This, in turn, demanded the expertise of the Swedish School of Textiles, with their expertise in textile design and engineering. These institutions embrace a range of design courses that have benefited from the project dissemination. Each partner brought an average of five students to the project. All partners introduced a range of industrial collaborators offering support to the project who also wish to benefit from the multidisciplinary training developed.

These exchanges grew out of prior successful Leonardo and Leonardo Multiplier projects in the area of performance sportswear design. Hamk University had been the lead applicant in the Leonardo bids with the lead academic area of expertise coming from the University of Derby. With the functional clothing design expertise now based at the University of Wales, Newport, this partner has since provided expert involvement in assessment, short courses and master classes at the Swedish School of Textiles, in the area of performance sportswear design. This collaboration has led to the subsequent signing of a Socrates agreements between these institutions. This IP, led by Hamk University, has enabled the three institutions to come together for the benefit of staff and students, in addressing the new generation of smart functional clothing design that is emerging with the performance sports community as an early adopter.

Rationale

The partners perceived need for training to address the new revolution in the clothing and textile industry, with the emergence of smart textiles and wearable technology that is opening up new global markets. These opportunities need to be understood by designers, and the future product development team, in order to bring appropriate products to market for the benefit of the breadth of society. Traditional industries need to think 'outside the box' and be open to new types of collaboration. Traditional manufacture cannot continue in Europe. A new generation of designers/product developers is needed to build on the well-established design base in Europe. Textile and clothing designers need to look beyond 'fashion' alone and become equipped to communicate with the sophisticated ICT, electronics and related industries. Emerging garment design and manufacture demands high technology operations, using advanced materials, and forming and joining techniques to create high-performance garments from innovative textiles. For example, smart textiles can incorporate conductive fibres within a range of constructions, fabric assemblies and finishes; can incorporate sensors and switches to monitor aspects of health and wellness, positioning, predominant posture, and speed as well as interfacing with mobile communications devices. Bringing commercially viable wearable technology to a breadth of user groups demands the integration of science, technology and creative design. Design embraces interaction design, concerned with the interactions between people, products and the technological information systems that support their use.

Background

Despite enormous commercial potential, this is a field in which there has been little existing higher level training anywhere in the world for designers in the application of emerging technologies, in smart technical textiles, for functional clothing and footwear. A principal constraint is in the limited availability of appropriately trained and experienced academic staff. A shared 'language' is needed between fashion, textile, graphic design with new media design, aspects of human physiology, textile technology, computing, electronics and new technologies in the future clothing manufacturing chain. In an increasingly globalised world, this language is trans-cultural as well as trans-disciplinary. In order to achieve design outcomes that are 'fit for purpose' future textile and clothing designers must liaise with technologists in a development team that adopts a product design approach in addressing end-user needs from technical, aesthetic and cultural view points.

Description of Programme

IP Aim

To bring together staff in partner institutions to share best practice and to build on their complementary strengths and expertises in providing collaborative training modules that promote an interdisciplinary mix of knowledge and skills for this new design subject area, that addresses a breadth of clothing needs in society.

IP Objectives

To upgrade and enhance the skills and mobility of students and teaching staff of Higher Education Institutions in Europe; and to encourage the creation of a basis for future development, through common curricula and courses/modules; agreements on credit transfer and mutual degree recognition, and reciprocal access to Higher Education.

Emphasis has been placed on the need to adapt constantly to changes to:

- Boost research and development
- Develop functional intellectual relationships between universities in Europe and to provide a framework for staff development in participating universities.
- Develop collaborative links between Higher Education Institutions, and their industrial partners that can ultimately lead to mutually beneficial economic co-operation.
- Communicate the results of the project to other stake-holders in Higher Education and to design related industries.

In particular the programme has been expected to:

- Introduce generic technologies related to technical textiles, functional clothing, electronics and related topics relevant to the embedding of smart attributes in a functional 'clothing system'.
- Provide students with a design methodology, driven by end-user needs, for the application of smart textiles in clothing categories such as functional sportswear, corporate wear and inclusive design.
- Build on the shared expertise of the partner institutions: textile design and engineering (Swedish School of Textiles) technical clothing and footwear (HAMK University, Finland), the application of smart technologies in relation to end-user needs (University of Wales, Newport).
- Collaborate with local, regional and international trade partners who wish to engage in this new hybrid industry.

- Prepare students for interdisciplinary work experience, employment and/or further study.

Partner Contributions

The partner institutions represented essential elements in the mix of this emerging design area. The team leaders from each institution took responsibility for relevant expertise within the interdisciplinary mix. The team leaders were committed to promoting the mutual exchange of ideas and expertise and development of a shared 'language'.

University of Wales, Newport

User-needs driven design methodology: The Smart Clothes and Wearable Technology Research Centre at the University of Wales, Newport, has developed a design methodology that provides a framework for the linking of technical textiles, clothing and electronics. This process informs design research and development of wearable products within the areas of sports, corporate wear and inclusive design. It incorporates the following topics concerned with form and function. Under 'Form', the subheading 'Aesthetics' looks at issues to do with colour, proportion, style, fabrication and comfort *etc* while 'Culture of the Activity' looks at the peer group needs of the identified end-user. Under 'Function', the subheading 'The Needs of the Body' looks at human physiology, with regard to work load, moisture management, protection, movement, anthropometry, 'feel good factor' *etc*, while 'The Demands of the Activity' looks at aspects such as location, expected environmental conditions, duration, and issues to do with safety and security. Reference is also made to 'Commercial Realities'. This methodology guides the student in requirements capture of technical, aesthetic needs to inform the design brief.

Design critical path: the University of Wales, Newport, also provided students with an overview of the key stages within the design research and development process for textile based wearable technologies from fibre production through to product launch.

This critical path embraces a basic explanation of textile structures, assemblies and finishes, garment cutting and materials selection, novel manufacturing methods, garment finish and point of sale promotion. Issues with regard to sustainability, garment aftercare and disposal were introduced. The University of Wales, Newport, also provided the necessary studio space and made contact with local and regional industry partners.

Swedish School of Textiles

This partner has provided core information on smart textiles. Expert talks, seminars and group workshops were delivered on the merging of technical textiles and electronics. This institution is known for it's wealth of textile resources in terms of knit, print and woven technology. It has textile design and textile engineering courses and research in the development of smart textile applications for clothing and interior design. Highly innovative prototypes have been exhibited at trade events and conferences such as Avantex, Frankfurt. The Professor of Smart Textile Design and an electronics expert provided input to the IP. Additional local support, in Wales, was provided by Wireless Edge who gave a seminar on communications.

HAMK University, Finland

Hamk University was the lead partner with experience, and local support in coordinating a European Union bid that contributed to the success in obtaining the programme funding. Hamk was responsible for the overall programme administration and in coordinating the final reporting. This institution also provided expertise in terms of garment technology in the application of smart materials in functional clothing. Staff from Hamk provided the day to day monitoring of, and technical support for, the student teams with regard to their progress in terms of garment prototyping. Local students within the teams, from Newport, were invaluable in helping the visiting student's access services and equipment.

Pedagogical Methods

The intensive programme was run in stages over a three-week period. The students were invited to make up cross-disciplinary teams, mixing participants from the three institutions focusing on the topics of sport, corporate and inclusive design. The staff participants used lectures and presentations to introduce the generic subject of smart clothes and wearable technology. Presentations were made by industry representatives on specialist topics. Seminars and brainstorming were used to identify student areas of interest and to determine their individual responsibilities/contributions within the teams. Study visits were made to trade events, and to carry out customer and market research, as appropriate, to support the live project work, teamwork and guided individual study. Students were encouraged to make regular visual and verbal presentations, representing their individual and group contributions to the teams, to both peers and staff. Final dissemination was made to a wider audience including project staff, interested staff and students from outside the school and to industry representatives. These presentations were recorded for further dissemination. Newport's European Office was represented.

Work Plan

STAGE 1
- Launch of project.
- Introduction to design brief.

STAGE 2
- Delivery of taught element.
- Guided independent study.
- Trade field trip(s).

STAGE 3
- Live project work: design development with support from industry partners re technologies, technical textiles, garment engineering *etc.*
- Delivery of taught element.
- Guided independent study.
- Trade field trip(s).

STAGE 4

- Preparation for team presentations.
- Presentation: team verbal and visual presentations to effectively 'sell' concepts back up by 3D samples as appropriate.
- Dissemination to wider audience of staff, students and trade partners.

STAGE 5

- Critique and feedback.

Learning Materials

The students, from disparate study backgrounds, benefited from reference to available learning materials that have been developed by the Smart Clothes and Wearable Technology Research Team supported by the Knowledge Exploitation Fund (KEF). These learning materials, on CD Rom, introduced to students to the user-needs driven design methodology through six individual modules that embrace the following topics:

Identification of end-user needs: to inform an effective design brief; who is the 'customer' from technical, cultural and aesthetic view points.

The demands of the body: basic human physiology, with regard to work load, moisture management, protection, movement, anthropometry, 'feel good factor' with end-uses such as sportswear, corporate wear, inclusive design etc.

Commercial realities: the nature of this emerging new market - individual student teams selected a focus (sport/corporate wear/inclusive design *etc*) to look at the competition, brand leaders, main trade events, size of market, gaps for innovation *etc*.

Smart textiles: introduction to fibres, material structures, properties, finishes *etc*.

Functional clothing: aspects to do with sizing, cutting for movement, new manufacturing methods, garment engineering *etc*.

Wearable electronics: introduction to what is available in the market, basic technical terminology *etc*.

Dissemination

Information on the project has disseminated in all partner countries by using connections to local networks and through the involvement and interests of related companies. Students who participated have built and maintained an international network and have benefited from the new knowledge provided by the IP in exploiting their new knowledge and skills in further project work and/or in employment. This project has raised the profile of this unique area of study and attracted further international exchange students to Newport.

Evaluation

This IP has improved the quality of education and training staff participating in the IP. It has brought together interested staff in partner institutions to share best practice and to build on their complementary strengths and expertises in providing collaborative training modules that promote an interdisciplinary mix of knowledge and skills for this new design subject area that addresses a breadth of clothing needs in society.

The IP has provided a test project to set the foundations and raise awareness in this new design area. It could be implemented as part of regular study programmes at BA level within local institutions. It provides the basis for MA and Postgraduate programme development and initiates interest in the subject for MA recruitment and/or subsequent postgraduate study. It has directly contributed to informing the development of an MA/MFA concept paper in the design of Smart Clothes and Wearable technology at the University of Wales, Newport, and promoted awareness in terms of potential recruitment. It may be extended to further short intensive programmes for dissemination to industry partners and to technology teachers.

Direct beneficiaries include staff and students:

- University of Wales, Newport: Undergraduate level design students; BA, Year 2.
- HAMK University: Clothing and footwear design; Years 2 and/or 3.
- Swedish School of Textiles: Undergraduate students from textile design and textile engineering; Year 2 and 3.

Conclusion

Traditional manufacture cannot continue in Europe. A new generation of designers and product developers is needed to build on the well-established design base in Europe. Textile and clothing designers need to look beyond 'fashion' alone and become equipped to communicate with the sophisticated ICT, electronics and related industries. Emerging garment design and manufacture demands high technology operations, using advanced materials, and forming and joining techniques to create high-performance garments from innovative textiles.

A shared 'language' is needed between fashion, textile, graphic design with new media design, aspects of human physiology, textile technology, computing, electronics and new technologies in the future clothing manufacturing chain. In an increasingly globalised world, this language is trans-cultural as well as trans-disciplinary.

This IP has demonstrated the potential to strengthen the role of education and training in the field of this new specialist training area based on the Lisbon process. This type of training could contribute to the enhancement of the capacity of specialist courses in universities in Europe to educate and train designers for a new and increasingly globalised field of the application of technical textiles in "Smart Clothes and Wearable Technology".

Further Information

The Smart Clothes and Wearable Technology Research Centre has been responsible for a new publication to support this type of cross-disciplinary study:

Smart Clothes and Wearable Technology
Edited by J.McCann and D.Bryson
Woodhead Publishing in Textiles
ISBN 978-1-84569-357-2
2009

University of Wales, Newport

Prifysgol Cymru, Casnewydd

Linking Research and Teaching in Higher Education
Simon K. Haslett and Hefin Rowlands (eds)
Proceedings of the Newport NEXUS Conference
Centre for Excellence in Learning and Teaching
Special Publication, No. 1, 2009, pp. 137-145
ISBN 978-1-899274-38-3

Undergraduate field-based project training exercises and Masters' level vocational training projects in Applied Environmental Geoscience, using study sites in South Wales.

Peter John Brabham

School of Earth and Ocean Sciences, Cardiff University, Cardiff, CF10 3YE.
Email : Brabham@cardiff.ac.uk

Abstract

Applied environmental geoscience is principally a field-based discipline and field training is a student's most significant learning environment. Field-based project training for Undergraduate Degrees must be focussed towards providing the student with all the skills necessary to undertake an individual level 6 (HE3) investigative research project, which is required by Quality Assurance Agency (QAA) credit specification criteria and accreditation bodies. Field-based project training for vocational Masters Degrees is fundamentally different. Vocational Masters' degrees must be designed to provide students with the professional training required by industry. This paper will discuss how both these objectives are achieved at Cardiff University using many relevant field sites in South Wales.

Introduction

The School of Earth and Ocean Sciences at Cardiff University has a diverse portfolio of staff, with wide ranging research interests. At Undergraduate level the School offers four Undergraduate subject pathways; Geology, Exploration Geology, Marine Geography and Environmental Geoscience. This paper concentrates on the importance of field-based teaching in environmental geoscience for both Undergraduate and taught Masters Degrees. As a response to changing market demand, a three-year B.Sc. degree scheme in Environmental Geoscience commenced in 1996. This scheme was expanded in 2004 to include a 4-year MESci option. There is also a popular one-year taught Masters community, with a MSc degree in Applied Environmental Geology that commenced in 1996, which was supplemented in 2005 with an MSc course in Environmental Hydrogeology. The various courses available in Environmental Geoscience are shown in Figure 1.

The South Wales area is an ideal location to train students in applied environmental geosciences for four reasons:

1. South Wales has a varied geology; it is surrounded by the Lower Palaeozoic rocks of West and Mid Wales. South Wales itself comprises Carboniferous rocks of the South Wales Coalfield and the younger Triassic/Jurassic rocks of the Vale of Glamorgan. All of which can be interpreted in terms of changing palaeo-environmental conditions.

2. The geological structure of South Wales is mainly formulated by the Variscan Orogenic event, followed by a long period of erosion with Tertiary rocks lying above an unconformity visible in the Vale of Glamorgan. The landscape expression of the geological structure has been modified by

the Quaternary Ice-ages and the present Holocene period of temperate climate with rising sea levels. Critically, the last major ice-age, the Devensian, had a southerly limit which ran east-west though the area, resulting in both glacial and periglacial landscapes available for study. Post-glacial landscapes are further modified by recent river action. Many of the present South Wales valley slopes are unstable and South Wales has one of the highest densities of urban landslides in the UK (Brabham, 2004). The Severn/ Loughor Estuaries and Bristol Channel offer world class areas for coastal environmental research and the effects of changing sea level.

3. Since the late 18th century the area has been a major driver in the industrial revolution. The chief extractive industries being coal, iron and limestone mining with associated iron, steel and tinplating manufacture. The rapid industrial growth resulted in the sudden expansion of towns and ports, with associated infrastructure such as railways, coke works, gas works and uncharted landfill sites. The Lower Swansea Valley was at one time the greatest metallurgical smelting location on Earth, leaving a legacy of toxic chemicals in dumps and groundwater. Rapid port expansion resulted in extensive land reclamation schemes, principally constructed using made-made materials of unknown origin and chemistry. Coal mining has left a legacy of uncharted mine workings, polluted groundwater, mining subsidence and unstable coal tips, culminating in the tragic events of Aberfan in 1966. Over the past 50 years there have been considerable developments in modern industries such as oil refineries, petrochemical works and two enormous steelworks at Llanwern and Port Talbot.

4. In the post-industrial period, there has been a decline in most of these industries. Due to the total decimation of deep coal mining and the introduction of North Sea gas, the vast majority of industrial sites such as town gas works, iron works and mine sites have become derelict and are now in demand for urban brown field redevelopment. The Aberfan disaster was a global turning point in environmental awareness and today no dangerous conical coal tips are extant in South Wales. The Cardiff Bay barrage is one of Europe's major urban land regeneration schemes. The cities of Cardiff, Swansea and Newport all are presently undergoing major dockland redevelopments. Other vast land reclamation schemes include Ebbw Vale, Llanwern steelworks and Llandarcy oil refinery. The South Wales Valleys is designated a European area of social deprivation that has seen many multi-million pound European Union-funded infrastructure programmes, particularly land stabilisation and road building projects (Brabham, 2004, 2005).

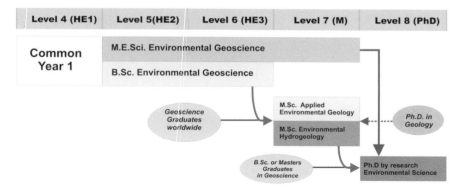

Figure 1. The matrix of courses available in Environmental Geosciences at Cardiff University.

Over the past decade there has been a considerable local demand by geo-environmental, engineering companies and government agencies for skilled professional environmental geoscientists to service the regeneration of this area.

Field-based learning and teaching integration at Undergraduate level 6

There are three fundamental aims in learning and teaching for B.Sc. Environmental Geoscience degrees:

1. To provide students with the ability to understand wide-ranging environmental concepts across all scientific disciplines; geology, chemistry, physics, biology with competence in numeracy and information technology, all of which are required skills of a modern professional geoscientist (Brown, 2004).
2. To provide students with a broad academic knowledge base of geoenvironmental issues of past, present, political, global and local significance.
3. To train students in how to design a research project to answer an environmental question, gather field data (both primary and secondary), statistically analyze or visualize their data using information technology and how then to critically evaluate their data (in the context of other peer reviewed published research) to reach an environmental conclusion (adapted from Mistry *et al.*, 2006). Students must be able to write a fully-referenced individual project report and also be able to give a confident oral presentation of their findings (Gedye and Chalkley, 2006).

The entry requirements to study an Undergraduate degree in Environmental Geoscience at Cardiff are 280-300 points at A-level (or equivalents), where one A-level must be a science. If Geography is the only chosen science A-level, then many students are ill-equipped with the necessary core science (chemistry, physics, and biology) and the mathematical skills required to become a quantitative Environmental Geoscientist. Also many students will have little previous experience of field-based science. A common year 1 course for all students, tries to address this issue by providing an introduction to key field skills and a broad knowledge base over wide aspects of geoscience. In reality, degree scheme choice takes place at the start of year 2. In this way students have experienced all aspects of geoscience in year 1 and, therefore, have a much better idea of their chosen career pathway.

A field-based multi-stage training programme must be designed at levels 5, 6 and 7 to fulfil HEFCW level descriptors (HEFCW, 2004). When teaching students at Undergraduate level in Environmental Geoscience, all staff involved must endeavour to fight against modular compartmentalization of knowledge, to achieve the full integration of research-led teaching, e-Learning, field training skills and assessment into one integrated teaching and learning package that satisfies all credit specification criteria. Applied Environmental Geoscience is principally a field-based discipline and field training is a student's most significant learning environment (Giles *et al.*, 2008). Figure 2 shows how this objective is achieved, with regards to obtaining all the skills necessary to undertake a quantitative scientific enquiry at level 6.

Level 4 (HE1)	Level 5(HE2)	Level 6 (HE3)	Level 7 (M.E.Sci)
Common Year 1	Data Analysis	Environmental Geoscience Field-based Project	Environmental Geoscience ResearchProject
	Geographical Information Systems		
	Field Skills Training		

Figure 2. Project training in Environmental Geoscience.

Figure 3. Geographical locations of project training exercises used at level 5.

The year 2 (level 5) programme of three inter-related modules is absolutely key in successful project training in Environmental Geoscience. The data analysis module provides training in project design, sampling, numerical analysis, graphical techniques and report writing. The Geographical Information Systems (GIS) module trains the students in geo-spatial data analysis, a vital component of any modern environmental geoscience study (Brown, 2004; Brabham 2004, 2005). These two modules are cross-referenced by the third and most vital component - the field skills training programme. Consequently, it is essential that all staff involved in teaching these three modules communicate, with a common learning objective, using consistent terminology and referencing.

The field skills training programme is essentially a series of one-day practical field-based projects covering numerous aspects of environmental geoscience. All projects involve day visits within a 40 mile radius of Cardiff. Class sizes range from 25-50, therefore, all sites must be easily accessible by coach and limitations on equipment usually result in students collecting field data in teams of 3 or 4. The locations used in South Wales are shown in Figure 3.

At each of these geographical locations there is a specific project objective outlined and, using problem-based learning exercises, field data is collected to try and achieve that objective. It is absolutely essential that the deliverable coursework component addresses a specific environmental question, which is clearly outlined and is also logistically achievable within the given timeframe. Students undertake a quantitative sampling strategy to try and answer that environmental question. The details of the individual field exercises are as follows:

- Basic geological mapping (2-3 days): Cribarth Mountain, Fforest Fawr Geopark. An exercise in basic geological mapping skills, rock recognition, structural map-ping and geomorphology. This exercise is now published as a guided walk by the Geopark [WWW1]. Deliverable: a geological map and sketch cross-section of the study area, based on simple geological units and structure.
- Geo-hazard assessment (rockfalls): Mumbles peninsular. Proposed road widening scheme in folded Carboniferous Limestone strata. Assessment of likely geo-hazard from rock falls due to the 3D structural geology relationship with the road cutting. Deliverable: a predicted hazard zonation map along the footprint of proposed new road widening scheme.
- Geo-hazard assessment (rotational landslides): Mynydd-yr-Eglwys landslide, Rhondda. Geomorphological mapping and landslide assessment. Deliverable: a reconnaissance geomorphological map of landslide with annotations (Figure 4).
- Water quality measurements (alkaline environments & dispersion): limestone quarry, Black Mountain. Mapping of surface water pH away from a lime dump as it diffuses into background values. Deliverable: quantitative chemical graphs

of pH versus distance away from polluting source.

Figure 4. The outdoor classroom, Rhondda Valley landslides

- Water quality measurements (acid mine drainage): Glyncorrwg , Afan Valley. Mapping of polluted mine water emanating from abandoned mine adits into a reed bed system and then into the local river system. Deliverable: quantitative chemical visualizations of spatial pH/Temp/electrical conductivity variations from point sources of pollution, through reed bed system, to river confluence (Figure 5).

Figure 5. Level 5 training (mapping acid minewater chemistry, Glyncorrwg).

- Water quality measurements (industrial pollution): Pluck Lake, Lower Swansea Valley. Mapping lake chemistry and study of metallurgical slag material found in local area. Deliverable: quantitative

chemical analysis of pH, dissolved oxygen and electrical conductivity around lake edge. Observations of sulphide mineralization composition of slag material in hand specimen.

- Water quality measurements (coastal salinity ingress): Swansea Marina/Tawe river barrage, 3D mapping of saline/freshwater plume through vertical depth sampling of water column. Deliverable: graphs and visualizations of vertical layering of water quality using dissolved oxygen and electrical conductivity measurements.

- Coastal geology and sea level rise: Wentlooge Levels, assessment of Holocene geological sequence and likely effects of climate change. Deliverable: geological sketch map and cross section.

- Holocene environmental change: Porthkerry Park, Barry. Drilling of a 7m core though coastal estuarine sediment sequence, providing training in core logging and environmental analysis. Deliverable: Fully annotated borehole log with environmental interpretation (Figure 6).

Figure 6. Masters' Project Training 1 (Drilling in Porthkerry Park, Barry).

- Recent environmental change: Porthkerry Park, Barry. Vegetation mapping; assessment of deciduous tree diversity and age. Investigation if present forest is purely natural or largely influenced by recent human management. Deliverable: quantitative vegetation traverse with associated statistical tests to assess whether forest should be designated a Site of Special Scientific Interest (SSSI) based on age and diversity.

- Recent environmental change: Llanrhidian salt marsh and sand dune systems. Walk over survey to assess the present environmental conditions of study area, then comparing this with historical air photography, the migration of the dune systems and salt marsh can be assessed. Deliverable: a proposal for a project plan monitoring recent environmental change of the area, with a logistically-achievable field-sampling strategy clearly described (Figure 7).

Figure 7. Explaining concepts of recent environmental change, Gower coast.

Following this intensive programme of training at level 5, students are positively encouraged to design their own individual Environmental Geoscience project at level 6. An interesting point is that for a geological exploration project, a student travels to a study area to find out what is there and is trained to make a map, there is no temporal component. With environmental projects, a one off "snapshot" does not tell you that much. Environmental factors change with time, e.g. landslides and water pollution tend to be seasonal, linked to rainfall. It is essential that environmental geoscience students fully appreciate this fact and design projects with a temporal component. Students are encour-

aged to collect field data during the summer vacation, thus allowing a further six-month sampling window to monitor possible temporal (or seasonal) changes in measured environmental parameters.

The project module at level 6 is worth 30 credits and counts for around 18% of the BSc degree. Failure of this 30 credit project module can effectively mean that a student does not obtain enough credits at level 6 to obtain an Honours degree. Every effort should be made by students and staff to avoid this scenario (Simm and McGuinness, 2004).

At level 7 (MESci), the project is again a major component of the degree. Usually students undertake a more academic (less applied) research project in year four and are assigned to a member of research staff as their research mentor. These projects may be field or laboratory-based and are usually linked to ongoing research programmes and PhD studentships within the School. MESci research projects are designed primarily as frontier research training for students to go on further to PhD research programmes.

Project Training at Taught Master's level

The taught Masters' Degree in Applied Environmental Geoscience has been in existence for 12 years and the Masters' in Environmental Hydrogeology for 4 years. Average combined class sizes are 35 and over 300 taught postgraduate students have successfully achieved a Masters' qualification, studying full time for one year, or part time on day release over three years.

Both courses are vocational and highly focussed; they include a large input from local professional geoscientists and are totally divorced from undergraduate teaching. They provide specific training in industrial legislation, best laboratory/field practice and industry standard software. They are not unfocussed research degrees based around the academic blue-sky research carried out by the school (Kneale, 2005).

The format of both Level 7 courses is of an initial intensive 7 month (October–April; stage 1) taught programme of lectures and training courses with examinations, followed by a 5 month (May–September; stage 2) individual research project. The popularity of the taught Masters' courses stems from the fact that wherever possible students are placed for the stage 2 component with professional companies, thus providing a relevant real-world applied project rich in data. Frequently the companies pay a basic salary or at least cover student expenses throughout stage 2.

Many of the industrial co-supervisors are alumni of the Masters' course and approximately 50% of projects are based in the South Wales area. Every student produces an extensive thesis based on 5 months' work, all of which are held in the University library. This is a vast resource of local geo-environmental information. Figure 8 shows a map of the spatial distribution of Masters' projects undertaken in the South Wales region.

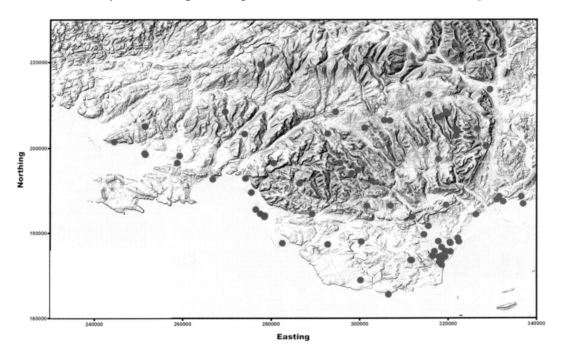

Figure 8. Map of locations of Masters' level dissertations in South Wales (1996-2008).

Figure 9. Project training exercises at taught Masters' level.

By cataloguing past projects and utilising the data within them, we are able to develop new MSc and BSc project training exercises. Access to long term datasets for monitoring temporal environmental change is essential for training students at Masters' level.

Field-based training at Masters' level is highly focussed on three substantial exercises in stage 1 (Figure 9).

Figure 10. Masters training in surveying techniques, Cardiff Bay.

An initial desk study project involves access to an electronic library of historical mapping/air photography. The student has to unravel the site's historical industrial evolution and predict any potential contamination hazard. Sites chosen are current developments and presently the International Sports Village development area of Cardiff Bay is used. This exercise is followed by two dedicated project training exercises (carried out in December and March) incorporating field data collection (Figure 10), where students write a professional industry-style report on their findings. Projects are performed in a simulated professional company environment; with the aim of providing many of the skills employers require (project/time management, initiative, working under pressure, team working, achieving project deadlines; Gedye and Chalkley, 2006). Individual feedback is given to students after marking project exercise 1, with the aim that students can significantly improve their report-writing style for project training 2. Students are not allowed to progress onto stage 2 of the course unless they have satisfactorily passed stage 1. We have found that by using this two stage strategy that students are fully capable of writing the substantial stage 2 dissertation project, having resolved any fundamental issues during stage 1.

Conclusions

"One of the principal purposes of modern higher education is to produce graduates who are able to succeed in the workplace and who can go forward to make worthwhile contributions in the organisations in which they are employed" (Gedye & Chalkley, 2006, p. vii). In the post industrial era in South Wales, employability has moved away from the mining industries into geo-environmental and geotechnical companies. The courses at Cardiff University have responded to this demand by also changing their focus. An essential part of any undergraduate geoscience degree and a student's future employability is the ability to carry out a field-based research project and report on its findings. South Wales has many interesting sites that can be used both for wide ranging undergraduate geoscience training or more specific professional vocational training at Masters' level.

Successful vocational Masters' courses benefit greatly from engagement with professionals in geo-environmental consultancies, local authorities and government agencies. These people can provide guidance on desired course content and also offer relevant case study lectures. By placing students with such companies, highly relevant real-world, data-rich projects can be developed with mutual benefit. These Masters' level dissertations provide a wealth of geo-environmental information that can then be used to develop undergraduate training exercises. Another spin-off of academic-professional collaboration is that some Masters' projects develop further into industrially-sponsored PhD studies. Over the past decade, seven applied environmental geoscience PhD projects studying sites in

South Wales, have been successfully managed by the research group. These have covered topics such as methane gas generation, landfill site hydrogeology, landslides and groundwater contamination (Brabham *et al.*, 2005). These projects could be considered as an example of "teaching-led research", where initial MSc projects have acted as catalysts to larger research programmes.

ACKNOWLEDGEMENTS

The author wishes to thank the staff that contribute to field-based training at the School of Earth & Ocean Sciences at Cardiff University, at both Undergraduate and Masters' level. In particular, he would like to acknowledge the vital role played by two recently retired colleagues, who initially set up the teaching programmes in field-based environmental geosciences at Undergraduate and Masters' level; Dr. Tony Ramsay and Professor Charles Harris. Acknowledgement must also be given to the site managers who allow their sites to be annually invaded by large student groups, in particular, Mr Pritchard, warden of Porthkerry Park and the rangers of the Fforest Fawr Geopark.

REFERENCES

BRABHAM, P. J. 2004. The Rhondda Valleys: Using GIS to visualize a variety of geological issues in an intensely-mined area. In: NICHOL, D., BASSETT, M. G., and DEISLER, V. K. (eds) *Urban Geology in Wales*. Cardiff: National Museum of Wales, Geological Series, No. 23, pp. 222-233.

BRABHAM P. J. 2005. The Rhondda valleys: Using GIS to visualize the rise and fall of coal mining and its industrial legacy. In: BASSETT, M. G., DEISLER, V. K. and NICHOL, D. (eds) *Urban Geology in Wales II*. Cardiff: National Museum of Wales, Geological Series, No. 24, pp. 193-204.

BRABHAM, P. J., GEORGE, A., PARIS, E., HARRIS, C., LING, S. 2005. Geophysical investigations and monitoring at landfill sites in South Wales. In: BASSETT, M. G., DEISLER, V. K. and NICHOL, D. (eds) *Urban Geology in Wales II*. Cardiff: National Museum of Wales, Geological Series No.24, pp. 156-164.

BROWN, K. 2004. Employability of Geography graduates in the GIS and GI related fields. *Planet*, No. 13, pp. 18-19.

GEDYE, S., CHALKLEY, B. 2006. Employability within Geography, Earth and Environmental Science. *GEES Learning and Teaching Guide*. Plymouth: The Higher Education Academy (Geography, Earth and Environmental Science Subject Centre).

GILES, D., WHITWORTH, M., POULSOM, A. 2008. The development of fieldwork problem based exercises in the applied sciences. *Planet*, No. 20, pp. 37-40.

HEFCW [Higher Education Funding Council for Wales], 2004. *Higher Education in Wales, Credit Specification and Guidance*. Cardiff: Higher Education Funding Council for Wales.

KNEALE, P. 2005. Enthusing staff delivering taught Masters' programmes. *Planet*, No. 14, pp. 13-15.

MISTRY, J., WHITE, F., BERADI, A. 2006. Skills at Masters' level in Geography higher education: teaching learning and applying. *Planet*, No. 16, pp. 9-14.

SIMM, D., M^cGUINNESS M. 2004. Crisis resolution of student-led research projects at distant locations. *Planet*, No. 13, pp. 8-11.

WWW1 (2009) Fforest Fawr Geopark. URL - http://www.breconbeacons.org/geopark.

University of Wales, Newport | Prifysgol Cymru, Casnewydd

Linking Research and Teaching in Higher Education
Simon K. Haslett and Hefin Rowlands (eds)
Proceedings of the Newport NEXUS Conference
Centre for Excellence in Learning and Teaching
Special Publication, No. 1, 2009, pp. 147-155
ISBN 978-1-899274-38-3

Internet accounts of natural disasters: undergraduate student analysis of the Indian Ocean tsunami of 2004.

Simon K. Haslett[1] and Edward A. Bryant[2]*

[1]Centre for Excellence in Learning and Teaching, University of Wales, Newport, Lodge Road, Caerleon, South Wales, NP18 3QT, United Kingdom. Email: Simon.haslett@newport.ac.uk

[2]Faculty of Science, University of Wollongong, Wollongong, NSW 2522, Australia.
Email: Ebryant@internode.on.net
(*retired)

Abstract

Natural disasters provide topical learning opportunities for undergraduate students. However, due to the time is takes for peer-reviewed accounts to enter the academic literature, internet-based news reports and blogs offer a timely source of eyewitness accounts that may be utilised as an e-learning resource. This paper describes an undergraduate geography exercise concerning the Indian Ocean tsunami of 2004, and provides examples of eyewitness accounts harvested, and scientific interpretations made, by students. Together, these combine to provide a relatively detailed account of the nature and character of the tsunami event and the associated physical processes and impacts. As well as providing an example of a research-based exercise within the research-teaching nexus classification, the paper also questions pedagogic issues surrounding the use of these types of internet sources.

Introduction

The scientific study of natural disasters is problematic as it is not possible to predict with accuracy the timing and location of their occurrence, which makes direct observation of hazard processes and impacts difficult. Eyewitness accounts are one of the only media that may describe the active processes that occur during such events and, historically, interviews and eyewitness reports in newspapers have been invaluable in this regard. With the advent of the internet, eyewitness reports have become rapidly available to a wide audience, and blogs in particular enable eyewitnesses to write about their experiences and observations immediately after, and sometimes during, disasters. Researchers are able to examine these accounts to construct sequences of events and establish the nature of processes without having to undertake field work to interview survivors. Students studying natural disasters may also find internet-based accounts a useful e-learning resource to help them gather information as an aid to understanding the processes and impacts of natural disasters. Indeed, many blog sites now have pages dedicated to indexing blogs about natural disasters, which makes internet searching relatively straightforward (e.g. Blogged, 2009; Blogtoplist, 2009; Wordpress, 2009).

This paper reports on an exercise created in 2005 by the lead author for Year 2 (level 5 or intermediate level) undergraduate geography students studying a module in Coastal Science, and was undertaken by successive student cohorts until 2008. It was created as an exercise that enabled students to engage with a recent topical coastal disaster as part of their studies, but before peer-reviewed material appeared in the academic literature. The disaster that stimulated the development of the exercise was the Indian Ocean tsunami on 26th December 2004; but, later in 2005, the storm surge associated with Hurricane Katrina in the Gulf of Mexico offered a further example. Indeed, it has been acknowledged that the Indian Ocean tsunami of 2004 resulted in a new way of global communication using real-time media, changing the way geography is communicated (Atkins, 2006). In addition to describing the exercise, a compilation of student reports is provided as an example of the valuable information that may be gathered for research purposes, and also to illustrate the significance of internet-based accounts as an e-learning resource for undergraduate students.

This exercise is also an excellent example of how research and teaching may be linked in the study of topical events, such as natural disasters. Students were aware of the tutor's research interests related to the topic and were enthusiastic about undertaking coursework that related to the research area and proved to be an exciting learning opportunity. Students were also able to draw on recently published and unpublished material provided by the tutor (SKH) and student cohorts were able to attend three guest lectures given on the topic by EAB at the institution during research visits to the UK over a number of years. The exercise helped to promote a community research culture within the department and the results also informed the authors' research, to which the students felt they had contributed. This exercise is also discussed in terms of Healey's (2005) classification of the research-teaching nexus.

The Exercise

This section presents the formative exercise brief and guidance given to students.

"Tsunami are waves that are produced by a number of different mechanisms, including displacement of the sea-floor by movement along a fault (associated with an earthquake) or a submarine slide, volcanic activity, and asteroid impact. They have also been called tidal waves and seismic sea waves, but these are inappropriate as tsunami are unrelated to tides and those created by asteroid impacts are cosmogenic rather than seismogenic. The word tsunami itself is not ideal, as it is Japanese for harbour wave, and these waves are not confined to harbours.

The impact of tsunami on coastal populations and settlement is well-known, with prehistoric (Smith and Dawson, 1990) as well as very recent examples (e.g. the Asian tsunami of 2004, Papua New Guinea in 1998 and others: see Gonzalez, 1999). The influence on coastal evolution however, is only now being appreciated; both in terms of erosion and deposition, and some coastlines are now considered to be strongly influenced by repetitive tsunami (Bryant et al., 1996).

In keeping your studies current and up-to-date it is important, and interesting, to undertake studies in recent topical events and it, therefore, seems entirely appropriate to make some examination of the Asian tsunami that affected the Indian Ocean on the 26th December 2004. However, there has not been enough time since the event for a thorough scientific investigation by the academic community and very few academic articles have been published (e.g. Briggs, 2005) on the coastal impacts of the event (the seismic activity has been covered to a greater degree). Therefore, it would be very interesting and good experience to examine eyewitness accounts of the tsunami wave hitting the coast for details of the wave characteristics and types of physical impacts that resulted. You are, unusually, invited in this practical to examine non-academic sources, such as interviews in newspapers, magazine, and so-called 'blogging' sites on the Internet, where people have recorded their personal observations and experiences. It might also be interesting to compare eyewitness accounts of this tsunami, with those of historic events, such as the 1607 flood in the Bristol Channel (Bryant and Haslett, 2003).

You are not required to attend the time-tabled practical slot, instead you will do this exercise independently using the Internet. It will probably be easiest to use an Internet search engine, such as www.google.com, but I expect there will be an enormous amount of material retrieved. It would be best to give your self a time limit of an hour or so, to find a few eyewitness accounts that you could examine in a little more detail. Referring to your lecture notes, you should record:

1. *Source of the account:* give the full bibliographic reference to the article or internet site (with a hyperlink).
2. *Geographical location being described:* be as precise as possible as to where the account relates (can you get latitude/longitude coordinates?). Also, an estimate of the time would be useful.
3. *"Direct quotes containing relevant material":* here you can, exceptionally, cut and paste from the Internet, but make sure you read it first!
4. *Your interpretation of the direct quotes:* i.e. what are the eyewitness accounts describing in terms of tsunami characteristics (e.g. withdrawal of the sea, physical appearance (e.g. dazzling, foamy, frothy, noisy, etc), wave height, wave velocity, inland penetration; number of tsunami waves, etc) or physical impacts on the coast (e.g. erosion, deposition, vegetation loss, building damage, loss of life, etc).

Prepare a short report of up to a few pages on your findings and interpretation written using Microsoft Word, structured using points 1-4 above. This is not an assessed practical, so don't worry if you can't find anything substantial; it's the research experience of searching, evaluating and interpreting that I hope will be the outcome you benefit from in doing this, and also the knowledge gathered. The material will also be useful for the exam at the end of the module."

Internet Accounts

Approximately 80 students undertook the exercise between 2005-2008 and sourced many accounts from a mixture of internet news and blog sites. Table 1 presents 20 examples of extracts of the internet accounts and the corresponding interpretations made by students. They have been ordered with regard to their description of the tsunami itself and the physical processes and impacts associated with it. Locations have not been given, but the internet addresses (URL's) are given to allow readers to read the accounts in full.

Table 1. Twenty extracts of accounts of the 2004 Indian Ocean tsunami harvested by undergraduate geography students along with extracted examples of their interpretations of the accounts.

No.	Internet account	Student interpretation
1.	I was on a ferry between the island of Pulau Weh and Banda Aceh. I noted that the ship bounced a little but I didn't pay any attention to it. I was on the deck and an Indonesian guy pointed to the island saying "tsunami". (http://news.bbc.co.uk/1/hi/world/asia-pacific/4145859.stm)	This eyewitness notes that the ship she was on "bounced a little", and therefore was not greatly affected by the tsunami wave. This is a common characteristic displayed by a tsunami wave as it travels across the open ocean, similarly to a wind wave, where its wave height is small, so would not cause, for example, boats at sea to be moved greatly.

No.	Internet account	Student interpretation
2.	At the moment I got into the water the lagoon started to drain out - in particular on the far right hand side of the bay (as you look out to sea). Within seconds it was too shallow to ski, so i climbed back into the boat. (http://phukettsunami.blogspot.com/2004/12/first-hand-story-luke-simmonds.html)	The sea withdrew, here it seems particularly on one side of the bay.
3.	… it was like someone had pulled the plug on the ocean, crags and outcroppings of rock inside the sea were visible … (http://news.bbc.co.uk/go/pr/fr/-/1/hi/world/south_asia/4138913.stm)	… describes a typical tsunami characteristic. There is an initial rise in water and then a rapid withdrawal leaving the sea floor exposed. This description also suggests the strength and force of the ocean's pull.
4.	They also noticed that all of the water had gone away. Or at least - most had receded out of the bay. …Suddenly - in front of our eyes - the bay begin (sic) to fill. Rapidly. As if someone had turned on giant faucets - and it just seemed to rush in. In about 10-15 minutes this entire HUGE bay filled in. And then we saw the swell. (http://phukettsunami.blogspot.com/2004/12/surviving-tsumani-part-1-first-letter.html)	The sea withdrew due to the earthquake, as seen by the water disappearing from the beach. This was followed by the water returning over a 10-15 minute period, after which the tsunami wave hit.
5.	… it took maybe four seconds from the point when I was aware of it to the point when it hit the hotel … (http://news.bbc.co.uk/go/pr/fr/-/1/hi/world/south_asia/4138913.stm)	Although these are not specific velocity measurements the quote does indicate the speed of the second wave.
6.	We were in the ski boat facing towards the shore, when the water passing underneath us began to pull the boat around and towards the shore. Almost out of nowhere there was a huge wall of water, behind us at the beach. We were at the bottom of a 10 meter wave that stretched the entire length of the beach, maybe 1km. (http://phukettsunami.blogspot.com/2004/12/first-hand-story-luke-simmonds.html)	As the sea returned it drew the boat toward the shore. The wave was 10m in height and stretched the entire length of the beach c. 1km
7.	… swell after swell of water rose above the walls of the beach here in Thailand. The water rose about 18 feet / 6-7 meters - and basically destroyed everything below that mark for the first 3-4 blocks of the towns it hit. (http://phukettsunami.blogspot.com/2004/12/surviving-tsumani-part-1-first-letter.html)	The first wave was c. 6m in height.

No.	Internet account	Student interpretation

8.
We were roused from our lounge chairs by the pool to see a slow but extremely high surge of water which gently came forward to flood the beach. The surge was not strong at this point, although it was enough of a warning for most people to get off the beach. The same surging action repeated itself about two or three times. Within seconds, though, the surges of water became more forceful. Then the volume of water started increasing and decreasing. The back current pulled it back some 50m, and emptied the entire bay in about 10 seconds. Then the water began to rush in with equal speed, and ever increasing height, until the third and strongest wave which hit the clubhouse pool forced us to flee for our lives.

(http://news.bbc.co.uk/1/hi/world/asia-pacific/4132317.stm)

There is a mention of not just one tsunami wave, but several. This is typical of a tsunamigenic event, where not just one tsunami wave will be created, but a series of tsunami waves are created.

This account provides timings for the earthquake's tremors and the arrival of the resulting waves. Rather than as a towering breaking wave, the tsunami is described as a 'surge' of water which engulfs the coast. A sequence of waves, of varied sizes, were generated by the seismic activity. The phenomenon of the water receding before the waves hit the shore, typical of tsunami waves, is clearly described.

9.
It happened in cycles. There would be a surge and then it would retreat and then there would be a next surge which was more violent and it went on like that. Then there was this one almighty surge. I mean literally this was the one which was picking up pickup trucks and motorcycles and throwing them around in front of us.

(http://www.cnn.com/2004/WORLD/asiapcf/12/26/asia.quake.eyewitness/index.html)

The mention of several tsunami waves is consistent with a typical tsunamigenic event. Also the first waves do not necessarily have the most energy.

10.
The water receeded slight - and then, again with a vengence. Rushed forward - rose again - and the 18 feet wall rolled over the front of the beach - the shops and everything in its path … But it wasn't over. It just keep coming and coming. It would receed - and then come again - rushing over the seawall … Four hours - it keep this up - battering the sea front. Yes the sun kept shining. A very deceptive paradise … As the waves would retreat for 10-15 minutes, many people would try to make a run for it … For two hours - the waves ebbed and flowed - crossing over the edge - pushing and pulling items. But none were as strong as the first two tidal waves - that so destructively threw cars on top of each other - overturned busses - and washed out every stick of furniture – and people's belongings - from nearly every first floor room at the 20 block long beach … After about three hours - the waves stopped coming over the edge.

(http://phukettsunami.blogspot.com/2004/12/surviving-tsumani-part-1-first-letter.html)

The first 2 waves were the largest and caused great damage. After that the waves continued to for 2-4 hours (the account is unclear). The waves would retreat for long periods of time c. 10-15 minutes. Tsunamis do not produce large breaking waves, rather the sea level rises and falls again with a period of 12-20 minutes

No.	Internet account	Student interpretation
11.	… seconds later another white wall rounded the other side of the island, the waves surging towards each other … (http://news.bbc.co.uk/2/talking_point/4146031.stm)	… establishes the strength of the wave and also shows that the tsunami had been diffracted by the island and were beginning to reform, as they had passed the obstruction (the island).
12.	Then, as quickly as the water came up, it was gone, leaving fish flopping on the floor of the lobby and seaweed draped everywhere … I looked out to sea in the opposite direction … there was another wave coming right back at us, even bigger than the first, and even worse, full of air conditioners, refrigerators, water heaters, mattresses deck chairs, and even people … When the 2nd wave hit, it was like titanic, and we desperately tried to hang on as the dangerous debris smashed its way through the lobby again. this was followed by two more waves, which were slightly smaller, and then silence. (http://phukettsunami.blogspot.com/2005/12/survivor-dave-lowe.html)	A second large wave came from the opposite direction, followed by two smaller ones before a period of calm.
13.	I think I was relatively lucky that I was very close to the ocean - that meant that only water hit us. But if I had been 150m (500 feet) inside the coastline I would have been hit by flying debris, by 250 cars, by brick walls, by reinforcement bars. I would not have drowned, I would have been beaten to death. (http://news.bbc.co.uk/1/hi/world/south_asia/4138913.stm)	This account gives an idea of how far the water reached inland. Physical impacts such as sweeping away cars and buildings indicate the power of the tsunami surge. The writer identifies the way that the nature of the threat changed with distance from the shore.
14.	Great big swathes of the beach are completely washed away, the peninsula has huge gaps where hotels used to be … (http://news.bbc.co.uk/1/hi/world/asia-pacific/4126183.stm)	… suggest that the tsunami caused erosion …
15.	… I was on the first floor of the building in the restaurant – and it was like a bomb hit it. I saw part of it just get taken off … (http://news.bbc.co.uk/go/pr/fr/-/1/hi/world/south_asia/4138913.stm)	Not only does this show the power of the wave, in being able to damage concrete buildings but also the noise volume of the wave, by liken the damage to a "bomb" he suggests that it was loud and deafening.
16.	…the island had been cut in half, a river of water was now bisecting it, both ends of the island had lost 50 meters of land (and had come within 10 meters of washing away reception) and coconut trees were being washed out to sea. for the next 6 hours, we rode out wave after wave as the sea gradually calmed down … (http://phukettsunami.blogspot.com/2005/12/survivor-dave-lowe.html)	The tsunami had eroded away 50m of land at either end of the Island and had cut the island in half with a river of water. The waves continued for 6 hours before being calm.

No.	Internet account	Student interpretation
17.	… within seconds we were waist deep in this horrible grey mud. (http://news.bbc.co.uk/1/hi/world/asia-pacific/4126183.stm)	… deposition of sediment which the tsunami washed ashore.
18.	… I stood up to look at the sea and was stunned to see a huge whirlpool in front of my apartment. (http://www.cnn.com/2004/WORLD/asiapcf/12/27/more.emails/)	This description describes the large "eddies" which can develop along a coastline that has experienced a tsunami.
19.	I actually saw the seaplane getting sucked under by the vortexes and eddies that were 20 feet across … (http://phukettsunami.blogspot.com/2005/12/survivor-dave-lowe.html)	… wave created vortexes and eddies that were 20 feet in diameter.
20.	… when I looked outside, I could see that the ocean was now level with our island, and to my horror, a wall of water, boiling, frothing, angry as hell, was bearing straight down at us…there was a strange smell in the air, like death, and a weird mist that looked like thick fog … (http://phukettsunami.blogspot.com/2005/12/survivor-dave-lowe.html)	The wave was fierce and large, bearing down on them.

Discussion

Study of a natural disaster

The internet accounts harvested by the undergraduate geography students offer an insight into the character of the Indian Ocean tsunami in 2004 and the physical processes and impacts that were associated with it. These accounts back up theoretical modelling that existed at the time. They also allude to present difficulties in modelling flows generated by tsunami. Firstly, account 1 clearly indicates that out at sea, away from the coast, the tsunami was not very noticeable, which, as the student interpretation alludes to, is a common attribute as tsunami only grow in height close to the shore as they begin to shoal. Accounts 2-4 describe how the sea receded prior to the tsunami, which account 4 suggests then happened quite rapidly. So there was very little response time between first seeing the tsunami and taking evasive action (account 5). Accounts 6 and 7 suggest initial tsunami wave heights of 6-10 m, but that in some places it appeared as a surge rather than a distinct wave form (account 8). However, as is common with tsunami, there was more than one tsunami in the wave train, and accounts 8-10 record the cyclical nature of the event which, as the student interpretations indicate, was of a periodicity of 10-20 minutes, and that the first tsunami to hit was not necessarily the largest within the wave train. Also, the speed of the backwash is also suggested in account 8. The four hour duration related in account 10 is not unusual for great tsunami events.

Interestingly, it is possible to detect descriptions of more subtle wave modification processes within the internet accounts, as rightly interpreted by some of the students. For example, accounts 11 and 12 describe what appear to be either refracted or diffracted tsunami waves, which may wrap around islands, headlands or other promontories (Haslett, 2008). Account 12, and 13, also make reference to sediment transport by the tsunami as debris, such as refrigerators, were clearly visible in the water. The mention of debris as being the likely cause of death is unique for this event. These articles would have been a constituent of an assemblage of sediment particles transported inland by the tsunami, as account 13 clearly indicates that the density of transported sediment (i.e. debris) increased landward. Examples of the source of sediment and debris is indicated by

153

accounts 14-16, which describe significant coastal landform erosion and the destruction of buildings. These facets are typical of great tsunami events Indeed, account 17 describes mud transported onshore by the tsunami. The high density of muddy water defied attempts at modelling the wave and flows using existing theory.

Accounts 18 and 19 describe vortices created by tsunami in the water column. Bryant (2008) argues that high-velocity tsunami flow is capable of creating vortices that are able to severely, but locally, erode landforms. These accounts, reported here, suggest that this may indeed be possible. Lastly, account 20, is remarkably similar to historic accounts of possible tsunami examined by the authors in the UK. For example, a comparison with the following contemporary account describing a catastrophic flood event in the Bristol Channel in 1607 shows a number of similarities: '… the element huge and mighty hilles of water tombling over one another … it dazzled many of the spectators that they imagined it had bin some fogge or mist coming with great swiftness towards them ….' (Bryant and Haslett, 2003, p. 164), both describing the sea in a similar way and both mentioning fog.

Research-teaching Nexus

In terms of Healey's (2005) classification of the research-teaching nexus, this may be considered a research-based exercise as it 'emphasises students undertaking inquiry-based learning'. It may also serve as an example of research-informed teaching, in that the tutor's research interest informs the curriculum content as well as integrating use of technology in teaching and learning as suggested by a growing body of pedagogic research output (Haslett, 2009).

The inquiry skills employed by the students in undertaking this exercise were varied. Most students had already taken a geographical research methods module prior to the exercise, so were relatively familiar with textual research. They had also experienced IT training as part of a geographical skills module. Once accounts were located on the internet, using search engines, students had to read them and judge the appropriateness and suitability of the content and to decide if it matched the exercise brief. From these lay accounts, students then had to interpret the scientific information contained within them and 'translate' them into scientific interpretations. As the examples in Table 1 indicate, this was achieved to varying degrees of success, but in many instances the use of correct scientific terminology and relating observations to concepts and theory is clear. An indicator of the success of this exercise is that a number of students went on to undertake Honours dissertations in the research field in Year 3 of their studies.

Academic and pedagogic use of internet sources

Regarding the use of internet sources in scientific research, this exercise suggests that they appear to be useful in the absence of published peer-reviewed material. However, observations made by the tutor regarding student engagement with the exercise suggests that future pedagogic research should evaluate the practicalities of using internet sources, such as language (students may have to use online translation facilities), geography (accessibility of computers by eyewitnesses at disaster locations), and to consider issues of the authenticity and personal agenda of blog authors (Johnson & Kaye, 2004). Also, internet-based exercises like this, might positively address issues surrounding student disability (inclusion), e-learning, and transferable skills. The exercise may also be an example of a novel and innovative way of teaching and learning, utilising socio-technological advances and harnessing interest, and relatively untapped skills, of students in terms of internet use and social networking. Finally, given the exercise was largely self-directed, pedagogic self-development of students might also be worthwhile exploring (Knight, 2006).

The wider application of internet-based news accounts and blogs beyond geography, and in other learning situations and environments (e.g. field trips, visits, film screenings, exhibitions) should also be acknowledged. Indeed, it may be appropriate, as some are already doing, to use web-based blogs, rather than paper-based reflective diaries, as e-learning resources and items of student assessment. The use of such technology would help to create a dynamic and interactive forum for discussion and student learning, enhancing student participation and experience of online learning (Oravec, 2003).

Conclusions

This paper presents an example of how research and teaching may be linked in the study of natural disasters. The internet accounts harvested for an exercise related to the Indian Ocean tsunami in 2004 enable a detailed picture to be created of the event, including the nature and character of the tsunami and the physical processes and impacts that it had on coastlines. The exercise is an example of a research-based exercise within the research-teaching nexus classification, and also serves as an example of research-informed teaching. The use of internet sources in the study of natural disasters, and in other fields, has a number of benefits for students, in that it enables students to engage with eyewitnesses without the need to travel and interview them, but issues such as authenticity, language, eyewitness motivation and geography need to be consider further. However, the use of internet sources may be of benefit in terms of widening access for students to first-hand information, and also utilises relatively untapped online skills that students nowadays tend to possess.

ACKNOWLEDGEMENTS

We are grateful to successive cohorts of undergraduate geography students on the Coastal Science module in the Department of Geography at Bath Spa University for their enthusiasm to engage with this research. SKH would like to thank Dr David Simm (Bath Spa University) for discussions on the use of blogs.

REFERENCES

ATKINS, P. 2006. Online: Geography in the blogosphere. *Geography Review*, 20, p. 41.

BLOGGED 2009. *Blogs about: natural disasters.* http://www.blogged.com/about/natural-disasters/ (accessed 7th may 2009).

BLOGTOPLIST 2009. *Blogs about "natural disasters".* http://www.blogtoplist.com/rss/natural-disasters.html (accessed 7th may 2009)

BRIGGS, J. (ed.), 2005. The Indian Ocean tsunami: geographical commentaries one year on. *Geographical Journal*, 171, 369-386.

BRYANT, E. 2008. *Tsunami: the underrated hazard.* Chichester: Praxis.

BRYANT, E. A., HASLETT, S. K. 2003. Was the AD 1607 coastal flooding event in the Severn Estuary and Bristol Channel (UK) due to a tsunami? *Archaeology in the Severn Estuary*, 13 (for 2002), 163-167.

BRYANT, E. A., YOUNG, R. W., PRICE, D. M. 1996. Tsunami as a major control on coastal evolution, southeastern Australia. *Journal of Coastal Research*, 12, 831-840.

GONZALEZ, F. I. 1999. Tsunami! *Scientific American*, May, 44-55.

HASLETT, S. K. 2008. *Coastal Systems (2nd edition).* London: Routledge.

HASLETT, S. K. 2009. Unpicking the links between research and teaching in Higher Education. *Newport CELT Journal*, 2, 1-4.

HEALEY, M. 2005. Linking research and teaching: exploring disciplinary spaces and the role of inquiry-based learning. In: Barnet (ed.) *Reshaping the University: new relationships between research, scholarship and teaching.* London: McGraw Hill/Open University, pp. 67-78.

JOHNSON, T. J., KAYE, B. K. 2004. Wag the blog: how reliance on traditional media and the internet influence credibility perceptions of weblogs among blog users. *Journalism and Mass Communication Quarterly*, 81, 622-642.

KNIGHT, J. 2006. Investigating geography undergraduates' attitudes to teaching, learning and technology. *Planet,* 16, 19-21.

ORAVEC, J. A. 2003. Blending by blogging: weblogs in blended learning initiatives. *Journal of Educational Media*, 28, 225-233.

SMITH, D. E., DAWSON, A. G. 1990. Tsunami waves in the North Sea. *New Scientist*, 4th August, 46-49.

WORDPRESS 2009. *Blogs about: Natural Disasters.* http://en.wordpress.com/tag/natural-disasters/ (accessed 7th May 2009).

University of Wales, Newport

Prifysgol Cymru, Casnewydd

Linking Research and Teaching in Higher Education
Simon K. Haslett and Hefin Rowlands (eds)
Proceedings of the Newport NEXUS Conference
Centre for Excellence in Learning and Teaching
Special Publication, No. 1, 2009, pp. 157-165
ISBN 978-1-899274-38-3

Hazard management in Tunisia: water supply for agriculture.

Jennifer Hill and Wendy Woodland

Department of Geography and Environmental Management, School of the Built and Natural Environment, Faculty of Environment and Technology, University of the West of England, Frenchay Campus, Bristol, BS16 1QY, United Kingdom. Email: Jennifer.hill@uwe.ac.uk; Wendy3.woodland@uwe.ac.uk

Abstract

The primary aim of this paper is to evaluate two contrasting techniques of water management for agriculture in Tunisia in terms of environmental sustainability. Analysis indicates that traditional rainwater harvesting advantageously partitions the continuum dividing hazards and resources through subtle manipulation of the environment. A potentially hazardous environment is rendered secure by resourceful water management based on community action and cumulative knowledge. By contrast, dam irrigation establishes carrying capacity more forcibly through centralised control in order to place society within world markets. An almost total break from environmental variability is made in the short term, but this can lead to disequilibrium over longer durations. Maintenance of traditional methods can reduce the negative impacts caused by modern programmes and support their positive characteristics. A secondary focus of the paper is to highlight the integration of the research presented here into undergraduate teaching, learning and assessment.

Introduction

Responding largely to the Earth Summit of the United Nations Commission for Environment and Development (1992), the Tunisian government developed a strategy (*La Stratégie de Gestion de L'Eau*) for the sustainable management and utilization of the country's water resources, including water management for agriculture (Ministry of Environment and Land Use Planning, 2001). This strategy aimed not only to ensure quality and availability of water to meet human consumption, but also to protect soil and water resources and to adapt to hazardous events such as floods and drought.

Tunisia contains three different climate zones: Mediterranean, semi-arid and arid, which experience differing water availability. Due largely to these differences in potential water resources, there exist a number of distinctive methods of water management for agriculture (Hill and Woodland, 2003). The northern Mediterranean region is dominated by modern reservoir-fed irrigation. In the semi-arid central part of the country modern dams have been constructed in the north of the zone, but rainwater harvesting and terraced wadi systems predominate towards the south. In the arid south, communities practice traditional rainwater harvesting within small hillside catchments.

This paper compares two contrasting agricultural water management techniques in Tunisia to examine their environmental sustainability: traditional small-scale rainwater harvesting and modern large-scale dam irrigation. It also highlights how students contributed to the research presented here and how the results have informed teaching within the Department of Geography and Environmental Management at the University of the West of England (UWE), specifically at second year undergraduate level.

Contrasting Water Management Techniques and Environmental Sustainability

The locations of the case study areas within Tunisia are highlighted in Figure 1.

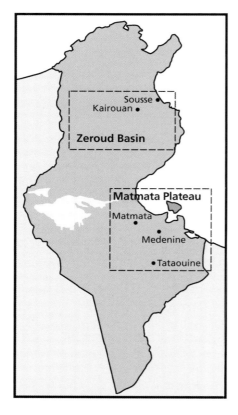

Figure 1. The location of the case study areas in Tunisia.

The Matmata Plateau, in the south of the country, exemplifies small-scale rainwater harvesting and the Zeroud Basin in the central steppe highlights modern, large-scale dam irrigation. The Matmata Plateau falls within the arid zone, with average annual rainfall varying between 100 mm to 250 mm. Actual evapotranspirative losses vary between 400 mm to 500 mm per annum resulting in a

negative annual water budget of 200 mm to 300 mm (Frankenberg, 1980). Valleys to the west of the Plateau are covered by loess deposits: aeolian sand and silt which easily form a surface crust, facilitating overland flow in catchments (Boers *et al.*, 1986a, b). The natural vegetation of alfa grass, with an average ground cover of 20%, affords little protection to the soils during high intensity rains (Chahbani, 1984). Central Tunisia can be divided into two geographical regions (Figure 2). To the west, the mountains of the Dorsale give way to the Plain of Kairouan in the east. The plain is covered in alluvial Miocene and Pliocene (clay-sand) deposits. Rainfall across the region varies between 200 mm to 350 mm per annum, but actual evapotranspirative losses reach 600 mm to 700 mm per annum resulting in a negative annual water balance of between 300 mm and 400 mm (Guillaud and Trabelsi, 1991). The climate supports semi-arid steppe vegetation. With lack of plant cover and steep gradients in the highlands, runoff is collected rapidly by wadis that descend from the Dorsale. The wadis are high energy, erosive systems that respond rapidly to high magnitude events.

Traditional rainwater harvesting

Macrocatchment rainwater harvesting has a long history in the Matmata Plateau, dating back many hundreds of years to the original Berber inhabitants (Ouessar *et al.*, 2004). Climate, topography and soils together make rainwater harvesting very effective. The majority of rain falls as high intensity-low frequency downpours. Overland flow is generated rapidly and it travels quickly over steep slopes, supplying water and soil to valley bottoms. Earthen retention dams (tabias) are sited progressively downslope to trap eroded material from the valley sides and this material is levelled to form agricultural fields (jessour). The soils on jessour tend to be deep and relatively fine in texture. They support crops such as drought-resistant annuals with a short growing season (wheat and barley) and perennial crops that can survive dry periods (olive trees). Water that is trapped behind tabias after rain events infiltrates into the soil where it creates temporary, phreatic water supplies. The rainfall multiplier effect of rainwater harvesting depends primarily on the ratio of runoff area to cropped area. On the western outskirts of Matmata, a ratio of 6:1 translates into field sizes approximating 0.6 ha and catchment sizes of around 4 ha (Hill and Woodland, 2003) (Figure 3).

A recent study in the Bou Hedma catchment (approximately 200 km north of Matmata) demonstrates the hydrological efficiency of such rainwater harvesting systems (Nasri *et al.,* 2004a). This catchment records an average annual rainfall of 141 mm

and annual losses by evapotranspiration of just over 1,000 mm. The system proved to be effective in reducing flood and erosion risk by decreasing hillslope runoff. Virtually all observed runoff during a four year observation period (September 1995-December 1999) was harvested by the system. The efficiency of the system meant that harvested water reached seven times the amount of precipitation for each rainfall event that exceeded 20 mm. Soil water content increased after each rainfall event and then decreased gradually in the months following, allowing farmers to plant and grow peas, olive trees and fig trees.

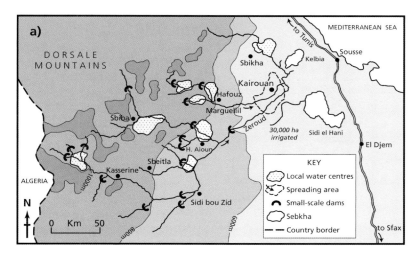

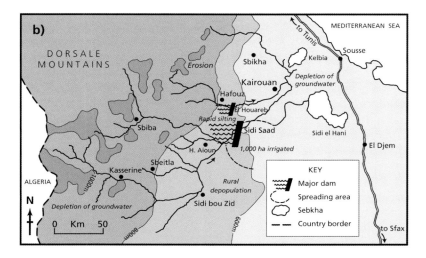

Figure 2 The Zeroud Basin, central Tunisia: (a) decentralized and (b) centralized water management (after El Amami, 1986).

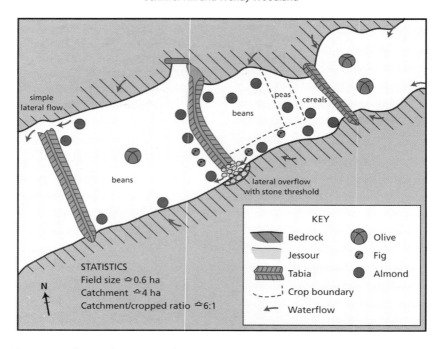

Figure 3. Plan view of a catchment on the western outskirts of Matmata. Average field sizes, tree spacings and catchment statistics are highlighted.

Tabias are equipped with overflows in order to promote effective water distribution and to allow some flexibility against climatic extremes. Lateral overflows are employed in 60% of the tabias in the Matmata Hills (Bonvallot, 1979). These are purpose-made breaches in the earthen bunds at valley sides that permit excess water to flow by gravity onto the terrace below, ensuring irrigation water with minimal erosive capability. The engineering of tabias, particularly the height of the overflow threshold, ensures that fields downslope are not deprived of water by higher fields, leading to crop failure. Equally, the height of the threshold prevents the build up of too much water after storms such that the root zone remains waterlogged for long periods. This enhances the agricultural potential by increasing root aeration and reducing soil salinization because water infiltrates efficiently and is used rapidly by crops (Rapp and Hasteen-Dahlin, 1990).

Small-scale hydraulic works prove sustainable in the face of extreme events. An example is their response to exceptional rains in March 1979. Between the 3rd and the 6th of March, many parts of the Matmata Plateau received rainfall approaching their average annual total. The average annual rainfall of Matmata, for example, is 222 mm, yet the area received 120 mm in one day (Fersi, 1978). These high intensity rains engendered catastrophic floods. The delegations of Tataouine and Beni Kheddache suffered the collapse of 70% to 80% of their agricultural bunds, whereas Matmata suffered damage of less than 10% (Bonvallot, 1979). Significantly, community work using local materials allowed a rapid response to the altered environment. These landscapes can be reworked effectively and they are thereby sustainable environmentally over long time frames and across climatic extremes.

Modern dam irrigation

The Kairouan Programme, initiated in 1975, centred on the construction of two large dams in the neighbouring Zeroud and Marguellil Basins. Its aims were to reduce flooding in the Kairouan Plain, to recharge of the Kairouan aquifer, to develop irrigated areas downstream of the dams and to supply the city of Kairouan with an improved water supply (Guillaud and Trabelsi, 1991; Kingumbi *et al.,* 2004). The Sidi Saad Dam, in the Zeroud Basin, came into service in 1982. By 1986, the dam was supplying water, via a system of gravity flow pipes, to irrigated perimeters up to 15 km away (Guillaud and Trabelsi, 1991). This led to a substantial rise in the acreage of olive and almond trees in the low steppe, and to an extension of market gardening using poly-tunnels for early winter fruit and vegetables.

Water flow in the Zeroud and Marguellil Basins had been regulated for centuries by means of a network of small barrages and 30 local dams. Such decentralised management maintained a number of spreading areas, which irrigated 30,000 ha and replenished local water tables (Figure 2a). The cost of these small-scale works has been estimated at only TD 6 million, as they utilised local equipment and 40,000 local labourers (El Amami, 1986). This heritage could have been used to sustain decentralised water systems, but following the severe floods of 1969, which caused 150 deaths on the Kairouan Plain (Guillaud and Trabelsi, 1991), the decision was made to construct a single large dam at Sidi Saad (Figure 2b). Costing TD 60 million, the dam initially supplied an irrigated area of 4,000 ha which has subsequently decreased to 1,000 ha (El Amami, 1986). Although proving itself in terms of flood control during the heavy rains of 1990 (Guillaud and Trabelsi, 1991), it has produced an irrigated area just one thirtieth of the size of the original, at ten times the cost.

With an obvious economic disadvantage compared to small-scale hydraulic works, how do such large-scale developments compare in terms of long-term environmental sustainability? High intensity downpours falling on exposed friable soils in the centre of the country mean that the large-scale developments are liable to rapid, but spatially and temporally unpredictable, sediment input. Based on reservoir siltation rates measured between 1982 and 1993, the probable service duration of the Sidi Saad Dam has been calculated as 87 years (Zahar, 2001). This figure falls notably short of the generational

history recorded by the dryland jessour systems. Additionally, the Sidi Saad Dam would face a drastic reduction of its predicted service duration if it were to experience rains of similar magnitude to those of autumn 1969. These rains generated 2,500 million cubic metres of water at Sidi Saad measuring station in just two months, more than the annual average for all Tunisian watercourses. The discharge reached 17,050 cumecs on 27th September, an immense figure when compared with the annual average of just three cumecs. An estimated 275 million cubic metres of solids were mobilised, which is equivalent to 14 years sediment supply (Cruette *et al.,* 1971). These figures must be compared with a flood spillway capable of evacuating 7000 cumecs and a storage capacity of 209 million cubic metres (Zahar, 2001). If the dam had been constructed prior to the rains, it would have been unable to contain the flood peak and would have been filled completely with sediment. Such sedimentation can also reduce aquifer recharge. The infiltration flow rate from the neighbouring El Haoureb dam (Figure 2b) has decreased from 650 L/s in 1989 to 310 L/s in 1998 as sedimentation in the dam has proceeded (Kingumbi *et al.,* 2004).

In Tunisia, large water storage schemes represent a mobilizable volume of 1,612 million m³ (Habaïeb and Albergel, 2004), with an average storage loss to sedimentation estimated at 1.6% per annum, associated largely with extreme events (Albergel *et al.,* 2003). This storage loss could well represent a serious threat to future agricultural development. The Sidi Saad reservoir will most likely have to be abandoned less than 100 years after construction (Zahar, 2001); compare this with the continued use of depressions for rainwater harvesting in the south of the country that have been farmed for generations.

The scale of the hydraulic works renders adaptive response to extreme events difficult. Dam walls are difficult and costly to raise to prolong life, unlike tabias when their jessour suffer rapid sedimentation. Dam structures must be sufficient to withstand high magnitude events from the outset, but predicting the vagaries of this marginal environment, where inter-annual variability of precipitation ranges between 30% to 40%, is notoriously difficult (see Nasri et al., 2004b; Cudennec et al., 2005).

With a reliable supply of water over the short term, the problem has arisen of over-watering crops. Irrigation water infiltrates into the soil and the excess not used by plants is drawn back to the surface by evaporation. This process can bring salts to the surface that reduce soil fertility and decrease yields. Salinization is aided by capillary rise from groundwater, which records a salt content of 1.5 g/l by the dam, increasing to 5 g/l near Kairouan (Besbès, 1978). The high salinity limits the utility of groundwater to crops as most suffer restricted yields between 1.5 g/l-3.5 g/l (Barrow, 1999). To combat salinization at the field level, farmers have moved away from basin flooding and furrow irrigation towards trickle irrigation. Perforated plastic pipes can be observed in many fields of the Zeroud and Marguellil basins, following crop lines and administering low rates of water application directly to plant roots. This minimises losses via surface runoff, evaporation and deep percolation and maximises delivery to the root zone.

Reviewing sustainability

The efficiency of minor hydraulic works in southern Tunisia is currently being main-tained, but a crucial development has reduced sustainability in the north: the abandonment of community based indige-nous knowledge, which demonstrated physical adaptability to a dynamic and often extreme environment. Adaptability is the precursor to reliability and it is under threat in large-scale developments. Such develop-ments possess rigid physical structures that are not easily adapted to the vagaries of climate. Modern large-scale developments have provided no more reliability over space and time than earlier small-scale works and they often result in less irrigated land per unit of water stored. Over long time frames modern developments are more susceptible to extreme events than community works.

The only difference is that modern dam developments can provide short-term yield maximisation but this requires greater volumes of water, often leading to insidious environmental degradation.

Conclusions

Combining traditional and modern approaches for agricultural sustainability

The aim of the contrasting water manage-ment techniques described in this paper is to equilibrate spatio-temporal inequalities in water resources. Rainwater harvesting stores water in the root zone below the catchment during wet seasons to cover water require-ments throughout growing seasons, whilst large dams store water above ground within the catchment to overcome annual and inter-annual deficiencies. There is a precarious equilibrium, however, dividing hydrological hazards and resources in Tunisia. Traditional management was able to physically partition the continuum between hazards and resources in favour of the latter through construction of jessour systems. Thus, a potentially hazardous environment of slope instability, flash flooding, soil erosion and drought was transformed into a secure environment by resourceful management. It was achieved by subtle manipulation of the landscape at micro and local scales using trial and error practical experience and drawing upon a community memory that allowed prediction of future success or failure. Collective community action and cumulative knowledge allowed high reliability farming. The environment was not perceived as risk-laden and, therefore, 'critical' but as reliable (Kasperson et al., 1996). The communities demonstrate a history of sustained produc-tion in difficult environments and it is likely that such adaptability and flexibility will continue to sustain agriculture into the future, if it can survive the lure of employment in the service sector of major cities.

Across Tunisia, new waves of proactive water conservation measures are being implemented (Ministry of Agriculture, 1998; Ministry of Development and International

Cooperation, 2002). One such example is a soil and water conservation programme, centred in the Governorats of Kairouan, Siliana and Zaghouan, which began in 2000. The project exemplifies the balance that can be achieved between large-scale centralised development and small-scale decentralised management based on modernised indigenous technology and undertaken with local participation. The programme has encouraged an increased uptake of field-scale water harvesting methods and it has helped local farmers to create a network of small hillside dams to collect surface runoff. By 2001, as part of this programme, 586 small reservoirs and 224 small hilltop dams had been completed throughout Tunisia (Ministry of Environment and Land Use Planning, 2001). These second generation works have reduced siltation rates in the large dams and, through basal seepage into sand, replenished local aquifers (Grünberger *et al.*, 1999; Montoroi *et al.*, 2002; Nasri, 2002). This encourages rural populations to remain settled as the groundwater reserves help reduce the risks of crop cultivation in an unpredictable environment.

Overwatering of crops by irrigation has been tackled by sectoral reforms that include adjustments to water tariffs and the implementation of financial incentives to encourage farmers to adopt new irrigation technologies. Farmers are encouraged to adopt low pressure drip or sprinkler irrigation, receiving a subsidy for between 40% and 60% of the cost of new equipment. This has resulted in water savings of 25% (Vidal, 2001).

The process of water development in the centre of the country appears to be coming full circle with a return to small-scale management to complement and sustain the large-scale hydraulic works (see also Woodland and Hill, 2006; Hill and Woodland, 2008). Such a dovetailing of different scales and technologies, integrated under a national planning structure, promotes a controlled but flexible approach to water management. This is crucial to long-term viability as it allows local voices to be heard in terms of hydrological requirements and it attenuates environmental extremes, turning hazards into resources on the desert fringe. A mix of modern and traditional management methods, integrating international negotiation across territories and local participatory community management, seems to have been acknowledged as the practical foundation to sustainable water supply in the new millennium.

Linking water management research to undergraduate teaching, learning and assessment

Teaching on undergraduate programmes in the Department of Geography and Environmental Management at UWE is underpinned by the practice of linking student learning and assessment to the research process. This concept is based on the premise that, if the relationship between teaching and research is managed positively, students will benefit, particularly through their interaction with deep learning. The importance of linking teaching and research is articulated by many practitioners in Geography, Earth and Environmental Sciences (see for example Healey *et al.*, 2003; Jenkins, 2003).

Fieldwork is a significant medium through which to link teaching and research. The data on catchment statistics from Matmata presented in this paper were collected by undergraduate students (overseen by staff) undertaking a second year overseas fieldwork module. The specific aim of the module was to teach a range of field methods, skills and techniques that would allow students to carry out empirical research. Students undertook group research exercises that charted a progressive pathway through the research process. The module was assessed via submission of an individually prepared research proposal, which could build easily on the concepts and skills gained from the rainwater harvesting and other exercises. Research into student responses to the module (Hill *et al.*, 2004) discovered that it helped almost all students in their initial dissertation preparations. For many, the module marked the realisation that the dissertation was a problem-solving exercise rather than an extended essay. When asked to indicate how the module had aided them in their preparations, with no prompting, students isolated particular aspects of the research process, including the necessity of establishing a broad context via reading; defining a research question; practical application of field techniques; and the need to remain critical throughout the research process.

The findings from the water management research presented here have subsequently been used as case study material in a second year optional module entitled Extreme Environments. The management of hazards and the utilisation of resources in hot deserts comprise part of the syllabus, and this includes water management for agriculture. The Tunisian case study is outlined in a lecture and an accompanying seminar encourages students to engage with the information, promoting consideration of ontology and epistemology.

To conclude, the research presented here is articulated into the syllabus in a number of ways, from the more basic research-led teaching (where module content is structured around the research interests of staff) to the more advanced research-informed teaching (where curriculum design, learning, teaching and assessment are informed by research inquiry) (Griffith, 2004). Learning and assessing through active student involvement in the research process at Level 2 seems to be an appropriate method of preparing students for their independent Dissertation at Level 3 and making them realise the contested and provisional nature of geographical knowledge.

REFERENCES

ALBERGEL, J., PEPIN, Y., NASRI, S., BOUFAROUA, M. 2003. Erosion et transport solide dans des petits bassins versants Méditerranéens. In: *Hydrology of the Mediterranean and Semi-Arid Regions*. Proceedings of the International Symposium, Montpellier, April 2003, IASH Publication 278, pp. 373-379.

BARROW, C. J. 1999. *Alternative Irrigation: The Promise of Runoff Agriculture*. Earthscan Publications Limited, London.

BESBES 1978. *L'inventaire des ressources en eaux souterraines de la Tunisie centrale*. Unpublished PhD thesis, Université Paris VI (Pierre et Marie Curie).

BOERS, TH. M., DE GRAAF, M., FEDDES, R.A., BEN-ASHER, J. 1986a. A linear regression model combined with a soil water balance model to design micro-catchments for water harvesting in arid zones. *Agricultural Water Management*, 11, pp. 187-206.

BOERS, TH. M., ZONDERVAN, K., BEN-ASHER, J. 1986b. Micro - Catchment - Water - Harvesting (MCWH) for arid zone development. *Agricultural Water Management*, 12, pp. 21-39.

BONVALLOT, J. 1979. Comportement des ouvrages de petite hydraulique dans la région de Médenine (Tunisie du sud) au cours des pluies exceptionelles de mars 1979. *Cahiers ORSTOM Série Sciences Humaines*, 16, pp. 233-249.

CHAHBANI, B. 1984. *Contribution à l'étude de l'érosion hydrique des loess des Matmatas et de la destruction des jessour. Bassin versant de l'Oued Demmer, Beni Kheddache, Sud Tunisien*. Unpublished PhD thesis, University of Paris I (Panthéon-Sorbonne).

CRUETTE, J., RODIER, J.A., DUBEE, G., GAULDE, R. 1971. Mesures de débits de l'Oued Zeroud pendant les crues exceptionnelles de l'automne 1969. *Cahier ORSTOM Série Hydrologie*, 13, pp. 33-64.

CUDENNEC, C., MOHAMED, S., LE GOULVEN, P. 2005. Accounting for sparsely observed rainfall space-time variability in a rainfall-runoff model of a semi-arid Tunisian basin. *Hydrological Sciences Journal*, 50, pp. 617-630.

EL AMAMI, S. 1986. Traditional versus modern irrigation methods in Tunisia. In: E. GOLDSMITH, N. HILDYARD (eds) *The Social and Environmental Effects of Large Dams*. Vol. 2, Wadebridge Ecological Centre, Cornwall, pp. 184-188.

FERSI, M. 1978. *Dossier pluviométrique de Matmata*. DRES, Tunis.

FRANKENBERG, P. 1980. Evapotranspiration, bilan de l'eau et variabilité des précipitations en Tunisie en relation avec l'agriculture. *Méditerranée*, 40, pp. 49-55.

GRIFFITHS, R. 2004. Knowledge production and the research-teaching nexus: the case of the built environment disciplines. *Studies in Higher Education*, 29, pp. 709-726.

GRÜNBERGER, O., MONTOROI, J-P., ALBERGEL, J. 1999. *Evaluation par bilan isotopique de la recharge d'un aquifère induite par le fonctionnement d'une retenue collinaire. Premiers résultats sur le site d'El Gouazine (Tunisie centrale)*. Volume des abstracts, Colloque International sur l'apport de la Géochimie Isotopique dans le Cycle de l'Eau. ENIS, Hammamet, Tunisie, 6-8 avril, 1999, pp. 52-53.

GUILLAUD, C., TRABELSI, M. 1991. Gestion des resources hydriques en Tunisie centrale: les projets Sidi Saad et El Haoureb. Hydrology for the Water Management of Large River Basins. Proceedings of the Vienna Symposium, August 1991. *IAHS Publication,* 201, pp. 129-138.

HABAÏEB, H., ALBERGEL, J. 2004. Vers une gestion optimale des ressources en eau: exemple da la Tunisie. In Séminaire Int. *Hydrologie des Régions Méditerranéenes.* Documents Techniques en Hydrologie. UNESCO, Paris, pp. 187-193.

HEALEY, M., BLUMHOF, J., THOMAS, N. 2003. The research-teaching nexus in Geography, Earth and Environmental Sciences (GEES). *Planet,* Special Edition 5, pp. 5-13.

HILL, J., WOODLAND, W. 2003. Contrasting water management techniques in Tunisia: towards sustainable agricultural use. *Geographical Journal,* 169, 342-357.

HILL, J., WOODLAND, W. 2008. Traditional agricultural water management in Tunisia: contributions to environmental sustainability. In : E. ROOSE, J. ALBERGEL, G. DE NONI, A. LAOUINA, M. SABIR (eds) *Efficacité de la gestion de l'eau et de la fertilité des sols en milieux semi-arides.* AUF, EAC and IRD, Paris, pp. 86-91.

HILL, J., WOODLAND, W., SPALDING, R. 2004. Linking teaching and research in an undergraduate fieldwork module: a case study. *Planet,* 13, pp. 4-7.

JENKINS, A. 2003. Designing a curriculum that values a research based approach to student learning in Geography, Earth and Environmental Sciences (GEES). *Planet,* Special Edition 5, pp. 2-5.

KASPERSON, J. X., KASPERSON, R. E., TURNER II, B. L. 1996. Regions at risk: exploring environmental criticality. *Environment,* 38, pp. 4-15.

KINGUMBI, A., BESBES, M., BOURGES, J., GARETTA, P. 2004. Transfer evlaution between dam and aquifers by the balance method in a semi-arid region. The El Haoureb case in central Tunisia. *Revue des Sciences de l'Eau,* 17, pp. 213-225.

MINISTRY OF AGRICULTURE 1998. *Stratégie du secteur de l'eau en Tunisie à long terme (2030).* Eau XXI. Ministère de l'Agriculture, Tunis.

MINISTRY OF ENVIRONMENT AND LAND USE PLANNING 2001. *National Report on Tunisia's achievements in the area of sustainable development and in implementing Agenda 21.* Ministry of Environment and Land Use Planning, Tunis.

MINISTRY OF DEVELOPMENT AND INTERNATIONAL COOPERATION (2002) *The Tenth Plan in Brief 2002-2006.* Ministry of Development and International Cooperation, Tunis.

MONTOROI, J-P. GRÜNBERGER, O., NASRI, S. 2002. Ground water geochemistry of a small reservoir catchment in central Tunisia. *Applied Geochemistry,* 17, pp. 1047-1060.

NASRI, S. 2002. *Hydrological effects of water harvesting techniques: A study of tabias, soil contour ridges and hill reservoirs in Tunisia.* Unpublished PhD thesis, Lund Institute of Technology, Lund University, Lund.

NASRI, S., ALBERGEL, J., CUDENNEC, C., BERNDTSSON, R. 2004a. Hydrological processes in macrocatchment water harvesting in the arid region of Tunisia: the traditional system of tabias. *Hydrological Sciences Journal,* 49, pp. 261-272.

NASRI, S., CUDENNEC, C., ALBERGEL, J., BERNDTSSON, R. 2004b. Use of a geomorphological transfer function to model design floods in small hillside catchments in semiarid Tunisia. *Journal of Hydrology,* 287, pp. 197-213.

OUESSAR, M., SGHAIER, M., MAHDHI, N., ABDELLI, F., DE GRAAFF, J., CHAIEB, H., YAHYAOUI, H., GABRIELS, D. 2004. An integrated approach for impact assessment of water harvesting techniques in dry areas: the case of Oued Oum Zessar watershed (Tunisia). *Environmental Monitoring and Assessment,* 99, pp. 127-140.

RAPP, A., HASTEEN-DAHLIN, A. 1990. Improved management of drylands by water harvesting in Third World countries. In: J. BOARDMAN, I. D. L. FOSTER, J. A. DEARING (eds) *Soil Erosion on Agricultural Land.* New York: Wiley, pp. 495-511.

VIDAL, A. 2001. *Case Studies on Water Conservation in the Mediterranean Region.* International Programme for Technology and Research in Irrigation and Drainage. Rome: FAO.

WOODLAND W., HILL J. 2006. Water management for agriculture in Tunisia: towards environmentally sustainable development. In: J. Hill A. Terry and W. Woodland (eds) *Sustainable Development: National Aspirations, Local Implementation.* Aldershot: Ashgate, pp. 229-251.

ZAHAR, Y. 2001. L'estimation probabiliste des durées de service futures des barrages en Tunisie. Essai de caractérisation et proposition d'une formule régionale. *Revue Internationalle de l'Eau,* 1, pp. 71-80.

Linking Research and Teaching in Higher Education
Simon K. Haslett and Hefin Rowlands (eds)
Proceedings of the Newport NEXUS Conference
Centre for Excellence in Learning and Teaching
Special Publication, No. 1, 2009, pp. 167-174
ISBN 978-1-899274-38-3

University of Wales, Newport

Prifysgol Cymru, Casnewydd

Developing customised dice games within an applied research project: linking research and knowledge transfer.

Mark Francis

Newport Business School, University of Wales, Newport, Allt-yr-yn Campus, Allt-yr-yn Avenue, Newport, NP20 5DA. Email: mark.francis@newport.ac.uk

Abstract

This paper provides an example of how applied research can be linked to knowledge transfer and Learning & Teaching outcomes. It explains how with careful design, the findings of an applied, case study-based research project in the Aerospace industry were exploited in the Enterprise domain in the form of four bespoke dice games developed for a knowledge transfer training exercise. It also explains how the main deliverable of this project (the design of a 'pull system' for increasing the throughput of material in the focal aircraft panel production plant) was successfully exploited in the form of a £70k implementation project that delivered a multiple return on this investment.

Introduction

The purpose of this paper is to provide an illustration of how research can be linked effectively to knowledge transfer. It draws upon an applied research project undertaken by the author and his research team from the Lean Enterprise Research Centre (LERC) in Cardiff University at the aerospace firm Bombardier Aerospace Belfast (BAB). This study was undertaken under the aegis of 'Workpacket 3' (WP3) of a programme called *Precision Concept Design Model of Manufacturing for Competitive Advantage* (PREMADE).

In preview, this paper has three sections. The first section explains the research context by detailing the design of the PREMADE programme; the background of BAB who were the lead case study organization; and the research methodology of WP3 project conducted at this firm. It also explains the design of the Drum-Buffer-Rope (DBR) pull system that was the output of WP3. The second section explains how this research project was then linked into the domain of

Enterprise by utilizing the collected WP3 data to develop a series of four bespoke dice games designed to simulate the DBR mechanism for a knowledge transfer training exercise. It also explains how the material was used to stimulate a £70k spin-off exploitation project. The last section provides a brief summary and conclusions.

The Research Context

PREMADE – Research Design

PREMADE was a three year applied research programme that started in 2006 and ended in April 2009. Its £2.5m of funding was provided by the UK Department of Trade and Industry, now called the Department of Business, Enterprise & Regulatory Reform (BERR). PREMADE involved a consortium of ten industrial and two academic partners; the latter being the Lean Enterprise Research Centre (LERC) from Cardiff University and the School of Mechanical and Aerospace Engineering at Queens University Belfast

(QUB). The project aim was to develop a digital manufacturing tool and wider supporting application methodology based upon the DELMIA software suite. This tool was to facilitate digital manufacturing assembly line layout and configuration for new products prior to their production. It was to embody Lean manufacturing and supply chain process design principles; hence becoming a Digital Lean Manufacturing (DLM) tool. The concept therefore was to develop a digital manufacturing environment that would enable competing assembly line configurations to be evaluated and optimised in terms of lead time and cost prior to undertaking any conventional physical layout activities, and hence ultimately increasing competitive advantage via time (responsiveness) and cost reduction for the firms concerned.

The high level research design and programme management framework of PREMADE involved five distinct 'packets' of work. Workpacket 1 (WP1) was the initial programme planning element that involved refining the individual workpacket deliverables and timescales. WP2 involved the functional development of the DLM tool components and supporting methodology. This was conducted at Bombardier Aerospace Belfast (BAB), who are a manufacturer of aircraft fuselages and nacelles and were the lead industrial partner in the PREMADE project. WP3 entailed the (internal) verification of this functionality by means of a test application within BAB, whilst WP4 formed the (external) validation of the generalised functionality in a new industrial setting. This was conducted at the aerospace component and sub-assembly firm called Langford Lodge Engineering Company Ltd in Crumlin, Northern Ireland. The last workpacket is the ongoing dissemination and commercial exploitation of the project deliverables by the academic partners, of which this paper forms a part.

Bombardier Aerospace Belfast – The Participant Organisation

Bombardier Aerospace Belfast (BAB) is an integral part of Bombardier Aerospace; the world's third largest civil aircraft manufacturer. Bombardier Aerospace is headquartered in Montréal, Canada, and employ more than 28,000 people worldwide. For the year ending January 31 2009, Bombardier Aerospace's revenues amounted to $10 billion. BAB by contrast employ over 5,000 people at six plants in Northern Ireland. They design, manufacture and support fuselage, engine nacelle and flight control surface structures for the parent firm's small and medium sized regional aircraft series, such as the Learjet, Challenger and Global Express ranges. These structures are assembled on a number of dedicated assembly lines in the Main Factory (final assembly hall) in Belfast before the resultant 'pods' (complete fuselages or nacelles) are shipped on; with final aircraft assembly being conducted at the parent firm's North American plant.

Metal Bond/Centre 04 (C04) is one of these six plants and is located approximately one mile from the Main Factory. C04 is an upstream fabrication facility that receives raw material such as sheet metal from external suppliers and produces a variety of aircraft panels. The facility produces both bonded (parts glued together using adhesive) and non-bonded panels. Panel production starts with the rolling of sheet metal into the panel shape/ curvature at large machines called the Farnham Rolls; the *gateway* work centre. These and most of the other main manufacturing resources used in panel production such as the Clean Line and Chemical Milling are *shared resources;* not being dedicated to any contract or value stream. Once produced, the panels are transported to a local BAB pre-assembly buffer area called the Flight Shed before being called off by the downstream Main Factory where they are then assembled into fuselage or nacelles 'segments' (concentric sections) as part of the final assembly process.

Workpacket 3: Methodology

The output of LERC's WP2 study was a diagnosis of the configuration and financial consequences of the current-state of the whole of BAB's Northern Ireland operation (Darlington *et al.*, 2008a, 2008b) which was embodied in a new form of representation called a Big Picture Financial Map (BPFM). The WP2 analysis enabled BAB's senior manage-ment team to objectively target the focal area within their operation that would most benefit from improved product flow characteristics. They decided that this would be in C04 because the BPFM had identified this as an area of particularly high inventory and operating expense. Coincidentally, C04 was a high profile problem area within the firm at that point in time because it was struggling to service its Main Factory customer. C04's production was not synchronised with final assembly, and it also suffered from significant rework and scrap rates. As a consequence, panels were not available when required. The firm's response to this had been to 'work harder'. However, this had not solved the problem. All it had achieved was to build more work in progress (WIP) panels; tying up more working capital and resulting in more damages – because many of these typically large and expensive panels had to be stored on the floor.

BAB were physically running out of space to store these panels, and the problem was poised to become acute within six months due to a large increase in order book demand. A project designed to reduce WIP whilst increasing responsiveness to this demand was therefore both urgent and important. It was subsequently decided that C04 would form the focal organisation for the LERC WP3 study, and the research question would be: *What design of pull-system will most significantly improve the flow of material through C04 by minimising lead time (total elapsed time from start to finish of the operation) and hence maximise throughput to the downstream final assembly area?*

WP3 consequently represents a pur-posively selected (Silverman, 2000) case study; a research strategy promoted by scholars such as Yin (2003) and Eisenhardt (1989) and advanced as an appropriate methodology for logistics and supply chain research by proponents such as Ellram (1996). Primary data collection instruments included semi-structured and unstructured interviews and various process mapping, audiovisual and observational techniques. Document and archival analysis were used for the secondary research with the data being ordered into a number of software tools that were used to support the design of the pull-system deliverable.

Workpacket 3: Results (Drum-Buffer-Rope Pull System Design)

A project team was formed comprising LERC and BAB staff from C04. Extensive data was collected and then analysed. As a conse-quence of this it was decided to reject the conventional Lean kanban approach to pull system design (see Bicheno, 2004; Womack and Jones, 1996) as inappropriate for a fabrication operation such as C04. Instead, the Drum-Buffer-Rope (DBR) technique drawn from the Theory of Constraints (Goldratt and Cox, 1984) was identified as the most effective approach for maximizing throughput in this context (Figure 1).

DBR is an unconventional approach to production scheduling. The 'Drum' is the constraint/ pacemaker resource whose 'beat' determines the throughput of the whole system (Bicheno, 2004). By definition, the Drum is the resource that is most highly loaded given the demand/product mix. Identifying the Drum for a complex opera-tions such as C04 involved the construction of a capacity planner, WIP monitoring tool and a software simulation of the material flows. The Laser Scribe machine was subsequently identified as the Drum.

According to the Theory of Constraints (TOC) a minute lost at the Drum is a minute lost for the whole system. An inventory 'Buffer' is therefore required to protect the Drum by ensuring that it never runs out of work. This is a *time based buffer* representing a pre-determined amount of time of the next items to be processed rather than a discrete number of or specific type of panel. The actual size of this Buffer is determined by the probability of failure upstream of the Drum. After analysing the C04 failure reports, a four day buffer was agreed.

The 'Rope' is a signalling device that links the Drum to the gateway work centre (the Farnham Rolling machine in C04) and is synchronised with the Drum. When the Drum processes a panel the Rope is used to send a signal to the gateway to release the material for the next panel to the first workstation. Similarly, if the Drum stops for any reason no signal is sent and therefore no more work is released into the system as this would merely build WIP/ queue size. In the case of C04, a ready-made physical rope device existed in

the form of overhead conveyancing 'flight bars' on which the panels were hung to transport them around the factory. The team could use this to signal material release. They could also use it to physically limit the amount of WIP by adding or removing the number of flight bars in circulation.

Given the above design the team conservatively estimated that its DBR implementation would result in a 20% lead time reduction as measured by WIP inventory from a starting position of 40 days worth. Working in conjunction with BAB's accountants this level of inventory reduction was costed to a $450k material and utility cost reduction, or $850k in fully absorbed standard costing terms.

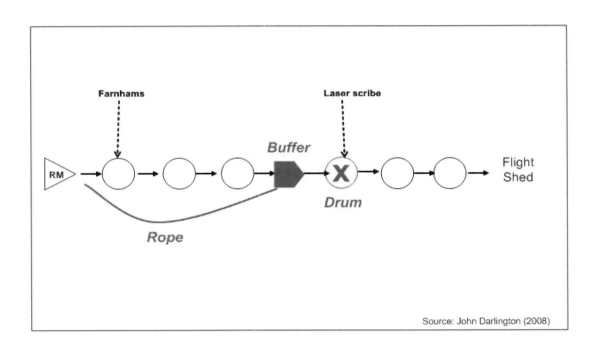

Source: John Darlington (2008)

Figure 1. Drum-Buffer-Rope Pull System design at C04
(note: simplification – fuselage panels only).

Linking Research to Enterprise

Knowledge Transfer at C04: Development of Bespoke Dice Games

There was, however, a dilemma. Regardless of the confidently forecast benefit, the LERC DBR design was 'owned' only by them. Both it and its underlying TOC principles were alien to the C04 management team, and importantly, their *in situ* performance measurement system (which was premised upon labour/unit cost 'optimisation' rather than throughput minimization). This issue is not unique. Indeed, when Goldratt conceived TOC he preempted this issue by offering a sequence of dice games to explain its fundamental principles. The problem encountered by the LERC team was that even after taking the BAB staff through these games during an initial training session designed to support the research project, they still didn't embrace the DBR approach. This seemed at least partly attributable to their seeming inability to interpret these generic games for the C04 context.

It was consequently decided to develop and test a series of bespoke dice games for C04 in order to overcome this problem. There were three objectives for this knowledge transfer exercise:

1. To better communicate the DBR pull-system design to the C04 management team to stimulate an implementation decision.

2. To act as a training aid to the project team of BAB staff that were actually to carry out this implementation – to better understand the 'counter-intuitive' system they were being tasked with implementing.

3. To act as a communication and training aid to help them explain the new system to their colleagues during the post-implementation effort (after the LERC team left).

To achieve the above the team drew upon the data previously collected as part of the applied research methodology. This included the capacity planner and simulation software that were used to identify the Drum. It also notably included an extensive Value Stream Map (see Womack and Jones, 1996; Rother and Shook, 1998) that was drawn using marker pens and sticky notes by the BAB team to describe the current-state of the C04 operation (see Figure 2). To recap, these tools had originally been deployed to inform the process improvement initiative (Rother and Shook, 1998; Womack & Jones, 1996) undertaken for discipline-based research. The innovation was, therefore, to additionally harness this data to inform the design of a pedagogical outcome.

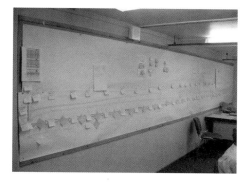

Figure 2. Undertaking value stream mapping at C04, Bombardier Aerospace Belfast.

A summary of the four resultant games is provided in Table 1. Space constraints prohibit a detailed description of them. However, the game setup position for Game #4 (DBR) can be found in the Appendix and illustrates two common denominators of these fabrication games compared to the three original linear-sequential final assembly TOC dice games on which they are based: (i) 'Y-shaped'/concurrent flow of Fuselage and Nacelle panels, (ii) Relevant C04 workcentres/resource names.

Pull System Implementation

BAB subsequently commissioned the implementation of the DBR designed during WP3. This was a spin-off exploitation project that was duly entitled *Pull System Implementation (PSI)*. At the time of writing PSI is nearing completion. Initial results are very promising and have already exceeded expectations. While the new pull-system has not yet been 'optimised', the latest results show a reduction in the total number of panels in C04 from 432 to 174 (59.7%). This reduction equates to 39.61 to 17.01 days worth (57.1%); which produced an increase in inventory turns from 9.09 to 21.16. PSI has been nominated by BAB for a worldwide Bombardier Aerospace process improvement prize and plans are in progress to roll it out to all six of BAB's Northern Ireland facilities.

Conclusions

The purpose of this paper was to provide an illustration of how research can be linked to knowledge transfer. After contextualizing the host PREMADE/WP3 research project it explained how the collected data and findings were exploited in the form of four bespoke dice games that were developed for a knowledge transfer training exercise. The paper explained how the main theoretical deliverable of the research project (the design of a pull-system) was also successfully exploited in the guise of a business case and proposal for a £70k implementation project that subsequently yielded a very strong return on investment for the commissioning firm.

No.	Name	Purpose
1	Balanced Plant	To demonstrate the phenomenon of *dependent events* and *statistical fluctuations* that arise when an attempt is made to balance capacity rather than flow in a plant; and how these influence the level of WIP and difficulty in meeting shipment dates.
2	Flexible Labour	To reinforce the message that an unbalanced plant will provide increased throughput and more reliable delivery dates compared to a balanced plant, but that flexible labour (capacity) alone is not the optimum nor practical solution to the problems facing C04.
3	Bottleneck (Drum)	To illustrate the impact of a bottleneck workstation on WIP, lead-time and throughput of the plant. It therefore introduces the concept of the bottleneck as 'Drum' ('pacemaker') for Game #4.
4	Drum-Buffer-Rope	To illustrate the positive impact of the DBR pull-system as a response to the operational challenges facing C04; and to explain the mechanics of how this would operate.

Table 1. Summary of bespoke C04 dice games.

This need not be the end of the story. The richness of the material developed during this exercise lend themselves to further exploitation; for example utilising the PREMADE material and dice games to realise the university's goal of research informed curriculum. Such a development would represent 'multiple bangs for the research bucks' and underlines the value of applied research as a device for achieving both discipline-based and pedagogical outcomes.

ACKNOWLEDGEMENTS

The author would like to thank his research team at the Lean Enterprise Research Centre, Cardiff Business School without whom neither the PREMADE project nor this paper would have been possible. He would also like to thank Bombardier Aerospace Belfast for the research access provided and extend this thanks to his PREMADE colleagues at Queens University Belfast.

REFERENCES

BICHENO, J. 2004. *The New Lean Toolbox: Towards Fast, Flexible Flow*. Buckingham: PICSIE Books.

CURRAN, R., BUTTERFIELD, J., COLLINS, R., CASTAGNE, S., JIN, Y., FRANCIS, M., DARLINGTON, J., BURKE, R. 2007. Digital lean manufacture (DLM) for competitive advantage. In *Proceedings of 7th AIAA Aviation Technology, Integration and Operations Conference (ATIO)*, Belfast, 18-20 September.

DARLINGTON, J., FRANCIS, M., FOUND, P. 2008a. Flow accounting: effective performance assessment for the lean enterprise. In *Proceedings of the 13th International Symposium on Logistics,* Bangkok, Thailand, 6-8 July.

DARLINGTON, J., FRANCIS, M., FOUND, P. 2008b. Flow accounting in application: big picture financial mapping in the aerospace industry. In *Proceedings of the 13th International Symposium on Logistics,* Bangkok, Thailand, 6-8 July.

EISENHARDT, K. M. 1989. Building theories from case study research. *Academy of Management Review*, 14 (4), pp. 532-550.

ELLRAM, L. M. 1996. The use of the case study method in logistics research. *Journal of Business Logistics,* 17 (2), pp. 93-138.

GOLDRATT, E. M., COX, J. 1984. *The Goal*. Gower: London.

ROTHER, M., SHOOK, J. 1998. *Learning to See: Value Stream Mapping to Create Value and Eliminate Muda*. Brookline (MA): The Lean Enterprise Institute.

SILVERMAN, D. 2000. *Doing Qualitative Research*. London: Sage Publications.

WOMACK, J., JONES, D. T. 1996. *Lean Thinking: Banish Waste and Create Wealth in Your Corporation*. New York: Simon & Schuster.

YIN, R. K.2003. *Case Study Research: Design and Methods (3rd ed.)*. London: Sage Publications.

APPENDIX

C04 Dice Game #4 (Drum-Buffer-Rope) - Illustrative Material

Purpose of the Game. To illustrate the impact of the DBR pull-system as a response to the operational challenges facing C04; and to explain the mechanics of how this pull system would operate.

Checklist of Equipment Needed (based on the standard game setup)

○ 9 x Players

○ 9 x *Workstation/ Score Sheets*

○ **12** x Dice (standard, 6 sided) {to represent workstation capacity}

○ 2 x Raw material containers

○ 1 x Shipped/ finished goods container

○ Approx. 100 x Colour#1 counters (eg red) {to represent Nacelle panels}

○ Approx. 100 x Colour#2 counters (eg blue) {to represent Fuselage panels}

Objective

Capacity in this game is embodied in the dice. There is only one dice at the LASER SCRIBE 'drum', and the average score of a standard six-sided dice is 3.5. Over 20 days we could, therefore, expect a target throughput of 70 counters (3.5 x 20). The objective of this game is therefore **to ship 70 counters** (any combination/ colour) over the course of the 20 days of the game. Game layout is shown in Figure 3.

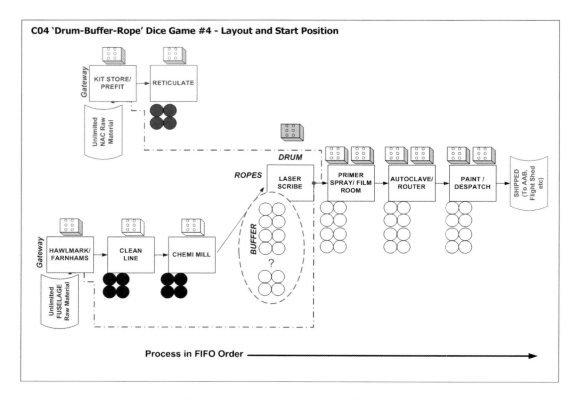

Figure 3. Setting up the game (layout).

Linking Research and Teaching in Higher Education
Simon K. Haslett and Hefin Rowlands (eds)
Proceedings of the Newport NEXUS Conference
Centre for Excellence in Learning and Teaching
Special Publication, No. 1, 2009, pp. 175-197
ISBN 978-1-899274-38-3

ABSTRACTS

This section presents abstracts of other papers presented at the Newport NEXUS Conference 2009 for which a full written paper is not available. The abtsracts are organised by symposium.

SYMPOSIUM - EDUCATION FOR SUSTAINABLE DEVELOPMENT AND GLOBAL CITIZENSHIP

Teaching ethics and sustainability.

Gideon Calder

Department of Health & Social Sciences, University of Wales, Newport, Caerleon Campus, Newport, NP18 3QT, United Kingdom. Email: gideon.calder@newport.ac.uk

Teaching environmental ethics in a broader curriculum is often hard work. This may seem unexpected: at face value, issues like sustainability have a kind of edgy urgency which few others share. But pedagogically, ethics runs smoothest when it tackles questions close to the individual agent: a difficult choice, the weighing of a dilemma, the experience of being pulled in different directions by conflicting reasons or priorities. Environmental questions put a strain on this system. The bigger the issues get – say, climate change – the harder it is to render them in the usual vocabulary of the ethical dilemma. This is accentuated by the fact that ethical theory has traditionally been neglectful of social structures and environments (built or natural). This paper will suggest that what we learn from teaching ethics, we learn about ethics as a whole: it might be easier to 'run with' when agent-centred, but overdoing this will close off big issues and crucial questions. Using work by Warwick Fox and Alasdair MacIntyre, it suggests that we think better about values questions when we think about them *environmentally*, in specific senses of this term.

SYMPOSIUM – PROFESSIONAL DEVELOPMENT

Innovations in cultivating personal development and self awareness.

Ariana Faris and Norma James

School of Health & Social Sciences, University of Wales, Newport, Allt-yr-yn Campus, Newport, NP20 5DA, United Kingdom. Email: ariana.faris@newport.ac.uk ; norma.james@newport.ac.uk

The research question comes in two parts. The first question is how we might improve the delivery acquisition of self knowledge and general learning experience of students in the context of personal development training on a counselling course. The second is how might Coopera-tive Enquiry and action research methods contribute to the creation of an enhanced learning environment within such a context? We have used such a methodology and world cafe design working with students on the pg counselling programme at Certificate and Diploma stages of the course. The students were engaged in a collaborative process whose outcome was to produce a personal development group work design and then evaluate it over the course of one academic year. Early outcomes indicate that the Diploma students who had some experience of personal development prior to the research, reported that their learning was enhanced and that the cooperative process has contributed to increased participation. Early indicators for Certificate students who had little or no prior experience of personal development group work have evaluated their participation in the action research as generally very positive. However the evaluations of their group work design and experience has been mixed.

Overall the research which is still in process would indicate that cooperative enquiry and action research methodologies result in student led designs in which students who have some experience of personal development groups report an increase in participation and learning.

Supporting tomorrow's managers: creating a team coaching culture to support the Personal Development Process.

Alan Robinson

Newport Business School, University of Wales, Newport, Allt-yr-yn Campus, Newport, NP20 5DA, United Kingdom. Email: alan.robinson@newport.ac.uk

Changing the way in which we offer learning opportunities owes much to the increasing demand for flexibility in where and how learning takes place. For many, formal programmes of learning are usually part of a much bigger journey of personal development. Not only do we need to be more creative regarding the way in which we generate learning opportunities but we also need to ensure that learners have access to effective support whilst undertaking this journey. In order to respond to this there needs to be a fundamental change in the way in which we, as academics, approach our roles as facilitators of learning. We need to move away from being the "sage on the stage" and to act as more of a "guide on the side". This paper illustrates the creation of a coaching culture providing a highly effective means of helping students address this holistically, during their formal studies and beyond. As part of this, academics work as a team providing an informed and co-ordinated approach to personal development. This paper will also explore how coaching as a process can act as an equally important developmental tool with both staff and students, helping students to appreciate how formal learning fits into their wider personal learning agenda. All aspects will be illustrated through a case study based on a postgraduate learning experience.

Elemental things.

Jane Davison

Newport School of Art, Media and Design, University of Wales, Newport, Caerleon Campus, Newport, NP18 3QT, United Kingdom. Email: jane.davison@newport.ac.uk

When Paul Ramsden was asked by the Universities Secretary to assess the main challenges for the future of higher education over the next 10-15 years, he concluded that we need to explore new models of curricula that encourage interdisciplinary learning throughout the student lifecycle.

This paper will present the findings of a Learning and Teaching Award to investigate how interdisiplinary learning is understood within different subject areas at undergraduate level, particularly in relation to:

- Supporting ESDGC
- Enhancing employability skills
- Developing students' creativity

The data collection process was divided into two parts, the first included interviews with 18 representatives of both the HE Academy Subject Centres and the QAA subject benchmarking groups. The second stage focused on interdisciplinary learning at programme level, through a review of published documentation from eight HEIs in England and Wales.

To coincide with the Nexus Conference, academic staff from a range of disciplines within Newport School of Art, Media and Design have been invited to contribute to an exhibition in the Ffloc Gallery entitled "Elemental Things". The work on show will reflect the findings of the study, and will explore opportunities for collaboration across a broad range of subject areas.

Entrepreneurship in Higher Education

Richard Jeans and Emma Williams

Research & Enterprise Department, University of Wales, Newport, Allt-yr-yn Campus, Newport, NP20 5XA, United Kingdom Email: richard.jeans@newport.ac.uk; emma.williams7@newport.ac.uk

Governments across the globe are seeking to achieve a more competitive economy in which enterprise, entrepreneurship and innovation are the drivers of growth. In an increasingly high skilled workforce, graduates are a key to national growth and hence HEI's are ideally placed to expose students to environments which foster entrepreneurial mindsets. (NESTA 2008)

This has been recognised at Newport and the development of Entrepreneurship and Innovation is a key feature of the University's Strategic Plan, Learning and Teaching, and Research and Enterprise Strategies (2008-2012). However, to date, initiatives to embed entrepreneurship skills in the curriculum have been fragmented, short term and uneven. The presenters will report on a Learning and Teaching Award that investigates best practice in embedding entrepreneurship training in the curriculum across undergraduate programmes. They will describe the project and report on progress to date, initial findings and future plans. Attendees will be invited to share their own ideas, best practice and suggestions that might contribute to the development of Enterprise and Entrepreneurship skills in students.

Developing pedagogy and curriculum through action research.

Janet Pinder

Centre for Community & Lifelong Learning, University of Wales, Newport, Caerleon Campus, Newport, NP18 3QT, United Kingdom. Email: janet.pinder@newport.ac.uk

Through the use of a research based case study, the paper illustrates how alternative curriculum, linked directly to pedagogy and methodology emerging from action inquiry can direct the development of an appropriate curriculum and teaching approach, engage learners and recruit marginalised members of society in addition to ensuring engagement, retention, progression and achievement.

The case study is the BeWEHL (Bettering Education, Wellbeing, and Lifelong Learning) project, funded between 2000 and 2006 by the Welsh Assembly Government as a research based project. The project benefited from support from the European Social Fund (2002 – 2006), which allowed the research findings and curriculum developed to be tested in a development situation alongside the ongoing research. The project is now core funded by the University.

An overview of the methodology used to secure engagement and develop curriculum is presented in addition to addressing the high levels of both academic and personal student support required when working with marginalised communities and individuals. As well as the student experience, the educational and employment outcomes of engagement are highlighted alongside a discussion focused on the validity of alternative, innovative and reflexive approaches to addressing student needs as opposed to more traditional approaches and policy frameworks. The presentation will be led by staff from the BeWEHL project as well as students.

A voice of my own: supporting students toward academic literacy

Nicola Woods and Rachel Stubley

Newport School of Education, University of Wales, Newport, Caerleon Campus, Newport, NP18 3QT, United Kingdom. Email: nicola.woods@newport.ac.uk; rachel.stubley@newport.ac.uk

There is increasing concern that the levels of literacy achieved by graduate students has declined over recent years and the salient perception is one of 'deteriorating standards' (Street 2004). As we plan our L&T strategies, respond to the demands of our stakeholders (including employers) and, most importantly, ensure the best educational opportunities for our students, it is vital that we address the question of what we mean by academic literacy and, once defined, consider how best to go about developing the literacy levels of our students.

Adopting a critical ethnographic approach with a focus on academic literacies (Lea and Street 1998), the research seeks to elicit expectations and interpretations that both students and tutors have regarding academic writing. The paper reports on the first stage of research including focus groups with students, involving discussion and reflections on issues such as the following: What do we mean by a 'good essay', What are students' aims and understanding in drafting and constructing a piece of writing (and do these reflect the aims and understanding of tutors)? Do we encourage students to think about their writing processes? Discussion focuses on academic writing as social practice and the importance of both recognising students' existing skills and embedding support for writing into the students' broader educational experience.

How to encourage International students studying finance modules on MBA programme adopting a deep approach to learning?

George Salijeni

Newport School of Education, University of Wales, Newport, Caerleon Campus, Newport, NP18 3QT, United Kingdom. Email: george.salijeni@newport.ac.uk

In "How to encourage International students studying finance on an MBA programme to adpat a deep approach to learning" the author looks at the challenges encountered by international student enrolled on this programme who have little or no accounting/ financial background. Students bring feelings of tension and anxiety to their studies (Richardson et al 1972 cited Joyce et al (2006, P457) and in most cases students are motivated by fear of failure rather than the understanding of the module (Haggis), 2003). Consequently they adopt a surface approach to learning which entails them to memorise the contents of the modules. This approach will do little to help students to enhance their lifelong learning skills and personal development. In contrast, if these students adopt an active or deep approach to learning, which encourages them to understand the underlying meaning, use analytical skills and independent thinking (Warburton,2003) the whole picture would be reversed. They are likely to understand and develop as a person (Marton and Saljo, 1984). As most of the international students have different cultural backgrounds, the project will look at culture (Hofsteded, 1984) as an instrument in conditioning the whole process of encouraging a deep approach to learning. To do this, the perception of, and approach to, learning among international students will be assessed. I will use group learning to foster a deep approach to learning.

SYMPOSIUM – STUDENT ENGAGEMENT

Decline driven portfolio development.

Claire Westlake

Strategic Planning Department, University of Wales, Newport, Caerleon Campus, Newport, NP18 3QT, United Kingdom. Email: claire.westlake@newport.ac.uk

Newport Business School receive a number of applications that do not convert into enrolments and the school was keen to investigate why, after being attracted enough to apply to the University, prospective students go on to either decline the offer that they received or withdraw their application completely.

Telephone interviews were conducted with a sample of declining and withdrawing applicants in two phases to discover the reasoning behind the decision to decline or withdraw their application. These interviews focused on the effect the application process and contact with

Newport Business School as well as investigating what they preferred about the course and University they ultimately decided upon.

Student engagement.

Graham Rogers[1], Gary Pritchard[2], Tony Ruckinski[3] and Lawrence Wilson[4]

[1]University of Wales, Newport, Caerleon Campus, Newport, NP18 3QT, United Kingdom. Email: graham.rogers@newport.ac.uk

[2]Newport School of Art, Media & Design, University of Wales, Newport, Caerleon Campus, Newport, NP18 3QT, United Kingdom. Email: gary.pritchard@newport.ac.uk

[3]Learning and Information Services, University of Wales, Newport, Caerleon Campus, Newport, NP18 3QT, United Kingdom. Email: tony.rucinski@newport.ac.uk

[4]Student Support Services, University of Wales, Newport, Caerleon Campus, Newport, NP18 3QT, United Kingdom. Email: lawrence.wilson@newport.ac.uk

The aim of this project is to understand more fully the reasons for student engagement and non-engagement with the University and their course, and to propose action that enables and supports students so that they engage more effectively with their programme of study.

Out with the old, in with the New ......Space.

Allan Theophanidies

Information & Library Services, University of Wales, Newport, Caerleon Campus, Newport, NP18 3QT, United Kingdom. Email: allan.theophanides@newport.ac.uk

The University of Wales, Newport has built up a reputation for unique e-Learning developments over the past four years ever since moving from a commercial VLE to an in-house developed managed learning environment platform (myLearning Essentials, or mLE). This decision enabled tools to be developed as and when required including Instant Messaging, course/module group text messaging as well as personal timetabling schedules, and all included without having to wait or rely on upgrades from a vendor.

After integrating a Blogging/Forum/Gallery application a few years ago, 2007 saw the University take its first venture into the mainstream social networking domain through developing a Facebook plugin called myNewport which allowed students and staff to access the e-Learning platform (mLE) through their own profile.

This was seen as the first step into not only trying to appeal to the increasing 'digital native' student psyche, but also as an experiment on whether students were willing for an educational institution to enter their 'virtual world' - something which has recently been contested in Academia as pointless given users want to keep their private and academic lives separate.

'Out with the old, in with the New...space' presents a case study giving an insight into how far educational institutions can go in developing ideas and 'riding on the coat tails' of the latest digital trends; especially with regards embracing students' digital identity and using social networking for retention and promotion to students.

Experiential pedagogy: the key to student engagement.

David Gibson

NICENT Teaching Fellow, Queen's University Management School, Queen's University Belfast, 63 University Street, Belfast, BT7 1NN, United Kingdom. Email: david.gibson@qub.ac.uk

David Gibson will address the possibilities of developing new teaching strategies to turn lectures into interactive learning experiences to increase Student engagement both in and outside the classroom, whatever the subject area. David will explore a range of pedagogic possibilities and the link to formative and summative assessment. He will provide examples of how appropriate Pedagogy can not only enhance the learning experience of the students but lead to greater knowledge and skills development within the subject area. He provides a structure and self assessment tool for educational development as academics must develop strategies to engage students in addition to imparting relevant knowledge in their subject areas.

David is the only UK National Teaching Fellow In Enterprise Education as recognised by the Higher Education Authority, based upon the ability to engage students within sixty seven subject areas at Queens, a Russell Group research University. As a result enterprise is now embedded within 100% of the Curriculum in 100% at the University and longitudinal studies have revealed the positive impact on students academic and careers performance based on interactive experiential learning experiences. David has numerous teaching awards and his work has been implemented in China and India and was recently recognised within. David is the author of "the Efactor"(Pearson 2006) an interactive learning which is now a core text in over 200 International Universities and is a keynote speaker throughout the world

SYMPOSIUM – TECHNOLOGY ENHANCED LEARNING

Reading, seeing and hearing: learning through podcasting and vodcasting.

Jo Smedley

Newport Business School, University of Wales, Newport, Allt-yr-yn Campus, Newport, NP20 5DA, United Kingdom. Email: jo.smedley@newport.ac.uk

Exploring innovative uses of modern technologies in subjects which historically use more text - based delivery approaches presents challenges for staff and students. This paper, featuring work supported by JISC TechDis HEAT3 funding, discussed the learning methodologies with case study applications in law and economics, featuring staff experiences and student expectation in this approach to learning engagement

Evaluating fieldwork/practice placement evaluation tools.

Lana Morris and Alun Griffiths

School of Health & Social Sciences, University of Wales, Newport, Allt-yr-yn Campus, Newport, NP20 5DA. Email: lana.morris@newport.ac.uk; alun.griffiths@newport.ac.uk

This project aimed to review the school evaluation tool used to evaluate the placement experiences of students from the BA (Hons) Youth and Community Studies and BA (Hons) Social Work programmes.

Our poster presentation explores the process of evaluating the existing evaluation tool and its subsequent refinement as a result of a UK wide literature review on current tools used to evaluate social work and youth work placement experiences and our findings from a series of focus groups with local social work practitioners. Our presentation will also consider some of the barriers of involvement experienced in relation to the participation of youth work practitioners', and the extent to which the current evaluation tool which was approved by the regional partnership Social Care in Partnership- South East (SCiPSE) comprising 10 local authorities in South East Wales is fit for purpose for youth work placements.

The development of institutional repositories and their use in supporting teaching and learning.

Angharad James

Information and Library Services, University of Wales, Newport, Caerleon Campus, Newport, NP18 3QT, United Kingdom. Email: angharad.james@newport.ac.uk

This paper will begin by discussing the development of repositories as part of the Open Access movement. The current institutional repository landscape will then be described, identifying the number of repositories in existence (around 1300 worldwide), where they are located and they types of material they hold. The variety and quantity of freely available academic research held within repositories will be emphasised. As will the huge growth in repository content in recent years.

The benefits of repository use will be discussed from the perspective of students, researchers, academics and institutions. Academics who deposit material will benefit from increased visibility of their research, broadening research networks and peer recognition. Intuitions benefit from raising their research profile both nationally and internationally. Students (and academics) benefit from free access to high quality research.

Services for accessing repository content will be explored, such as the *Intute Repository Search*, *OpenDOAR* and *Google Scholar*.

The paper will also examine the activities of the Welsh Repository Network. The WRN is a JISC funded project (delivered via the Repository Support Project) that provided all Welsh Higher education institutions with the necessary hardware and technical expertise to develop an institutional repository. Wales is now unique as the only country to have 100% coverage of repositories in Higher Education institutions.

The University of Wales, Newport Repository will be demonstrated and plans for its development will be discussed. The opportunity will be taken to encourage deposit from those undertaking research at the University

GAMEZ MEANZ LEARNZ!* or How to make making games make learning.

Mike Reddy[1] and Emma Westecott[2]

[1]Newport Business School, University of Wales, Newport, Allt-yr-yn Campus, Newport, NP20 5DA, United Kingdom. Email: mike.reddy@newport.ac.uk

[2]Games Research Fellow, Synergy International Film School Wales, Newport School of Art, Media and Design, University of Wales, Newport, Lodge Road, Caerleon, Newport NP18 3NT, United Kingdom. Email: Emma.westecott@newport.ac.uk

To be shown is good. To do is better. To play is best. This presentation will explore how the creation of serious games can take constructionist involvement to a further level by capturing the essential elements of a community of practice. This distillation of a discipline, by systems thinking, provides an opportunity to link concept, context and concrete in an Activity Theoretical framework.

Video podcasts as a learning support resource for Geography.

Jenny Hill[1] and Mandy Nelson[2]

[1]Department of Geography and Environmental Management, School of the Built and Natural Environment, Faculty of Environment and Technology, University of the West of England, Frenchay Campus, Bristol, BS16 1QY, United Kingdom. Email: Jennifer.Hill@uwe.ac.uk

[2]Quality Assurance Agency, Southgate House, Southgate Street, Gloucester, GL1 1UB, United Kingdom. Email: m.nelson@qaa.ac.uk

The use of ICT to support geography teaching and learning in Higher Education has grown markedly over recent years (Lynch *et al.* 2008). Whilst there is the potential for this technology to enhance student learning, there is equally a need to investigate, via empirical investigation, its effectiveness in mediating the student learning process. In particular, few formal studies exist on the effectiveness of podcasting in engaging students and influencing their learning (Edirisingha & Salmon 2007, France & Wheeler 2007, Winterbottom 2007). It is important, therefore, to examine the utility of podcasting technology in supporting specific module aims and learning outcomes, and in promoting a positive student experience and learning response. The research presented here examines undergraduate student perceptions of the learning utility of video podcasts, with particular reference to their understanding of exotic ecosystems. Podcasts have been made available to students via the Faculty intranet and they have been accessed either on-line or downloaded to appropriate mobile technology. The effectiveness of the technology in student engagement and learning is being assessed by questionnaire, focus groups and summative assessment. Preliminary results are presented here concerning i) student engagement with the technology: location(s) and time(s) of use, method(s) of use, enjoyment; and ii) their perceived value as a learning resource: positive (immediacy, flexibility, repeatability, attention holding?) and negative (easy to ignore, difficult to access, difficult to interact with?).

The creation of technology-enhanced mentorships and their effect in improving perceptions of social inclusion and skills in older people and in new undergraduates.

Julian Green

School of Health and Social Sciences, University of Wales, Newport, Caerleon Campus, Newport, NP18 3QT, United Kingdom. Email: julian.green@newport.ac.uk

This paper illustrates a key area of research that the School of Health and Social Sciences at University of Wales, Newport is currently proposing: an examination of the impact of various online and mobile technologies on issues of social inclusion within a community, as well as skill transferability between younger and older mentors.

The Technology Enhanced Learning and Learning Support (TELLS) team within the School will initiate the first stages of an e-learning programme of supportive mentorships, constituting a longitudinal study into issues which benefit perceptions of social inclusion and the effective transference of a skills set. Samples will be drawn from a group of older people who are in or approaching retirement and domiciled in the surrounding areas of Newport in South Wales, and a group of Newport first year undergraduate students new to the academic environment who will be starting the academic year in September 2009. The project is framed around the idea of a mutual mentoring programme, in that an older person will be paired with a younger student at the University.

It is envisaged that the partnership between student and older persons will also be mutually beneficial through, for example, the transference of skills, such as technological support in using social networking sites and webcam video conferencing clients. In addition, it is foreseen that the relationship should also help to foster transference of skills from the older mentor in the form of 'life' skills, such as time management and organisational empowerment.

The best of both worlds: bringing the benefits of online communities into the virtual learning environment.

Nick Swann

Newport School of Education, University of Wales, Newport, Caerleon Campus, Newport, NP18 3QT, United Kingdom. Email: nick.swann@newport.ac.uk

The internet is a natural part of many people's lives, and most students now entering HE have never known a time without access to ICT. For these people, the sense of dichotomy between 'real' and 'virtual' is not as clear as it might be for older generations: the 'virtual' world is 'really' experienced. This extends to the sense of community found in online groups, and indeed since the earliest days of mass up-take of the internet the bonds of friendship in virtual worlds have seemed as real as those in any other.

A strong sense of community amongst students has for many decades been associated with better performance and better retention, but how does this transpose into an online student community and can similar benefits be brought into the Virtual Learning Environment? Drawing on in-depth interviews with students with a variety of distance learning experience, this paper examines the sense of community (if any) found in such scenarios, and possible ways of using this to enhance learning and teaching on- and off-line.

Digital writing.

David Longman, Kerie Green, Lynne Jones and Barbara Kurzik

Newport School of Education, University of Wales, Newport, Caerleon Campus, Newport, NP18 3QT, United Kingdom. Email: david.longman@newport.ac.uk; kerie.green@newport.ac.uk; lynne.jones@newport.ac.uk; Barbara.kurzik@newport.ac.uk

This paper is a report of our Learning and Teaching Award project undertaken during the academic year 2008-09 and outlines our approach to developing sustainable and purposeful PDP tools for use within teacher education courses. This is based on a process described by QAA as "a structured and supported process undertaken by an individual to reflect upon their own learning, performance and/or achievement, and to plan for their personal, educational and career development."

This work is stimulated by the ongoing debate initiated by Estyn in "Transforming Schools" (2007) and the Furlong Review of ITT in Wales (2006) in which it is observed that the lack of structure for professional development impacts on retention and development of staff. It is a strategic aspiration that professional development begins with initial teacher training and continues to "…develop and nurture staff through effective … professional development systems." (Estyn, p29).

The presentation will be illustrated with live examples of the tools as used by students. These include literacy and numeracy audits to generate specific learning targets; records of established capabilities, talents, knowledge and skills and areas for development; SMART target setting tools; and the construction of a CV and portfolio.

Boundaries and bouncing

Gilly Salmon

Beyond Distance Research Alliance, Floor 18 Rm 1813, Attenborough Tower, University of Leicester, University Road, Leicester, LE1 7RH, United Kingdom. Email: gilly.salmon@le.ac.uk

Professor Gilly Salmon shares approaches to transferring

- learning innovation to practice,

- pilots to mainstream

- technology research to impact on student experiences.

Not for the fainthearted.

It's good to talk: Interactive assessment and feedback.

Rosemary Eaton

Newport Business School, University of Wales, Newport, Allt-yr-yn Campus, Newport, NP20 5DA, United Kingdom. Email: rosemary.eaton@newport.ac.uk

As a new lecturer I have found getting a response from students, particularly in the lecture theatre environment, a challenge. This makes it difficult to assess the extent to which students absorb and understand the information presented to them.

Following some research on a range of technological systems, I identified the Interwrite PRS response system (http://www.interwritelearning.com/products/prs/infrared/detail.html; http://www.interwritelearning.com/products/prs/radio/detail.html) with the aim of providing innovative ways to enhance the student experience in the lecture theatre and the classroom.

In the lecture theatre Interwrite PRS can be used with PowerPoint response questions slides, enabling interaction with students and instant confirmation of whether learning objectives are being achieved.

It can be used similarly in the classroom and can also be used for a variety of objective testing questions (MCQ, True/False, numeric and short answer). As a lecturer in accounting, several of the professional qualification subjects I teach are tested in this way and using Interwrite PRS provides a quick way of checking homework answers, confirming understanding of learning objectives and offering progress tests.

The use of this system assists the lecturer in identifying areas where students need additional help in their learning and also in the design of a range of appropriately targeted learning materials.

Speaking our minds: issues in designing learning with reflection and reflective practice.

Richard Pountney

Sheffield Hallam University, City Campus, Howard Street, S1 1WB, Sheffield, United Kingdom. Email: r.p.pountney@shu.ac.uk

This paper examines attempts to describe the learning and teaching practice on a postgraduate course in education and problematises why this is difficult and in many ways unsuccessful. It forms part of a larger project to explore the intentions and outcomes of interventions designed to bring about reflection and reflective practice as part of professional development planning (PDP) and the use of e-portfolio. It takes a perspective on this of being 'a problem of the present' and considers the potential conflicts and fragmentation that may arise as a result of the divisions in interpretation of the metanarrative of reflection and reflective practice within one course, the institution and the academy. This has impacted on learners' understanding of the purpose and benefits of reflection and its relation to professional practice, making it difficult for them to build this successfully into their learning. The author questions the practicality of continuing this struggle given the current educational discourse on planning and developing curricula. It is argued that it may be possible for courses to maintain substantial links with the shifts towards an enhancement-led approach in which practice is validated as dynamic and changing rather than reified in documentation

Greater Expectations Project.

Alison Oldfield

Future Lab, 1 Canons Road, Harbourside, Bristol, BS1 5UH, United Kingdom. Email: alison.oldfield@futurelab.org.uk

Greater Expectations is a Futurelab research and development project that explores the principles and issues that matter to young people in their lives and learning, asks how they can feel empowered and motivated to achieve their aspirations and learn about their entitlements, and examines what role digital technologies can play in that process.

Through desk research, field work and support from a partner network, the 3-year project will develop and deliver a free-to-use, learner-centred resource that aims to support young people to learn about and pursue the aspirations and issues important to them. To accommodate for a wide range of users that focuses primarily on young people but secondarily involves parents, teachers, and other children's professionals, this resource will connect users with tools, resources and inspiring examples that illustrate how young people can be confident, engaged and supported agents of change and how technology can enable and facilitate that to happen.

This presentation will outline the project's aims and research process and findings from the first year's activities, as well as plans for and current understanding of the resource

SYMPOSIUM – INTERNATIONAL SCHOLARSHIP

A Finnish experience.

Sharon Rees

Newport School of Art, Media and Design, University of Wales, Newport, Caerleon Campus, Newport, NP18 3QT, United Kingdom. Email: sharon.rees@newport.ac.uk

For the last four years, BA Hons Fashion Design have been involved in an Erasmus Exchange involving staff and students with Hameenlinna Fashion and Textile School at the HAMK University of Applied Sciences in Finland. The sharing of good design practice with the added social and cultural collaboration has confirmed the global language of fashion design transcends the limitations of any national speech.

The staff exchange has exploited the teaching expertise at each institution to enhance and broaden the subject curriculum and aimed to encourage and improve the standard of spoken and written English on the fashion programme at Hameenlinna. The fashion design and trend prediction projects tested the abilities of staff and students to communicate beyond the normal language barriers. The universal language of fashion design illustration, with pattern and garment construction became the basis of communication, an 'internationally recognised language' and confirmed that 'a drawing is indeed worth a hundred words'. Fashion design and manufacture is a global industry and this experience illustrated the necessity to communicate 'beyond words' and the freedom of expression that could be achieved with good practical design abilities in both two and three dimensions.

The Erasmus exchange programme continues to foster the collaborative nature of fashion design and also the recognition that the components that complete the fashion design product may originate from many parts of the globe. The experience has proven that effective and practical communication is key to the successful completion of the 'critical path' of any design product.

Erasmus exchange experiences with Masaryk University Faculty of Sports Studies.

George Rose

School of Health and Social Sciences, University of Wales, Newport, Caerleon Campus, Newport, NP18 3QT, United Kingdom. Email: george.rose@newport.ac.uk

An Erasmus exchange programme between Newport's Department of Health and Sport and the Faculty of Sports Studies, Masaryk University, Brno in the Czech Republic has been in existence for six years. A recent staff visit to Brno provided opportunity to deliver lectures, seminars, and participate in practical sessions with Czech and Erasmus students in the English Language.

Brno is a quiet city surrounded by lush countryside and is home to exceptionally friendly and hospitable people very appreciative of foreign visitors. Cross institution comparisons demonstrated cultural learning differences and similarities across sport and health related degree programmes at undergraduate and post graduate levels. An understanding of Czech teaching approaches and resources has encouraged exchange of good practice particularly in the areas of technology enhanced learning and learning resources such as the laboratory environment. An understanding of the learning environments native to exchange students has allowed a greater appreciation of the challenges faced when adapting to new cultures.

The visit coincided with the International Conference for Sport and Quality of Life, an opportunity to present research and lead an English speaking symposium. Successful relationships were forged with a view to explore future comparative research studies in the field of exercise of physiology.

Young people today face problems and issues that transcend national borders and challenge professional boundaries: developing collaborative European partnerships and multidisciplinary perspectives on working with young people.

Mark Edwards

School of Health and Social Sciences, University of Wales, Newport, Caerleon Campus, Newport, NP18 3QT, United Kingdom. Email: mark.edwards@newport.ac.uk

This paper originates from willingness by academics in three European higher education institutions to collaborate on a practice framework for working with young people. Student experiences acquired during work practice in the three home institutions is used as a base for critical reflection and analysis. Processes required for creating effective partnerships with other higher education institutions in Europe are presented and the development of a collaborative proposal for an Erasmus Intensive Programme is discussed. Arguments for closer professional collaboration and the need to cross both national and professional boundaries are developed while acknowledging the challenges to the partners of working within a multi-disciplinary context.

SYMPOSIUM – RESEARCH-INFORMED TEACHING

Research-informed teaching explored.

Hefin Rowlands

Research & Enterprise Department, University of Wales, Newport, Allt-yr-yn Campus, NP20 5XA. Email: hefin.rowlands@newport.ac.uk

The University of Wales, Newport is continuing its journey on the integration of research & enterprise with Learning & teaching activities. The Research & Enterprise strategy provides a University wide framework for developing and further embedding research and enterprise activities within the activities of academic Schools and Departments. The Learning & Teaching strategy describes the learning environment as a self perpetuating triangle of learning & teaching – research – knowledge transfer and further supports and enhances the above linkages.

This presentation will explore the teaching-research nexus and will provide an insight into practices and published case studies from across to world. The strategic drivers and frameworks for defining the research informed teaching concept will be considered and finally the links to existing practices and future activities at Newport will be explored.

Demystifying the academic: the role of internships in the Research - Teaching NEXUS

Claire Mashiter

Centre for Research Informed Teaching, University of Central Lancashire, Preston, Lancashire, PR1 2HE, United Kingdom. Email: CFMashiter@uclan.ac.uk

The Robbins report of 1963 highlighted the importance of 'partnership between the teacher and taught in a common pursuit of knowledge…' (Committee on Higher Education 1963 para 555 cited in Jenkins et al. 2007), a concept which is later referred to by Jenkins et al (2007) under the guise of 'research-teaching nexus', to enhance students' research skills and gain an understanding of how knowledge is generated. Yet it is the practical element of this partnership which is often overlooked, as academics focus on pedagogical concerns the student element of the formula is sidestepped, it may be a case of research to inform them, but do students know what research really involves and do they see its importance for their learning?

This paper looks at the first university-wide student internship programme at the University of Central Lancashire. The research utilised student and staff surveys before, during and after the process, combined with video interviews and case studies, to review the perception and understanding of research and look at how the internship affected their future research choices.

The work serves to illustrate the benefits of the programme for both staff and students, not only in terms of subject knowledge but indirect consequences of understanding the role of an academic and the significance of research for their learning. The paper tentatively suggests that whilst the research – teaching nexus has the academic as the centrifugal force, then the true benefits will never be seen by the students.

Diffusion: the UCLan Journal of Undergraduate Research.

Ryan Gibson

Centre for Research Informed Teaching, University of Central Lancashire, Preston, Lancashire, PR1 2HE, United Kingdom. Email: ROGibson@uclan.ac.uk

The Undergraduate Research Journal, although an established feature of many American universities, is relatively new in the UK. The first to venture into this field did so at subject level, starting with the Sciences and more recently extending to the Humanities and Social Sciences. However, in June 2008 the University of Central Lancashire took this a stage further with the launch of *Diffusion: the UCLan Journal of Undergraduate Research*, because *Diffusion* is a multi-disciplinary journal, which publishes on-line, twice yearly (June and December), outstanding undergraduate research papers from across the University of Central Lancashire as a whole.

With a third issue due for release in June 2009, the Editorial Team who produce this journal, have developed an editing policy to deal with this diversity. This presentation will share, from the perspective of an undergraduate Contributor and Member of the Editorial Team, both the experience of editing a journal on this scale and the benefits to be gained from the process.

Making an IMPACT: how the relationships between teaching and research are defined, differentiated and named within different disciplines.

Helen Day

Centre for Research Informed Teaching, University of Central Lancashire, Preston, Lancashire, PR1 2HE, United Kingdom. Email: HFDay@uclan.ac.uk

IMPACT is a series of books published by the Centre for Research-informed Teaching at the University of Central Lancashire that aims to showcase the different relationships between research and teaching in the different schools and disciplines within each faculty. So far in the Faculty of Arts, Humanities and Social Sciences three editorial teams within the Schools of 'Education and Social Sciences,' 'Language and International Studies,' and 'Journalism, Media and Communication' have consulted with staff and students, and collected and collated subject-specific and individual examples of the research-teaching nexus and used these to shape their own publications. This discussion paper explores the different ways these three groups chose to define, differentiate and name the numerous relationships between teaching, learning and research that were included within the case studies, profiles, extracts and summaries of published materials, and editorial commentary. These will be compared with the models suggested by Healey (2005 in Jenkins, Healy and Zetter 2007), Brew (2006) and Rowland (2006) as well as the Centre for Research-informed Teaching itself.

The presentation will summarise the impact of this process and these publications on the pedagogies and strategies that can lead us beyond the teaching and research divide, pedagogies and strategies like collaborative learning, becoming critical and reflective practitioners, mentoring and academic support, engaging with research and teaching passions, designing curricula around inquiry-based approaches, involving undergraduates in research projects usually reserved (within Humanities and Social Sciences) for postgraduates, and widening the definition and understandings of the term 'research', to name but a few. I will end by asking participants how far this reflects or could impact upon their own experience. Despite the general perception that it is research that affects teaching, rather than the other way round (critiqued by Brew 2006), these texts reveal numerous examples of students and staff engaging in pedagogic research, teaching-informed research and practice-informed research as well as the more widely publicised research-informed teaching and curriculum development.

SYMPOSIUM – COMMUNITY AND LIFELONG LEARNING

Community and Lifelong Learning Symposium

Kirsten Merrill-Glover

Centre for Community and Lifelong Learning, University of Wales, Newport, Lodge Road, Caerleon, South Wales, NP18 3QT, United Kingdom. Email: Kirsten.merrill-glover@newport.ac.uk

The Community and Lifelong Learning Symposium is welcomed at Newport's Learning & Teaching conference serving to highlight the University's commitment to community education and meeting the needs of non-traditional learners. The presentations and papers within highlight some of the ongoing community-based education and research currently taking place across the five counties of South East Wales.

In the first paper Jeremy Gass, former Head of Community Learning within the University's Centre for Community and Lifelong Learning (CCLL) questions how and if community education promotes social justice. He considers the extent to which the University of Wales, Newport's Community University of the Valleys – East based in Tredegar has contributed to the promotion of traditional notions of social justice. In the next paper Ceri Jones, Research and Evaluation Officer within CCLL then considers the wider benefits of learning as manifested in the experiences of CUV-E students having accessed the Certificate of Higher Education (Combined Open Studies) programme and how their experiences have impacted on family life and changed perceptions of learning. Angela West, Family Learning Co-ordinator based in CCLL then continues the theme of family learning exploring the feasibility and challenges around embedding family learning within mainstream curriculum. Angela identifies the tension between an acknowledgment that parental involvement in children's education is instrumental in raising aspirations and attainment with the reality of short-term funding, limited resources and a lack of co-ordination.

Ceri Davies, Emma Gearing and Kelly Mc Carthy all Development Officers from CCLL's BeWEHL project based in Newport then present a research based case study illustrating how alternative curriculum linked directly to pedagogy and methodology emerging from action inquiry can direct the development of appropriate curriculum that engages marginalised groups and aids retention and progression. The final paper shifts emphasis to how modern technologies can support work-based learning. Dr Jo Smedley, Associate Dean for Learning and Teaching within Newport Business School highlights the importance of students being able to reflect on their experiences in the workplace. The presentation provides an insight into a project involving work-based learners during their year-long work placements as part of their undergraduate degree studies and their experiences and reflections of using hand-held technologies to support their work-based learning practice. The paper argues that modern technologies can capture work-based learning experiences through text, images, audio and video enabling frequent communication and support on reflective placement based assignments and work-based learning practice.

Community education: promoting social justice?

Jeremy Gass

Centre for Community & Lifelong Learning, University of Wales, Newport, Caerleon Campus, Newport, NP18 3QT, United Kingdom. Email: Jeremy.gass@newport.ac.uk

Drawing on the author's experience of the Centre for Community and Lifelong Learning's Community University of the Valleys-East (CUV-E) initiative, the paper will explore what, if any, contribution community education can make to social justice.

Craig and Burchardt (2008) caution that 'everybody is in favour of social justice' and point out that the meaning attributed to the term and the public policies they believe in as a result vary widely.

It will be argued that a commitment to a particular notion of social justice is one of the key values that underpin and inform the practice of CUV-E. This has more in common with the discourse of the Labour Party's Commission on Social Justice (1994) than that of the Conservative Party's Social Justice Policy Group (2007).

The extent of inequality in the Valleys area is widely recognised in various ways including its designation as an Objective 1 area, the Heads of the Valleys Initiative and the high proportion of Communities First areas. The extent to which, in this context, CUV-E has contributed to the promotion of social justice will be examined in relation to the concepts of distribution and recognition

I know I've changed, most of the time my kids talk to me like an adult now Making Learning normal: The impact on Families of Parental Involvement in Community Based Higher Education.

Ceri Jones

Centre for Community & Lifelong Learning, University of Wales, Newport, Caerleon Campus, Newport, NP18 3QT, United Kingdom. Email: ceri.jones6@newport.ac.uk

In 1995 Titus Alexander and Peter Clyne stated that 'Families are the main context of learning for most people. Learning within the family is usually more lasting and influential than any other. Family life provides a foundation and context for all learning. Their work placed the emphasis on the more practical elements of learning stressing the importance of informal learning and the benefits gained from families learning together. They argue that these two interlinked concepts not only underpin the learning of roles, but also help define responsibilities and strengthen relationships within the family, and influence how families manage and define interactions with external forces that impact on family life.

The paper is, in essence, based on these assumptions framed by the argument that the perception of learning, for parents actively involved in adult education, changes in significant ways and these changes also bring the realisation of alternative future choices. The range and acceptance of change and the belief in the long-term viability of alternative choices varied but without exception all the parents indicated some sense of adult education being a life changing process.

Embedding family learning.

Angela West

Centre for Community & Lifelong Learning, University of Wales, Newport, Caerleon Campus, Newport, NP18 3QT, United Kingdom. Email: angela.west@newport.ac.uk

This paper seeks to explore the concept of embedding family learning within main stream educational provision and examine feasibility, structures and strategic priorities. Consideration of current provision would suggest that family learning is a relatively well established aspect of the community and voluntary sector. However, Ofsted (2000) found it to be poorly resourced and coordinated. Equally, dependence upon short-term funding and a limited curriculum base negates consolidation and expansion of equitable provision

As a crosscutting theme, family learning attracts much deliberation regarding its role and relative value within formal education. Moreover there is no consistent approach to issues such as recognition of achievement, accreditation, monitoring, evaluation, progression, referral, signposting and tracking within this genre.

As professionals we recognise the family as a place of 'deep learning', Haggart (2000), and concur that parental involvement in the child's education is instrumental in raising aspirations and attainment at school. Family learning presents the opportunity to support a learning ethos in the home and contribute to the widening participation agenda. To this end it is essential to work collaboratively with key partners and community groups to ensure that skills and resources are pooled effectively to achieve common goals. A robust and inclusive strategy would set the agenda for family learning and promote active citizenship and community capacity building in its truest form.

Negotiating curriculum.

Ceri Davies, Emma Gearing and Kelly McCarthy

Centre for Community & Lifelong Learning, University of Wales, Newport, Caerleon Campus, Newport, NP18 3QT, United Kingdom. Email: ceri.davies@newport.ac.uk; emma.gearing@newport.ac.uk; kelly.mccarthy@newport.ac.uk

Through the use of a research based case study, the paper will illustrate how alternative curriculum linked directly to pedagogy and methodology emerging from action inquiry can direct the development of appropriate curriculum and teaching approach, engage learners and recruit marginalised members of society; in addition to ensuring engagement, retention, progression and achievement.

An overview of the methodology used to secure engagement and develop curriculum will be offered in addition to addressing the high levels of both academic and personal student support required when working with marginalised communities. In addition, the educational and employment outcomes will be highlighted with discussion focused on the validity of alternative, innovative and reflexive approaches to addressing student needs as opposed to more traditional approaches and policy frameworks.

Earning and learning: using modern technologies to support work based learning.

Jo Smedley

Newport Business School, University of Wales, Newport, Allt-yr-yn Campus, Newport, NP20 5DA, United Kingdom. Email: jo.smedley@newport.ac.uk

Work-based learning (WBL) is defined as "learning that is derived from doing a job of work and taking on a workplace role". It is not the experience of work itself that is paramount; rather it is the learning that an individual derives from that experience of work and from reflecting upon it. Accreditation is based on the demonstrable achievement of certain learning outcomes and usually involves learners in reflecting on their progress with feedback from employers or mentors. Supported by modern technologies, work-based learning experiences can be captured, through text, images, audio and video, enabling frequent communication and support on reflective placement based assignments and work-based projects, enabling a rich variety of submitted information and developing further the technological skills of the learners.

This presentation provides insight into a project involving work-based learners during their year-long work placements as part of their undergraduate degree studies and their experiences and reflections of using hand-held technologies to support their work-based learning practice. The outcomes from this project are contributing to the learning development approaches used in the Centre for Work Based Learning initiative, based in Newport Business School and linking with other Schools as determined from employer focused market research.

SYMPOSIUM – HAZARD AND GEOSCIENCE RESEARCH IN HIGHER EDUCATION

Shock waves and snow slab avalanches

Xinjun Cui[1] and Nico Gray[2]

[1]Newport Business School, University of Wales, Newport, Newport, NP20 5DA, United Kingdom. Email: xinjun.cui@newport.ac.uk

[2]School of Maths, University of Manchester, Manchester M13 9PL, United Kingdom. Email: nico.gray@manchester.ac.uk

Snow avalanches are a hazardous natural flow that poses a constant threat to inhabitants and infrastructure in the vicinity of mountains. Slab avalanches are the most common and most deadly ones, where layers of a snowpack fail and slide down the slop under the action of gravity. In mountainous regions, avalanche defences are often built to deflect the avalanche away from people and infrastructure, or to stop it before it reaches them. As the avalanche is deflected or stopped there are rapid changes in the avalanche height and velocity, this is known as granular shock waves. We apply classical oblique shock theory and use small scale experiments to investigate how weak, strong and detached shock waves are generated by a wedge and compare shock capturing numerical simulations on realistic topography to field observations from a deflecting dam in Flateyri, Iceland. These show that there is no one single set of upstream conditions that parameterizes the flow behaviour, but the solution evolves as the avalanche propagates along the dam in response to the deceleration imposed by the slope. Nevertheless the classical theory still yields important order of magnitude estimates for the flow velocity and thickness immediately upstream of the shock. The numerical method is extended to simulate the flow around arrays of rectangular obstacles, which are often placed in the run-out zone to slow the avalanche down. The results are also compared with small scale experiments.

A tale of two geological books from Canada.

Rob Fensome and Graham Williams

Geological Survey of Canada (Atlantic), Bedford Institute of Oceanography, PO Box 1006, Dartmouth, Nova Scotia, B2Y 4A2, Canada. Email: Rob.Fensome@NRCan-RNCan.gc.ca

The Atlantic Geoscience Society, based mainly in the Canadian Maritime Provinces, has a 30-year history of successful outreach activities and products, including geological highway maps, videos and teacher's workshops. In the late 1990s, a team of AGS members collaborated to produce a popular book on the geology of the Maritimes, which was published in 2001 as *The Last Billion Years (LBY)*. The first print run sold out in 6 weeks, and the book, now in its fourth printing, has become officially a Canadian "best-seller". Although not written as a text book, *LBY* has had a significant impact as an educational tool in schools and universities. Several factors have probably contributed to the *LBY*'s success, including extensive and dedicated artwork, quality photographs and an attractive layout. But perhaps more importantly, *LBY* succeeded because of the unusual process involved in compiling the text: it was originally drafted by a broad range of top researchers to provide state-of-the-art content, but underwent a hands-on editorial process to ensure that the book had a common narrative thread and a uniform style. *LBY*'s success gave us, its co-editors, the audacity to propose a similar book for the whole of Canada, a proposal that was eventually accepted as a principal Canadian contribution to International Year of Planet Earth. The book, entitled *Four Billion Years and Counting*, is now in advanced preparation and will be published within the next year.

SYMPOSIUM – INTERNATIONAL ACADEMIC SCHOLARSHIP

Knowledge transfer funding and support

Karen Turnbull

Research & Enterprise Department, University of Wales, Newport, Allt-yr-yn Campus, NP20 5XA. Email: karen.turnbull@newport.ac.uk

University of Wales, Newport has a successful track record of academic collaboration with private, public and third sector organisations. From the external organisation perspective such partnerships are a means of tapping into the academic knowledge base of universities. For the higher education sector such activities provide a range of opportunities which can enhance and inform research, learning and teaching. From the Government perspective, these partnerships are a mechanism to help drive future prosperity in Wales, the UK and the EU which is why a number of funding streams are available to support this activity.

Drawing upon fourteen year's experience of working at the academic and commercial interface and using case studies of good practice at Newport, this presentation will explore how knowledge transfer can be embedded into academia and highlight the funding streams available to universities. In addition it will examine the central function known as the "Industrial Liaison Office" which provides knowledge transfer support such as sourcing funding opportunities, assistance with the application process, customer relationship, contractual and intellectual property management.

Linking teaching and knowledge transfer.

Carolyn Roberts

Faculty of Education, Humanities and Sciences, University of Gloucestershire, Francis Close Hall, Swindon Road, Cheltenham, GL50 4AZ, United Kingdom. Email: croberts@glos.ac.uk

Case studies drawn from consultancy practice, rather than more traditional conceptions of 'research', can potentially be exciting and powerful ways of engaging students' interest, as they see that this type of inquiry has immediate outcomes in addressing societal problems. It can foster students' understandings of how research is applied, the politics behind securing funding for investigations, and the practical problems of working with real stakeholders beyond academia. Students immediately experience practical problem solving which requires compromise, the need to separate fact from opinion rapidly, and the pressure to develop high level communication skills. However there may be drawbacks. Some students may believe that superficial understanding of the context (and in scientific investigations, the science) is normally adequate, that economic considerations will typically overwhelm any other argument, and that legal disputes are always appropriate ways of resolving disputes. Moreover, the student involvement may of necessity not be experienced 'live'.

Drawing on a range of environmental consultancy work undertaken for Public Inquiries associated with development (for instance, quarries and toxic waste disposal), work for private and public clients experiencing major and minor flooding incidents, and work for the Police involving murder victims moving through rivers and canals, a new *nexus* of 'teaching' and 'consultancy' will be explored.

A critical analytical study of the benefits of Knowledge Transfer Partnerships (KTPs) to the teaching of Business and Management students.

Brian Telford, Hugh Coombs and Mike Porch

University of Glamorgan, Pontypridd, CF37 1DL, United Kingdom. Email: b.telford@glam.ac.uk

Part of the rationale of a Knowledge Transfer Partnership (KTP) is that the academic supervisor can use the experience in their teaching, for example through a case study. Thus, a KTP should be an ideal opportunity to link research with teaching. However, there is little evidence of this, as far as business and management teaching is concerned, in the literature. The aim of this paper is to establish the extent to which KTP-based research is used in teaching. An on-line questionnaire was developed, and emails inviting completion sent to 238 supervisors of current and recently (past 4 years) completed KTP projects in business schools obtained from the database on the KTP web site. In addition to completing the questionnaire respondents were invited to take part in interviews with the researchers with the results of these interviews being recorded, transcribed, and analyzed using NVivo. The paper suggests that the benefits of such activities are not fully exploited and that more could be made of the potential contribution to the student's learning experience. The use of case studies in the classroom was found not to be as developed as it could be as the main emphasis in the process was seen as delivering the outcomes of the project to the business partner. Anecdotes were used to bring teaching to life. Best practice in the use of KTPs to develop cases is also considered. Finally, the relevance of KTPs to research is outlined.

How the correlation between artist and the corporation functions in relationship to advertising practice and strategy.

Don Parker

Newport School of Art, Media and Design, University of Wales, Newport, Caerleon Campus, Newport, NP18 3QT, United Kingdom. Email: don.parker@newport.ac.uk

I have been exploring emotional attachments formed to brands in the light of brand marketing structures and examining whether critical steps in that process need to happen in order to create this attachment.

I have started to question existing conventional advertising and business models.

My current position is to pursue this academically and within my practice from this historical point (Thatcher/ Regan / Pinochet era), therefore key installations and events will be exploring the relationship between participant, object / event and the understanding of the way in which consumer decisions are made from an emotive and reactionary point of view

My current position is to understand the process and design of strategy for commercial development, which has informed my delivery of theory and practice on the BA (Hons) Advertising Design Programme at the University of Wales, Newport and as visiting Professor of Advertising Design at the School of Mass Communication, Shenzhen, China.

The delivery of the Programme is directly and constantly updated by my research and enterprise work with partners such as Body Shop, Identica, SAS Design and Johnson & Johnson. Much of the theoretical underpinning of the Programme is predicated upon my research practice with the example of my exploration of consumer behaviour in purchasing environments being used to develop student's positions on consumer theory.

One example of this being the development of a blog that maps directly onto my research, taking the traditional model of the Professor utilizing his student's undergraduate skills to inform his higher-level enquiry.

The Art and Design curriculum requires rapid and system wide development to firmly embed our research practice clearly and definitely into the University structure of delivery. The questions posed by academics in my field which contain a business and creative position will map more closely onto research funding council objectives, the need for targeted research and the desire to map this experience onto the delivery of Undergraduate teaching and learning.